Billing and Collections Best Practices

Billing and Collections Best Practices

Steven M. Bragg

WILEY

John Wiley & Sons, Inc.

Library of Congress Cataloging-in-Publication Data:

Bragg, Steven M.
  Billing and collections : best practices / Steven M. Bragg.
    p. cm.
  Includes index.
  ISBN 0-471-70224-2 (cloth)
  1. Collecting of accounts. I. Title.
  HG3752.5.B73 2005
  658.8'8—dc22

                                                            2004015545

Printed in the United States of America

10 9 8 7 6 5 4 3 2 1

Once again, to my wife Melissa. Thanks for minding the house and kids while I hide in the study to write another book!

About the Author

Steven Bragg, CPA, CMA, CIA, CPIM, has been the chief financial officer or controller of four companies, as well as a consulting manager at Ernst & Young and auditor at Deloitte & Touche. He received a Master's degree in finance from Bentley College, an MBA from Babson College, and a Bachelor's degree in Economics from the University of Maine. He has been the two-time president of the 10,000-member Colorado Mountain Club and is an avid alpine skier, mountain biker, and rescue diver. Mr. Bragg resides in Centennial, Colorado. He is the author of *Advanced Accounting Systems* (Institute of Internal Auditors, Inc., 1997), and the following books published by John Wiley & Sons, Inc.:

Accounting and Finance for Your Small Business

Accounting Best Practices

Accounting Reference Desktop

Business Ratios and Formulas

Controller's Guide to Planning and Controlling Operations

Controllership: The Work of the Managerial Accountant

Cost Accounting

Design and Maintenance of Accounting Manuals: A Blueprint for Running an Effective and Efficient Department

Essentials of Payroll

Financial Analysis

GAAP Implementation Guide

Inventory Best Practices

Just-in-Time Accounting: How to Decrease Costs and Increase Efficiency

Outsourcing: A Guide to Selecting the Correct Business Unit, Negotiating the Contract, Maintaining Control of the Process

Sales and Operations for Your Small Business

The Controller's Function: The Work of the Managerial Accountant

The New CFO Financial Leadership Manual

Contents

Preface

This book contains more than 200 best practices related to every phase of a company's billing and collections activities: creating credit systems, granting credit, creating and delivering invoices, applying cash receipts, managing the collections department, outsourcing collections work, and using a variety of collection techniques. Furthermore, one needs to measure a company's progress in achieving best practices, so a comprehensive list of billing and collections measurements are included in a separate chapter. Given the large number of best practices presented, the Appendix provides a summary of them for you. If there are any concerns about the meaning of any billing, credit, or collection terms, the Glossary contains a dictionary of relevant terms. In short, this is the go-to source for billing and collections improvements.

This book is designed for people in several parts of a company. The credit staff can use the chapters related to credit policies, procedures, systems, and credit granting techniques, while the accounting staff will find useful those chapters covering invoice creation, invoice delivery, and cash application. In addition, the collections staff has access to several chapters covering collection systems, outsourcing, management, and techniques.

This book is intended to be a buffet table of ideas from which one can sample. There is no clear set of billing and collection best practices recommended for all companies, all the time. Instead, given the wide array of industry-specific problems, one should skim through the book and select only those best practices resulting in the most obvious improvements. The Appendix, which summarizes all of the best practices, is a good place to conduct this review. However, a company's business plan will likely change over time, so it is worthwhile to refer back to this book occasionally to see what other best practices may have become applicable as a result of those changes.

Finally, one does not install a best practice merely by ordering that it be done. On the contrary, there is a plethora of ways in which a best practices implementation can fail. Read Chapter 1, Success or Failure with Best Practices, to learn what factors will affect a best practices implementation and how you can increase your odds of success.

Each best practice is followed by graphics indicating the cost and implementation duration for each item. A single stack of dollar bills represents an inexpensive best practice, with two or three stacks representing increasing levels of expense. Similarly, one clock represents a minimal implementation interval, with two or three clocks indicating increasingly lengthy periods before a best practice is likely to be completed.

In short, use this book to improve all aspects of your company's processes that ultimately relate to the successful collection of receivables from customers. This can result in a considerable reduction of a company's investment in accounts receivable as well as fewer bad debts, while also giving a considerable degree of structure to the credit, billing, and collections functions.

The foundation for this book is the author's *Accounting Best Practices*, which is now in its third edition. That book contains approximately 20 billing and collection best practices, all of which can also be found in this book. However, this book provides more than 180 additional best practices, giving the reader a much more in-depth knowledge of how these critical functional areas can be improved. For a general view of best practices covering the entire accounting function, read the author's *Accounting Best Practices*, or for a detailed view of inventory issues, try the recently released *Inventory Best Practices*, which includes almost 200 more best practices.

STEVEN M. BRAGG

Centennial, Colorado
December 2004

1

Success or Failure with Best Practices

This chapter is about implementing best practices.* It begins by describing those situations for which best practices are most likely to be installed successfully. The key components of a successful best practice installation are also noted, as well as how to duplicate best practices throughout an organization. When planning to add a best practice, it is also useful to know the ways in which the implementation can fail, so a lengthy list of reasons for failure is provided. Only by carefully considering all of these issues in advance can one hope to achieve a successful best practice implementation that will result in increased levels of efficiency.

Most Fertile Ground for Best Practices

Before installing any best practice, it is useful to review the existing environment to see if the implementation has a reasonable chance to succeed. The following bullet points note the best environments in which best practices can not only be installed, but also have a fair chance of continuing to succeed:

- *If benchmarking shows a problem.* Some organizations regularly compare their performance levels against those of other companies, especially those with a reputation for having extremely high levels of performance. If the performance levels of these other organizations and the company doing the benchmarking are significantly different, this can serve as a reminder that continuous change

---

* Adapted with permission from Bragg, *Accounting Best Practices, Third Edition* (Hoboken, NJ: John Wiley & Sons, Inc., 2003), Chapter 2.

is necessary in order to survive. If management sees and heeds this warning, the environment in which best practices will be accepted is greatly improved.

- *If management has a change orientation.* Some managers have a seemingly genetic disposition toward change. If a department has such a person in charge, there will certainly be a drive toward many changes. If anything, this type of person can go too far, implementing too many projects with not enough preparation, resulting in a confused operations group whose newly revised systems may take a considerable amount of time to untangle. The presence of a detail-oriented second-in-command is helpful for preserving order and channeling the energies of such a manager into the most productive directions.

- *If the company is experiencing poor financial results.* If there is a significant loss, or a trend in that direction, this serves as a wake-up call to management, which in turn results in the creation of a multitude of best practices projects. In this case, the situation may even go too far, with so many improvement projects going on at once that there are not enough resources to go around, resulting in the ultimate completion of few, if any, of the best practices.

- *If there is new management.* Most people who are newly installed as managers want to make changes in order to leave their mark on the organization. Although this can involve less effective best practice items such as organizational changes or a new strategic direction, it is possible that a renewed focus on efficiency will result in the implementation of new best practices.

In short, as long as management is willing to change and has a good reason for doing so, then there is fertile ground for the implementation of a multitude of best practices.

Implementing Best Practices

The implementation of any best practice requires a great deal of careful planning. However, planning is not enough. The implementation process requires several key components in order to ensure a successful conclusion. This section discusses those components.

One of the first implementation steps for all but the simplest best practice improvements is to *study and flowchart the existing system* about to be improved. By doing so, one can ascertain any unusual requirements that are not readily apparent and that must be included in the planning for the upcoming implementation. Although some reengineering efforts do not spend much time on this task, on the grounds that the entire system is about to be replaced, the same issue still applies; there are usually special requirements, unique to any company that must be addressed in a new system. Accordingly, nearly all implementation projects must include this critical step.

Another issue is the *cost-benefit analysis*. This is a compilation of all of the costs required to both install and maintain a best practice, which is offset against the benefits of doing so. These costs must include project team payroll and related expenses, outside services, programming costs, training, travel, and capital expenditures. This step is worth a great deal of attention, for a wise manager will not undertake a new project—no matter how cutting edge and high-profile it may be—if a sound analysis is not in place that clearly shows the benefit of moving forward with the project.

Yet another implementation issue is the *use of new technology*. Although there may be new devices or software on the market that can clearly improve the efficiency of a company's operations, and perhaps even make a demonstrative impact on a company's competitive situation, it still may be more prudent to wait until the technology has been tested in the marketplace for a short time before proceeding with an implementation. This is a particular problem if only one supplier offers the technology, especially if that supplier is a small one or has inadequate funding, with the attendant risk of going out of business. In most cases, the prudent manager will elect to use technology that has proven itself in the marketplace, rather than using the most cutting-edge applications.

Of great importance to most best practice implementations is *system testing*. Any new application, unless it is astoundingly simple, carries with it the risk of failure. This risk must be tested repeatedly to ensure that it will not occur under actual use. The type of testing can take a variety of forms. One is volume testing, to ensure that a large number of employees using the system at the same time will not result in failure. Another is feature testing, in which sample transactions that test the boundaries of the possible information to be used are run through the system. Yet another possibility is recovery testing—bringing down a computer system suddenly to see how easy it is to restart the system. All of these approaches, or others, depending on the type of best practice, should be completed before unleashing a new application on employees.

One of the last implementation steps before firing up a new best practice is to *provide training* to employees on how to run the new system. This must be done as late as possible, because employee retention of this information will dwindle rapidly if it is not reinforced by actual practice. In addition, this training should be hands-on whenever possible, because employees retain the most information when training is conducted in this manner. It is important to identify in advance all possible users of a new system for training, because a few untrained employees can result in the failure of a new best practice.

A key element of any training class is procedures. These must be completed, reviewed, and be made available for employee use not only at the time of training, but also at all times thereafter, which requires a good manager to oversee the procedure creation and distribution phases. Procedure writing is a special skill that may require the hiring of technical writers, interviewers, and systems analysts to ensure that procedures are properly crafted. The input of users into the accuracy of all procedures is also an integral step in this process.

Even after the new system has been installed, it is necessary to conduct a *postimplementation review*. This analysis determines if the cost savings or efficiency improvements are in the expected range, what problems arose during the implementation that should be avoided during future projects, and what issues are still unresolved from the current implementation. This last point is particularly important, for many managers do not follow through completely on all stray implementation issues, which inevitably arise after a new system is put in place. Only by carefully listing these issues and working through them will the employees using the new system be completely satisfied with how a best practice has been installed.

An issue that arises during all phases of a project implementation is *communications*. Because a wide range of activities may be going on, many of them dependent on each other, it is important that the status of all project steps be continually communicated to the entire project team, as well as all affected employees. By doing so, a project manager can avoid such gaffes as having one task proceed without knowing that, as a result of changes elsewhere in the project, the entire task has been rendered unnecessary. These communications should not just be limited to project plan updates, but should also include all meeting minutes in which changes are decided on, documented, and approved by team leaders. By paying attention to this important item at every step of an implementation, the entire process will be completed much more smoothly.

As described in this section, a successful best practice implementation nearly always includes a review of the current system, a cost-benefit analysis, responsible use of new technology, system testing, training, and a postimplementation review, with a generous dash of communications at every step.

How to Use Best Practices:
Best Practice Duplication

It can be a particularly difficult challenge to duplicate a successful best practice when opening a new company facility, especially if expansion is contemplated in many locations over a short time period. The difficulty with best practice duplication is that employees in the new locations are typically given a brief overview of a best practice and told to "go do it." Under this scenario, they have only a sketchy idea of what they are supposed to do, and so create a process that varies in some key details from the baseline situation. To make matters worse, managers at the new location may feel that they can create a better best practice from the start, and so create something that differs in key respects from the baseline. For both reasons, the incidence of best practice duplication failure is high.

To avoid these problems, a company should first be certain that it has accumulated all possible knowledge about a functioning best practice—the forms, policies, procedures, equipment, and special knowledge required to make it work properly—and then transfer this information into a concise document that can be shared with new locations. Second, a roving team of expert users must be commissioned to visit all new company locations and personally install the new systems, thereby ensuring that the proper level of experience with a best practice is brought to bear on a duplication activity. Finally, a company should transfer the practitioners of best practices to new locations on a semipermanent basis to ensure that the necessary knowledge required to make a best practice effective over the long term remains on-site. By taking these steps, a company can increase its odds of spreading best practices throughout all of its locations.

A special issue is the tendency of a new company location to attempt to enhance a copied best practice at the earliest opportunity. This tendency frequently arises from the belief that one can always improve on something that was created elsewhere. However, these changes may negatively impact other parts of the company's systems, resulting in an overall reduction in performance. Consequently, it is better to insist that new locations duplicate a best practice in all respects and use it to match the performance levels of the baseline location before they are allowed to make any changes to it. By doing so, the new location must take the time to fully utilize the best practice and learn its intricacies before modifying it.

Why Best Practices Fail

There is a lengthy list of reasons why a best practice installation may not succeed, as noted in the following bullet points. The various reasons for failure can be grouped into a relatively small cluster of primary reasons. The first is the lack of planning, which can include inadequate budgeting for time, money, or personnel. Another is the lack of cooperation by other entities, such as the programming staff or other departments that will be affected by any changes. The final, and most important, problem is that little or no effort is made to prepare the organization for change. This last item tends to build up over time as more and more best practices are implemented, eventually resulting in the total resistance by the organization to any further change. At its root, this problem involves a fundamental lack of communication, especially to those people who are most affected by change. When a single implementation is completed without informing all employees of the change, this may be tolerated, but a continuous stream of implementations will encourage a revolt. In alphabetical order, the various causes of failure are as follows:

- *Alterations to packaged software.* A common cause of failure is that a best practice requires changes to a software package provided by a software supplier; after the changes are made, the company finds that the newest release of the software contains features that it must have and so it updates the software, wiping out the programming changes that were made to accommodate the best practice. This problem can also arise even if there is only a custom interface between the packaged software and some other application needed for a best practice, because a software upgrade may alter the data accessed through the interface. Thus alterations to packaged software are doomed to failure unless there is absolutely no way that the company will ever update the software package.

- *Custom programming.* A major cause of implementation failure is that the programming required to make it a reality either does not have the requested specifications, costs more than expected, arrives too late, is unreliable, or all of the above! Because many best practices are closely linked to the latest advances in technology, this is an increasingly common cause of failure. To keep from being a victim of programming problems, one should never attempt to implement the most "bleeding-edge" technology, because it is the most subject to failure. Instead, wait for some other company to work out all of the bugs and make it a reliable concept, and then proceed with the implementation.

Also, it is useful to interview other people who have gone through a complete installation to see what tips they can give that will result in a smoother implementation. Finally, one should always interview any other employees who have had programming work done for them by the in-house staff. If the results of these previous efforts were not acceptable, it may be better to look outside the company for more competent programming assistance.

■ *Inadequate preparation of the organization.* Communication is the key to a successful implementation. Alternately, no communication keeps an organization from understanding what is happening; this increases the rumors about a project, builds resistance to it, and reduces the level of cooperation that people are likely to give it. Avoiding this issue requires a considerable amount of upfront communication about the intents and likely impact of any project, with that communication targeted not just at the affected managers, but also at all affected employees, and to some extent even the corporation or department as a whole.

■ *Intransigent personnel.* A major cause of failure is the employee who either refuses to use a best practice or who actively tries to sabotage it. This type of person may have a vested interest in using the old system, does not like change in general, or has a personality clash with someone on the implementation team. In any of these cases, the person must be won over through good communication (especially if the employee is in a controlling position) or removed to a position that has no impact on the project. If neither of these actions is successful, the project will almost certainly fail.

■ *Lack of control points.* One of the best ways to maintain control over any project is to set up regular review meetings, as well as additional meetings to review the situation when preset milestone targets are reached. These meetings are designed to see how a project is progressing, to discuss any problems that have occurred or are anticipated, and to determine how current or potential problems can best be avoided. Without the benefit of these regular meetings, it is much more likely that unexpected problems will arise, or that existing ones will be exacerbated.

■ *Lack of funding.* A project can be cancelled either because it has a significant cost overrun exceeding the original funding request or because it was initiated without any funding request in the first place. Either approach results in failure. Besides the obvious platitude of "don't go over budget," the best way to avoid this problem is to build a cushion into the original funding request that should see the project through, barring any unusually large extra expenditures.

■ *Lack of planning.* A critical aspect of any project is the planning that goes into it. If there is no plan, there is no way to determine the cost, number of employees, or time requirements, nor is there any formal review of the inherent project risks. Without this formal planning process, a project is likely to hit a snag or be stopped cold at some point before its timely completion. On the contrary, using proper planning results in a smooth implementation process that builds a good reputation for the project manager and thereby leads to more funding for additional projects.

■ *Lack of postimplementation review.* Although it is not a criterion for the successful implementation of any single project, a missing postimplementation review can cause the failure of later projects. For example, if such a review reveals that a project was completed despite the inadequate project planning skills of a specific manager, it might be best to use a different person in the future for new projects, thereby increasing his or her chances of success.

■ *Lack of success in earlier efforts.* If a manager builds a reputation for not successfully completing best practices projects, it becomes increasingly difficult to complete new ones. The problem is that no one believes a new effort will succeed, and so there is little commitment to doing it. Also, upper management is much less willing to allocate funds to a manager who has not developed a proven track record for successful implementations. The best way out of this jam is to assign a different manager to an implementation project, one with a proven track record of success.

■ *Lack of testing.* A major problem for the implementation of especially large and complex projects, especially those involving programming, is that they are rushed into production without a thorough testing process to discover and correct all bugs that might interfere with or freeze the orderly conduct of work in the areas they are designed to improve. There is nothing more dangerous than to install a wonderful new system in a critical area of the company, only to see that critical function fail completely because of a problem that could have been discovered in a proper testing program. It is always worthwhile to build some extra time into a project budget for an adequate amount of testing.

■ *Lack of top management support.* If a project requires a large amount of funding or the cooperation of multiple departments, it is critical to have the complete support of the top management team. If not, any required funding may not be allocated, and there is also a strong possibility that any objecting departments will be able to sidetrack the project easily. This is an especially common problem when the project sponsor has no clear project sponsor at all;

without a senior-level manager to drive it, a project will sputter along and eventually fade away without coming anywhere near completion.

■ *Relying on other departments.* As soon as another department's cooperation becomes a necessary component of a best practice installation, the chances of success drop markedly. The odds become even smaller if multiple departments are involved. The main reason is the involvement of an extra manager, who may not have as much commitment to making the implementation a success. In addition, the staff of the other department may influence their manager not to help out, and there may also be a problem with the other department not having a sufficient amount of funding to complete its share of the work. For example, an accounting department can benefit greatly if the sales department checks with the credit staff before attempting to make sales to high-risk customers. However, the sales staff may be driven more by the prospect of a large commission, and so will not cooperate in setting an effective credit policy.

■ *Too many changes in a short time.* An organization will rebel against too much change if it is clustered into a short time frame because change is unsettling, especially when it involves a large part of people's job descriptions, so that nearly everything they do is altered. This can result in direct employee resistance to further change, sabotaging new projects, a work slowdown, or (quite likely) the departure of the most disgruntled workers. This problem is best solved by planning for lapses between implementation projects to let the employees settle down. The best way to accomplish this lag between changes without really slowing down the overall schedule of implementation is to shift projects around within the department, so that no functional area is on the receiving end of two consecutive projects.

The primary reason for listing all of these causes of failure is not to discourage the reader from ever attempting a best practice installation. On the contrary, this information allows one to prepare for and avoid all roadblocks on the path to ultimate implementation success.

Summary

This chapter has given an overview of the situations in which best practices implementations are most likely to succeed, what factors are most important to the success or failure of an implementation, and how to successfully create and follow through on an implementation project. By following the recommendations made—not only those regarding how to implement, but also those regarding what *not* to do—a manager will have a much higher chance of success. With this information in hand, one can now confidently peruse the remaining chapters, which are full of billing and collections best practices. The reader will be able to select those practices having the best chance of a successful implementation, based on the specific circumstances pertaining to each manager, such as the funding and time available, as well as any obstacles, such as entrenched employees or a corporate intransigence pertaining to new projects.

2

Credit Policies, Procedures, and Systems

This chapter contains 22 best practices related to the organization of the credit function. The first five best practices address the creation and modification of a credit policy, as well as training employees in its use. The next four best practices describe three general types of credit scoring models and the use of credit reports, and the following eight cover the organization of a credit file and credit application, as well as when a credit application should be used. The final five best practices address communications with customers, credit-level review systems, late fee standardization, and the use of automation to give credit references. These best practices are summarized in Exhibit 2.1.

The best practices presented here are intended to bring a high level of organization to the credit granting process. Thus, the use of a credit policy, credit scoring model, customer filing system, and a standardized approach to the use of credit applications are highly recommended. Furthermore, the author has found that contacting customers to explain credit terms and payment procedures is a highly effective approach to keeping customer payment behavior in line with a company's credit policy.

2.1 Create a Credit Policy

One of the chief causes of confusion not only within the credit department but also between the credit and sales departments is the lack of consistency in dealing with customer credit issues. This includes who is responsible for credit tasks, what logical structure is used to evaluate and assign credit, what terms of sale are

---

Exhibit 2.1 *Summary of Credit Policies and Procedures Best Practices*

2.1   Create a credit policy

2.2   Modify the credit policy based on product margins

2.3   Modify the credit policy based on changing economic conditions

2.4   Modify the credit policy based on potential product obsolescence

2.5   Train the credit staff about credit procedures

2.6   Create a credit scoring model

2.7   Use a third-party credit scoring model

2.8   Create a credit decision table

2.9   Arrange for automatic notification of credit rating changes

2.10   Create a customer credit file

2.11   Include a requirement for multiple contacts in the credit application

2.12   Modify the terms of the credit application in the company's favor

2.13   Do not accept any order unless a credit application is completed

2.14   Require a new credit application if customers have not ordered in some time

2.15   Require a new credit application if credit limits are exceeded

2.16   Set a short time limit for the duration of credit reviews

2.17   Enter the last credit review date in the computer system

2.18   Call new customers and explain credit terms

2.19   Issue a payment procedure to customers

2.20   Create and periodically review a report showing credit levels exceeded

2.21   Uniformly administer late fees

2.22   Install an automated credit reference system

---

used, and what milestones are established for the collection process. Without consistent application of these items, customers never know what credit levels they are likely to be assigned, collection activities tend to jolt from one step to the next in no predetermined order, and no one knows who is responsible for what activities.

Establishment of a reasonably detailed credit policy goes a long way toward resolving these issues. A well-written credit policy should clearly state the mission and goals of the credit department, exactly which positions are responsible for the most critical credit and collection tasks, what formula shall be used for assigning credit levels, and what steps shall be followed in the collection process (although a true collections maestro might balk at the thought of using a boringly consistent methodology!). Further comments are as follows:

- *Mission.* The mission statement should outline the general concept of how the credit department does business: does it provide a loose credit policy to maximize sales, or work toward high-quality receivables (implying reduced sales), or manage credit at some point in between? A loose credit policy might result in this mission statement: "The credit department shall offer credit to all customers except those where the risk of loss is probable."

- *Goals.* This can be specific, describing the exact performance measurements against which the credit staff will be judged. For example, "The department goals are to operate with no more than one collections person per 1,000 customers, while attaining a bad debt percentage no higher than 2% of sales, and annual days sales outstanding of no higher than 42 days."

- *Responsibilities.* This is perhaps the most critical part of the policy, based on the number of quarrels it can avert. It should firmly state who has final authority over the granting of credit and the assignment of credit hold status. This is normally the credit manager, but the policy can also state the order volume level at which someone else, such as the Chief Financial Officer (CFO) or Treasurer, can be called on to render final judgment.

- *Credit-level assignment.* This section may be of extreme interest to the sales staff, the size of whose sales (and commissions) are based on it. The policy should at least state the sources of information to be used in the calculation of a credit limit, such as credit reports or financial statements, and can also include the minimum credit level automatically extended to all customers, as well as the criteria used to grant larger limits.

- *Collections methodology.* The policy can itemize what collection steps shall be followed, such as initial calls, customer visits, e-mails, notification of the sales staff, credit holds, and forwarding to a collection agency. This section can be written in too much detail, itemizing exactly what steps are to be taken after a certain number of days. This limitation can constrain an active collections staff from taking unique steps to achieve a collection, so a certain degree of vagueness is acceptable here.

- *Terms of sale.* If there are few product lines in a single industry, it is useful to clearly state a standard payment term, such as a 1 percent discount if paid in 10 days; otherwise full payment is expected in 30 days. An override policy can be included, noting a sign-off by the controller or CFO. By doing so, the sales staff will be less inclined to attempt to gain better terms on behalf of customers. However, where multiple industries are served with different customary credit terms, it may be too complicated to include this verbiage in the credit policy.

Cost: *Installation time:*

2.2 Modify the Credit Policy Based on Product Margins

Company management can cause significant losses if it attempts to loosen the corporate credit policy without a good knowledge of the margins it earns on its products. For example, if it earns only a 10% profit on a product that sells for $10 and extends credit for one unit on that product to a customer who defaults, it has just incurred a loss of $9 that will require the sale of nine more units to offset the loss. However, if the same product had a profit of 50%, it would only require the sale of one more unit to offset the loss on a bad debt. Thus, loosening or tightening the credit policy can have a dramatic impact on profits when product margins are low.

The obvious solution is to review product margins with management on a regular basis, whenever management wants to alter the credit policy, or when new products are about to be released. The concept can be taken a step further by altering the credit policy for each product family, so the credit limit is more closely aligned with product profit levels. This approach allows one to fine-tune a credit policy to maximize profits. At its most advanced level, one can consider the credit policy in advance for products that are still in the design stage. If a company is using target costing to more precisely define product costs during the design stage, this approach can be effective for linking credit policy with the product rollout to achieve maximum profitability upon product release.

Cost: *Installation time:*

2.3 Modify the Credit Policy Based on Changing Economic Conditions

When economic conditions within an industry worsen, a company whose credit policy has not changed from a more expansive period will likely find itself granting more credit than it should, resulting in more bad debts. Similarly, a restrictive credit policy during a boom period will result in lost sales that go to competitors. This latter approach is particularly galling over the long term, because customers may permanently convert to a competitor and not come back, resulting in lost market share.

The solution is to schedule a periodic review of the credit policy with senior management to see when it should be changed to match economic conditions. A scheduled quarterly review is generally sufficient for this purpose. To prepare for the meeting, one should assemble a list of leading indicators for the industry, tracked on a trend line, that show where the business cycle is most likely to be heading. This information is most relevant for the company's industry, rather than the economy as a whole, because the conditions within some industries can vary substantially from the general economy. If a company has international operations, then the credit policy can be tailored to suit the business cycles of specific countries.

Cost: 　　　　　　　　　　　Installation time:

2.4 Modify the Credit Policy Based on Potential Product Obsolescence

If a company manufactures or resells products with a short shelf life or that are subject to rapid technological obsolescence or fashion trends, completed products sitting in the warehouse may be subject to obsolescence in the short term. If so, a tight credit policy can result in limited product sales that leave excess quantities on hand. In such cases, the company is faced with the choice of scrapping the remaining inventory or selling it off at fire sale prices.

The alternative is to loosen the credit policy on those selected inventory items that are most likely to become obsolete in the near term. The logic is that, even if inventory is sold to customers with a questionable ability to pay for the goods, this at least presents higher odds of obtaining payment than if the company trucks the goods to the nearest dumpster.

To make this best practice work, the credit department must be kept regularly informed of the obsolescence status of inventory items, preferably on a daily or weekly basis. The easiest way to achieve this goal is to have the sales, marketing, and logistics staffs regularly flag potentially obsolete items in the inventory database and give the credit department online access to this information. When customers send in orders, the credit staff can call up this information in the computer system, verify the obsolescence status of the items ordered, and modify the credit policy as needed. If the company also has a credit scoring system (see the *Create a Credit Scoring Model best practice (2.6)*), it should consider linking this data feed from the inventory database into the scoring model, so the model automatically issues different credit recommendations based on the items being ordered.

Cost: 💰　　　　　　　　　　*Installation time:* ⏰

2.5 Train the Credit Staff about Credit Procedures

A new employee can have trouble adapting to the credit department, because he or she will not know how the credit scoring model works, how to handle a salesperson or customer demanding a higher credit limit, when and how to cut off credit, how to obtain a security interest in goods shipped, or how to process a credit application. Although these skills are not difficult to learn, someone dropped into the credit role with no experience will be much more likely to acquiesce to higher credit demands, misinterpret credit scoring results, or incorrectly process a credit application. The result is at least an increased level of department inefficiency and more likely an increased level of late payments for the collections staff to handle.

The solution is a training class for all new credit staff, covering all of the key credit areas just noted. Although outside organizations offer credit classes, it is best to conduct this training internally, because most companies have developed their own credit procedures and scoring models that may vary significantly from what is covered by an outside training organization.

The main problem with an in-house training class is finding the time to create and periodically update training materials or at least a set of procedures to use as the basis for the training class. One option is to use a consultant to create the training materials, although this person may have to be called in repeatedly to update the program. Otherwise, the best option is to schedule a training materials update on the department's annual calendar of events, and make sure that the internal staff completes the update.

Cost: 💰　　　　　　　　　　*Installation time:* ⏰ ⏰

2.6 Create a Credit Scoring Model

A common complaint of the collections staff is that there does not appear to be any reasoning behind the credit levels granted to customers, resulting in inordinately high credit levels for some customers who cannot begin to repay their debt. This results in considerable effort for the collections staff to bring in cash from those customers, as well as pleas to the credit department to lower credit to levels that have some reasonable chance of being repaid. This condition is caused by the approach of many credit departments to granting credit, which is that they grant the highest possible credit level to meet the latest customer order received. This approach is advocated heavily by the salesperson, who stands to receive a substantial commission if the sale is approved. Consequently, granting credit based on the size of a customer's order rather than its ability to pay leads to considerable additional collections work.

To solve the problem of an uncertain credit granting standard, one must create a procedure for granting credit that uses a single set of rules that are not to be violated, no matter how much pressure the sales staff applies to expand credit levels. The exact procedure will vary by credit department and the experience of the credit manager. As an example, a credit person can obtain a credit report for a prospective customer and use this as a source of baseline information for deriving a credit level. A credit report is an excellent source on which to base a standard credit level, for the information contained in it is collected in a similar manner for all companies, resulting in a standardized and highly comparable basis of information. Credit reports show the high, low, and median sales levels granted to a customer by other companies, giving the credit manager some idea of what other organizations consider to be an appropriate credit range for the customer. However, just using existing sales levels is not sufficient, because one must also consider the number of extra days beyond terms that a customer takes to pay its customers. This information is a good indicator of creditworthiness and is also contained in a credit report.

An example of how the "payment" information can be included in the calculation of a credit level is to take the median credit level other companies granted as a starting point and then subtract 5% of this amount for every day that a customer pays its suppliers later than standard payment terms. For example, if the median credit level is $10,000 and a customer pays an average of 10 days late, 50% of the median credit level is taken away, resulting in a revised credit level of $5,000. The exact system a company uses will be highly dependent on its willingness to incur credit losses and expend extra effort on collections. A company that is willing to obtain more marginal sales will adopt the highest credit level shown in the credit report and not discount the impact of late payments at all, whereas a risk-averse company may be inclined to use the lowest reported credit level and further discount it heavily for the impact of any late payments by the potential customer.

Another example is to set up a system whereby the amount of credit granted is a percentage of the customer's reported level of equity. The percentage is calculated by creating a credit score based on a variety of factors, such as the perceived riskiness of the country in which the customer is located, the presence of a clean audit report, positive cash flow, no family members in senior management positions, the possibility of significant repeat business with the customer, and so on. The exact set of criteria used will depend on the industry in which the company is located and fine-tuning of the system by the credit manager, who maintains it.

The range of standard procedures for granting credit levels is infinite. The main point is to have one consistent basis for creating reasonable customer credit levels, which gives the collections staff far less work to collect on sales exceeding the ability of a customer to pay. The procedure presented in this section involves using the information shown on a credit report, but other sources of information can also be used.

If a great many customers' credit levels must be tracked and updated, one should attempt to automate as many portions of the credit scoring system as possible. This may require building several interfaces to databases throughout the company in order to pull in key information. At a minimum, the system should access historical accounts receivable records, because past payment performance is one of the better indicators of how a customer will pay in the future. As a company grows and the credit scoring model becomes more central to its operations, more funds can be invested in automating the system. This tends to be an ongoing process that never totally results in complete system automation.

Cost:    Installation time:

2.7 Use a Third-Party Credit Scoring Model

Creating an in-house credit scoring model requires a great deal of time and also the creation of a database to accumulate and summarize scoring information. Many companies do not have the resources for such a system, although it can represent an excellent and tightly controlled way to grant credit to customers.

An alternative is to use the Dun & Bradstreet credit scoring model, called the "Credit eValuator Report." This report contains both a conservative and aggressive credit limit, a customer's payment performance trend, basic company details, and legal filings information. The report costs $35 per customer, with a discount if one purchases a subscription service with Dun & Bradstreet.

This is a good, low-cost approach for determining an approximate credit score, but it does not include variables that may be of considerable importance in a specific industry. Also, although the cost per report is low, this is not a viable scoring approach for small customer accounts.

Cost: *Installation time:*

2.8 Create a Credit Decision Table

Smaller companies usually do not create credit scoring models because they have too few customers to make it worth their time. However, without a scoring model, it is difficult to introduce any level of consistency to the credit granting process. The result is inordinately high or low credit levels for customers who have roughly the same credit characteristics.

An easy solution is to create and consistently use a credit decision table. This is a simple Yes/No decision matrix based on a few key credit issues. An example of how a decision table might work is as follows:

1. Is the initial order less than $1,000? If so, grant credit without review.
2. Is the initial order more than $1,000 but less than $10,000? Require a completed credit application. Grant a credit limit of 10% of the customer's net worth.
3. Is the initial order more than $10,000? Require a completed credit application and financial statements. If a profitable customer, grant a credit limit of 10% of the customer's net worth. Reduce the credit limit by 10% for every percent of customer loss reported.
4. Does an existing customer's order exceed its credit limit by less than 20% and there is no history of payment problems? If so, grant the increase.
5. Does an existing customer order exceed its credit limit by more than 20% or there is a history of payment problems? If so, forward to the credit manager for review. Use the same credit granting process listed in step 3.

6. Does an existing customer have any invoices at least 60 days past due? If so, freeze all orders.

This approach does not completely eliminate variability from the credit granting process, but it sets up clear decision points governing what actions to take for most situations, leaving only the more difficult customer accounts for additional review.

Cost: *Installation time:* 🕐

2.9 Arrange for Automatic Notification of Credit Rating Changes

It is an easy matter for a collections department to be completely blindsided by a sudden drop in a customer's credit rating, possibly resulting in bankruptcy and the loss of all accounts receivable to that customer. Although a company can track payment histories over time, talk to other suppliers of a customer, or periodically purchase credit records from a credit analysis group, all of these options require a continual planned effort. Many collections departments do not have the time to complete these extra tasks, even though the cost of being blindsided is high. They just take the chance that customers will continue to be financially stable.

Rather than undergo the embarrassment of losing an account receivable through the sudden decline of a customer, it is better to arrange for automatic notification of any significant changes to the credit standing of a customer. To do this, a company can contract with a major credit rating agency, such as Dun & Bradstreet. This organization can fax or e-mail a notification of key customer events, such as a change in the speed of the customer's payment, adverse legal judgments, or strikes, which may signal a decline in the customer's ability to pay its bills. With this information in hand, a credit manager can take immediate steps to shrink a customer's credit limit and put extra emphasis on collection efforts for all outstanding accounts receivable, thereby avoiding problems later on, when a customer may sink into bankruptcy.

The only problem with advance notification of a customer's credit is the credit agency's fee, which is typically in the range of $25 to $40 per notification. This fee is minor, however, in comparison to the potential loss of a major account receivable, but the cost may render this best practice uneconomical for smaller customer accounts.

Cost: Installation time:

2.10 Create a Customer Credit File

In a disorganized credit department, it is difficult to locate documentation on personal guarantees that customers may have sent the company in the past, resulting in unenforceable claims and bad debts. Furthermore, third-party credit reports may have been lost, requiring added expenses to purchase them again. Most commonly, customers asking for credit increases may have to fill out new credit applications, because the credit department has lost the original information. This is a particular problem if the accounting system crashes without a backup and the company loses its credit limit information.

A solution is to create a centrally located customer credit file. It should contain all credit applications, third-party credit reports, any personal guarantees, and financial statements, as well as contact and location information. Because this data can become voluminous over time, be sure to periodically purge unneeded records.

There are several variations on this approach. One is to store all of the credit files in a central location for easier access. However, depending on the circumstances, it may make sense to store relevant files next to the credit and collections staff who are directly responsible for those customers. It may also make sense to lock up these files or at least assign a single staff person to the task of extracting documents from and returning them to the files, thereby reducing the amount of misfiling. Finally, consider digitizing all of these documents, so employees can call up all relevant documents on their computers.

Cost: Installation time:

2.11 Include a Requirement for Multiple Contacts in the Credit Application

When a company begins doing business with a new customer, it may know a fair amount about the customer's finances, because of information listed on the credit application, but it probably knows nothing about whom to contact in case of collection problems. Consequently, the first collection contact tends to be a journey of discovery for the collections staff, determining where to call, whom to talk to, what fax number to use, and what e-mail address to access. This search greatly reduces the effective use of collections staff time as they deal with such investigatory issues.

A better approach is to modify the credit application or attach a contact request form to it, asking the customer to list a series of personnel: the name of the assigned accounts payable clerk, payables supervisor, controller, CFO, and perhaps even the president, including the phone number, fax, and e-mail address of each one. This information is invaluable for the collections staff in rapidly working collection problems up a customer's organizational ladder.

Storing this information can be a problem. If collection systems are entirely manual, just staple the completed list to the inside of the customer's account folder. Even with an automated system, there may not be enough fields in the computer to store all of the contact information for multiple users, which may force one into storing this information elsewhere, such as in a separate contacts database.

Also, have a system in place for updating this information because customer contacts change over time, perhaps by having a salesperson update the information once a year or so. If contact information is stored on a computer, consider using it to issue a standard report to all customers that lists the existing contact information, and asking them to update the report and return it.

Cost: *Installation time:*

2.12 Modify the Terms of the Credit Application in the Company's Favor

Too many companies create credit applications that are boilerplate models they copied from the Internet or purchased through an office supply store. The terms of these agreements may include loopholes that customers may exploit to avoid or delay payments.

The credit application is perhaps the only document that a credit department will persuade a customer to sign (they have to in order to be granted a line of credit!), so one should spend a considerable amount of time verifying that the application's terms enhance the company's ability to collect overdue receivables. At a minimum, the credit application should contain the following clauses:

- *Arbitration clause.* Include a binding arbitration clause in the credit application or some related document that customers must sign before doing business with the company. The steps followed in the arbitration process are similar to those used in normal legal proceedings, but they follow a more streamlined and compressed time schedule, with judgment being rendered by an arbitrator. A good arbitration clause is not designed to be totally one-sided in favor of the company, because the company should be mindful of its future relations with customers, who must perceive the process to be fair and unbiased. Also, consider specifying exactly what issues will be subject to arbitration and the steps both parties will follow during the process. Keeping the arbitration clause as specific as possible will keep the two parties from wrangling over how the arbitration is to be conducted, thereby shortening the period before the company achieves final resolution of the contested issue.

- *Credit venue provision.* When a company issues credit to a customer and the customer defaults, a question can arise regarding where a potential lawsuit will take place. If the company and its customer are located far apart, this becomes a serious issue, because one party must travel long distances to attend court. A creditor can ensure that it can sue in its state by including a creditor venue provision in the credit agreement, stating that any recourse to the courts will be settled in the company's state of residence.

- *Grant of a security interest.* Try to get customers to grant a security interest in goods shipped to them, rather than having the credit department try to negotiate this provision at a later date. Customers may cross out the provision, leaving the company no worse off than it was before. If this provision is signed, the credit department needs a procedure for perfecting any security interests received. Perfecting a security interest is time sensitive, because the first security interest publicly filed has priority over later claims.

- *Personal guarantee.* Company owners frequently have substantially more assets than their companies, so obtaining a personal guarantee is certainly worth a try. A customer who grants this guarantee is also more likely to obtain a larger line of credit. At worst, the customer will cross out this part of the application.

- *Reimbursement for collection fees.* The collection department may resort to the use of a collection agency or attorney to collect a past-due account. By having the customer agree in advance to reimburse the company for these added expenses, it may be possible to use the threat of this clause to accelerate customer payment.

■ *Reimbursement for NSF fees.* If a customer pays with a check that does not clear because there are not sufficient funds (NSF) in the account, the company will be charged a fee by the bank. The customer should agree in the statement to reimburse the company for this charge. Better yet, include a standard fee in the credit application that is even higher than the bank's fee, so the company can be reimbursed for its transaction handling costs.

If any provision is listed on the back of the credit application or on any page where the customer theoretically could not see it, include an extra signature line on that page of the application, thereby giving legal proof that the customer has acknowledged and agreed to the provision.

If the security interest or personal guarantee provisions are signed, the credit application becomes a valuable legal document, so make sure that a procedure is in place to appropriately store the application.

Cost: 💵   *Installation time:* ⏰

2.13 Do Not Accept Any Order Unless a Credit Application Is Completed

The credit application function can be a hit-or-miss affair, with some uncertainty regarding the order volume at which an application is required. This is a particular problem when a customer places a large number of small orders, none of which individually are cause for concern, but which in total can represent a serious credit risk. If the credit department is overwhelmed with work, it may not have the time to delve into the need for applications and will be content to let many seemingly smaller orders pass by with no credit review.

A solution for some situations is to require a completed credit application from all customers, irrespective of order size. This approach at least generates all paperwork needed to initiate a credit review, even if the credit staff does not choose to pursue a complete investigation. It has the added benefit of sometimes forcing customers into making an immediate payment rather than bothering with the hassle of completing an application. This approach works best in environments where most orders are relatively large.

This is not a valid best practice when order sizes are small, because the extra hassle may drive away small customers. Also, it is not useful when the credit staff is so small that it has no chance of ever reviewing all of the applications.

Cost: Installation time:

2.14 Require a New Credit Application If Customers Have Not Ordered in Some Time

If a customer has not placed an order recently, perhaps for a year or more, its financial situation may have changed considerably, rendering its previously assigned credit level no longer valid. This is a particular problem when the customer may be shopping through an industry to see who will accept an order and is forced back to the company when no other suppliers are willing to deal with the customer anymore. If the company's credit department simply dusts off the old credit review and allows the same credit limit, a bad debt could be lurking in the immediate future.

One solution is to require customers to complete a new credit application after a preset interval has passed, such as two years. This represents a significant additional workload for the credit staff, so only require this additional review if the old credit level was a sufficiently high one to represent a noticeable potential bad debt loss. Although the computer system can be designed to flag these customers for a credit review when new orders arrive, an alternative is to simply purge from the accounting database all customers with whom there has been no business in the past two years. Then, when an order arrives and the accounting system shows no customer record, the credit staff knows it needs to get involved.

Cost: Installation time:

2.15 Require a New Credit Application If Credit Limits Are Exceeded

When customers are delinquent in paying, it is common to see their receivable balances exceed their credit limits, especially when a company has a tight credit policy and only grants moderate credit limits. In these cases, the collections staff must constantly contact customers to hound them about payments. The usual threat is that all new orders will be held until the customers pay enough to bring the outstanding balance sufficiently below the credit limit for them to place more orders. This process is time-consuming and repetitive.

A simple alternative is a standard mailing to customers who have exceeded the credit limit, telling them of the overage problem and that they now have to fill out a new credit application in order to have the chance of obtaining a new, higher credit limit. If the attached credit application is sufficiently bulky, customers may well choose to make a payment rather than go through the ordeal of another credit application. In order to accelerate this process, consider converting the credit application into a portable document format (PDF) file and e-mailing it to the customer.

Cost: 　　　　　　　　　　　*Installation time:*

2.16 Set a Short Time Limit for the Duration of Credit Reviews

A thorough credit application contains a large amount of information to review, such as three to five trade credit references, possibly several bank references, and a verification of the customer's trade name, location, and credit history through a credit report. Waiting for callbacks on many of these items can require a multiday wait before the credit department has a full set of information on hand with which to reach a credit decision. In the meantime, a prospective customer may have tired of waiting and taken its business elsewhere, resulting in lost sales for the company.

A solution is to impose a maximum time interval for obtaining credit information. Once the time limit is reached, the credit department makes its credit decision, no matter how little information it may have obtained. Although this best practice may seem a dangerous one on the grounds that too much credit may be granted, the credit department needs to realize that it will obtain progressively less information as time goes by, with fewer callbacks from references after the first day or two. With a potential sale hanging in the balance, it is better for the credit staff to call the customer and ask for different references as soon as possible. If the credit report indicates that a potential credit problem may exist, then at least call the customer right away to explain the reason for a possible delay. Even under these circumstances, it may be better to grant a minimum level of credit just to get a small order in process than to force the customer to wait.

This approach mandates the smallest possible work queue for the credit staff, because they must be able to process applications with lightning speed. The credit manager will need to constantly monitor the workload in order to keep credit applications moving briskly through the system.

Cost: 💵   Installation time: ⏰

2.17 Enter the Last Credit Review Date in the Computer System

A reasonably organized credit department may require a credit analysis on every customer,but have no idea when the last review was conducted. Although one can always manually review a customer's credit file for this information, this represents an increasingly difficult filing problem as the number of customers grows over time. Furthermore, as time passes, the accuracy of the initial credit review declines, given ongoing changes in customers' financial condition. Thus, the importance of a periodic review becomes more critical just as a company's ability to find this information declines.

The solution is to conduct a complete review of all customer files, extract the date of the last credit review from them, and enter this information into the credit computer database. By doing so, one can match customer order volume to the last review date and easily see if a new credit review is in order.

It is necessary to have a spare date field available in the credit database in order to enter this information. Also, the credit file must be indexed to information in other tables, such as customer orders or sales volume, returns, bad debts, or late payments, in order to make this information relevant.

Cost: 💵   Installation time: ⏰ ⏰

2.18 Call New Customers and Explain Credit Terms

When a new customer receives its first invoice from a company, the standard sequence of events for the accounts payable staff is to enter the "pay to" information in the computer system, accept the corporate default payment days (such as 30), and press the ENTER key. By doing so, the customer has completely ignored the company's payment terms, not to mention any early-payment discounts that may have been added (and possibly negotiated at some length with the customer). This is a particular problem early in a company's relationship with a new customer, because the credit department is keeping an especially watchful eye on the payment situation at this stage. If payments arrive late, the business partners are off to a bad start.

The solution is to contact the customer at the beginning of the relationship and explain the payment terms. By taking the time to make this contact, the company has made the customer aware that the company takes payment terms seriously and expects them to be observed. This contact can take the form of a phone call, personal meeting, or letter. A phone call or personal meeting is the best alternative, because it gives the customer a chance to bring up any special payment issues that could interfere with timely invoice payment.

The key point is to make sure this contact is made with the correct person, or else the time invested in this best practice will serve no purpose. The best contact is the accounts payable manager. As an alternative, try the payables clerk to whom invoices will be sent; this is a less optimal choice, however, because account responsibilities may be shuffled among the clerks on a regular basis.

Cost: Installation time: 🕑 🕑

2.19 Issue a Payment Procedure to Customers

When a company sends an invoice to a customer, the customer assumes that the usual payment arrangements apply: the industry standard number of days to pay, ship back defective goods without notice, and call the company salesperson if there are any questions. If the company's systems are not set up to handle transactions in this manner, this can cause trouble.

A better approach is to develop a short payment procedure for new customers. It should certainly list the company's payment terms but then go further to list company contact information as well as the exact process for returning goods and how to claim a credit. The procedure can even extend to the use of an application form for payments via the Automated Clearing House (ACH) Network. This approach can greatly reduce the number of problems with which the collections staff normally deals.

Getting the procedure into the hands of all customers can take some work. It can go out with the next batch of invoices, or be delivered by the sales staff, or issued as a separate mailing. If any of the information on the procedure changes, the distribution must occur again, which can be a chore if the company has many customers.

Cost: 💵   Installation time: ⏰ ⏰

2.20 Create and Periodically Review a Report Showing Credit Levels Exceeded

Some accounting systems have no provision for automatically halting customer order shipments based on credit levels having been exceeded. This is especially common where either an enterprise resources planning (ERP) system has not been installed or there has been no provision to link different computer systems maintained by the credit, order entry, and shipping departments. When this happens, the shipping department has no idea that an order should be put on hold and blithely ships it, thereby increasing the amount of credit outstanding and the company's level of credit risk.

Several approaches to linking computer files can result in a mix of manual and automated systems to overcome this problem. At worst, one can manually match the accounts receivable file to the outstanding orders file to arrive at a customer's total credit usage, and then compare this number to credit limits to see which orders should not be shipped. At a higher level of automation where the credit, receivable, and order entry files are linked, the system can automatically sort through and report on this information.

Cost: 💵 💵   Installation time: ⏰ ⏰

2.21 Uniformly Administer Late Fees

Many companies debate the need for late-payment fees. The fees can irritate customers and are difficult to collect. The decision about whether to use these fees rests with company management. However, what is rarely considered is the legal consequence of not administering late-payment fees in the same manner among all customers of the same class. The Robinson-Patman Act prohibits price discrimination among customers in the same class. Thus, imposing a late-payment fee on one customer and not another can open a company to legal liability. Companies rarely think of this when they deliberately impose a late-payment fee on a particularly irritating customer, while using different criteria on other customers whose payments are also late.

This problem does not mean that late-payment fees should not be imposed at all. However, one must create a standard policy for the circumstances under which the fees will be imposed, and ensure that the procedure is followed uniformly across each class of customers. An acceptable policy could specify that a company automatically imposes a late-payment fee on all invoices more than 90 days old—period. However, if the collections manager is not consistent in occasionally waiving these fees after they are imposed, the company would still be breaking the law. Thus, proper compliance calls for regular training of the credit and collections staff in both imposing and subsequently handling the disposition of late-payment fees.

There are two additional problems with late-payment fees. One is that the maximum allowable interest rate that can be charged varies by state, so one must be aware of all state laws in this area in order to avoid being charged with usury. Second, customers are not legally required to pay a late fee unless they have agreed to it in advance, so wording should be included in the credit application warning of the late fee and the maximum amount or percentage that may be charged in the event of a late payment.

Cost: *Installation time:*

2.22 Install an Automated Credit Reference System

A large company's credit department may field dozens of credit reference requests per day. If it chooses to respond to them all, a staff person must look up the name of the targeted customer and inform the caller of the customer's high credit, past-due amount, general payment history, and so on. Even with all of this information available on-screen from a computer system, a large number of callers can take up a considerable amount of staff time.

For the small number of large companies that are subject to this problem, the installation of an automated credit reference system may make sense. Under this approach, callers are routed to a phone line that asks them for the customer's identification number, after which the system returns the customer's total amount past due, high credit, total owed, credit limit, payment terms, and number of years doing business with the company. This approach has the added benefit of removing all personal opinions from the information delivered. Because the system cannot express an opinion about a customer, the company also avoids any risk of being sued for libel by a customer.

The downside to this approach is its cost and installation time. The system will require an integrated voice-response system that is directly tied to the accounts receivable database. Assume a five-figure purchase and installation cost, plus two to three months for the installation.

Cost: *Installation time:* 🕰 🕰

3

Credit Granting Techniques

This chapter contains 31 best practices related to credit granting techniques. The first nine best practices involve the collection of information needed to grant credit or the most efficient way to grant credit (which can be of considerable concern when large numbers of customers apply for credit). The next 18 best practices describe a variety of restrictions on credit, including cash in advance, many types of guarantees, credit insurance, and three alternatives available for international sales. We finish the chapter with four approaches for identifying those customers whose credit levels should be most frequently reviewed. These best practices are summarized in Exhibit 3.1.

The credit granting process is a difficult one, balancing the need to do so efficiently while still finding a low-risk way to help the sales department make a sale. The best way to improve credit granting efficiency is through the centralization of credit granting with a single person, so work queues among employees are avoided.

The large number of best practices related to alternative types of credit are intended to give the credit manager a broad range of tools to use in finding a way to make a low-risk sale. No single technique is better than another. Instead, just be aware of the multitude of alternatives available and be willing to shift among them to find the best fit for a specific situation.

3.1 Automatically Grant Minor Credit Lines to New Customers

The sales staff will regularly bring a considerable volume of new customers to the credit department for a credit review. It can be overwhelming for the credit staff to handle a large number of review requests all the time. A common result is that all new customers are granted no more than a cursory review, resulting in an

Exhibit 3.1 *Summary of Credit Granting Best Practices*

3.1	Automatically grant minor credit lines to new customers
3.2	Assign new account processing to one person
3.3	Preapprove customer credit
3.4	Verify the existence of a prospective customer
3.5	Investigate unanswered questions on the credit application
3.6	Obtain credit reports on customers
3.7	Obtain additional credit application information through a customer visit
3.8	Join an industry credit group
3.9	Access the SEC filings of public customers
3.10	Refer a potential customer to a distributor
3.11	Require salesperson collection assistance in advance
3.12	Require partial cash-in-advance payments
3.13	Use COD terms sparingly
3.14	Combine COD terms with a surcharge
3.15	Offer a lease-purchase option to customers
3.16	Install a financing program for marginal customers
3.17	Perfect a security interest in personal property sold to a customer
3.18	Obtain a purchase money security interest in goods shipped
3.19	Enter into a consignment arrangement with a customer
3.20	Require senior lien holders to subordinate their liens below the company's lien
3.21	Require personal guarantees
3.22	Require intercorporate guarantees
3.23	Obtain a letter of credit
3.24	Obtain credit insurance
3.25	Obtain an export credit guarantee
3.26	Obtain a surety bond
3.27	Shorten the terms of sale
3.28	Review the credit levels of the top 20% of customers each year
3.29	Review the credit levels of all customers issuing multiple NSF checks
3.30	Review the credit levels of all customers who skip payments
3.31	Review the credit levels of all customers who stop taking cash discounts

elevated risk that excessively high credit lines will be granted to some customers who are less likely to pay the company within terms, or even go bankrupt.

A reasonable solution is to automatically grant all new customers a minor credit line, and then review the situation after some time has passed and more internal information has been compiled regarding customer ordering and payment habits. This system allows the credit staff to focus its attention on those customers who are clearly having trouble paying on time, as well as on those customers whose order volumes are increasing.

This best practice is most useful in cases when there are many new customers, when the credit department is understaffed, or when company products have such a high gross margin that a few bad debt losses will not cause a significant drain on company resources.

Cost: *Installation time:* 🕐

3.2 Assign New Account Processing to One Person

A common problem for new customers is obtaining rapid processing of their credit applications. One person may send a credit application form to a customer, while another processes the application, a third reviews it, and another sets up the new customer in the accounting system. With so many people involved, it is customary to put incoming paperwork in the work queue of the next person involved, resulting in an extremely slow credit processing interval. Although the end result may be correct credit analysis, the customer may have long since given up and purchased goods from some other company, rather than waiting for the interminable credit application process to be completed.

The solution is to assign sole responsibility for processing new customer credit applications to a single person within the credit department. By doing so, it is much easier for that one person to track the progress of a credit application, and also simpler for management to measure the processing time for applications. If a company is too large to have just one person be responsible for this function, break down the assignments by the first letter of the applying company's name, so that one employee is responsible for all companies whose names begin with A through C, the next for D through F, and so on.

Even with one person being responsible for applications, management should monitor the processing interval to ensure that applications are completed in the shortest possible time period. This can be done by having the assigned employees enter information about each application in the computer system, so managers can log into the credit database and determine which applications are being held up and why delays are occurring.

Cost: *Installation time:* 🕐

3.3 Preapprove Customer Credit

The collections staff suffers severely from credit that is granted *after* the sales force makes a sale to a customer. The typical situation is that a salesperson finds a new customer and makes an inordinately large sale to it; the salesperson then badgers the credit department to grant a large credit limit to the customer because a large commission is on the line. The credit staff yields to this pressure and allows more credit than is warranted, resulting in a difficult collection job for the collections staff.

An outstanding best practice for those companies wanting to avoid bad debt situations is to work closely with the sales staff to create a "hit list" of new customer prospects before any sales effort is made to contact them. The credit staff then reviews existing credit information about these customers, which is easily gleaned from credit reporting agencies, and calculates reasonable credit levels based on that information. These credit levels are given to the sales staff, which now knows the upper limits of what it is allowed to sell to each customer. This approach greatly reduces the pressure that salespeople are wont to bring on the credit staff for higher credit limits. A major by-product of this process is that the collections staff no longer has to deal with inordinately high accounts receivable with customers who have no way of paying on time.

The only problem with this approach is that a great deal of interdepartmental discipline is needed. The sales manager in particular must be able to carefully plan for upcoming sales campaigns and control the sales staff in following sales targets. In addition, this person must see the importance of setting up credit levels in advance and work closely with the credit department in granting appropriate credit levels. If this type of person is not running the sales department, it will be difficult to enforce this best practice.

Cost: *Installation time:* 🕐 🕐

3.4 Verify the Existence of a Prospective Customer

A company will occasionally receive what appears to be a valid purchase order for a modest dollar value from a new customer, ship product to the designated address, and never receive payment. The company has been the victim of fraud, because the customer company does not exist. Scam artists can frequently fly under the radar of credit departments by issuing bogus purchase orders for relatively small amounts that are unlikely to draw the attention of a credit analyst. Although these smaller scams do not usually cost a company much money, larger-volume scams can represent a significant impact on profitability.

A company should have a minimum threshold for a purchase order dollar amount, above which it always pulls a credit report on a new customer and sets up a credit file. The usual threshold amount is the point at which an order's prospective gross margin matches or exceeds the cost of a credit report. Depending on the size of volume discounts on credit reports, this is typically in the range of $25 to $45. By following this procedure, the credit staff can determine the existence of a company, which has already been researched by the credit reporting company. If this approach is used, be sure to ship the requested goods to the address listed on the credit report, not a different address listed on the purchase order.

An alternative approach is to look up the company name in a phone directory and see if it matches the phone number on the purchase order. If not, call the number in the phone directory and attempt to confirm the order. The same approach can be used for trade references, thereby avoiding a confirming callback to a fake reference.

Cost: *Installation time:*

3.5 Investigate Unanswered Questions on the Credit Application

A credit application does not resemble a college entrance test; it is short and to the point and should only take a few minutes to complete. And yet some customers persist in leaving many questions unanswered, such as somehow leaving out bank information, entering only a few of the required trade references, or not listing the names of any company principals. This withholding of information is a sure sign that the customer anticipates credit problems before the business relationship has even begun.

The answer is to reject all credit applications until they are completely filled out. Furthermore, flag all applications that were initially returned with incomplete or unanswered questions, and be especially careful in granting credit to these customers. Close monitoring of future collection problems against this initial credit application problem will likely convince the credit manager that no credit should have been granted at all!

Cost: Installation time: 🕐

3.6 Obtain Credit Reports on Customers

When a customer calls to ask for a delivery on credit, the credit department is operating from a clean slate; it has no idea whether the information the customer enters into a credit application is correct or not. Although a painstaking amount of labor can eventually verify this information, a large time penalty is required to do so. Meanwhile, customers must wait for the application to be completed, which may take days, sending frustrated customers elsewhere.

One solution is to purchase credit reports on customers. These reports list company locations, names, officer information, credit histories, legal problems, banking relations, financial information, and other data of great use to the credit department. The largest purveyor of these reports is Dun & Bradstreet (*www.dnb.com*), followed by Equifax (*www.equifax.com*). Report prices range from $40 to $125 for reports with varying amounts of information, with reduced pricing if one agrees to purchase a monthly subscription. Low-cost reports include only basic customer information, such as corporate names, locations, ownership, and corporate history, whereas the more expensive reports include a variety of financial and payment information. Equifax reports present information more graphically, but the two report providers issue essentially the same information. Both companies provide credit reports over the Internet.

The cost of these reports can certainly build up in a hurry if many customers require a review, so the credit manager should use some discretion in determining what credit level requires the use of a credit report. Also, be wary of entering into a subscription contract unless prospective report volume clearly justifies the subscriptions, which can add up to a significant expense over time.

Cost: 💵 💵   Installation time: 🕐

3.7 Obtain Additional Credit Application Information through a Customer Visit

Although customers will fill out credit applications in order to obtain a line of credit, they usually provide the bare minimum amount of information, partially on grounds of information privacy and also because they want to hide financial problems. When conducting a long-distance business relationship, it can be difficult to obtain additional information.

One possibility for customers with high credit requests is to visit them with the goal of obtaining additional information. During a personal visit, a customer is much more likely to hand over financial statements, even if only for a quick review. Also, ask for a tour of the premises, especially the production and warehouse areas. This tour can reveal the general level of machine utilization and the inventory level kept on hand (although this can be difficult to ascertain if outside warehouses are used). Also, look for the names of suppliers on any stored inventory and contact them as additional credit references. This visit is also a great time to build a relationship with a customer, who is much less likely to pay late if he or she knows you.

This approach can yield valuable additional information, but it is both expensive and time-consuming to visit customers, so use it only for those customers who want large amounts of credit.

Cost: 💵 💵   *Installation time:* ⏰ ⏰

3.8 Join an Industry Credit Group

Credit reports are an extremely useful way to obtain information about customer locations, business names, and general credit condition. However, they do not yield the most up-to-date information about a customer's immediate financial condition. It is entirely possible that a customer will enter a serious financial decline several months before any hint of its condition appears on a credit report. In the meantime, the company may have issued a substantial amount of credit to the customer, leaving the credit manager in a tenuous position.

An excellent solution is to join an industry credit group. These groups exchange information about specific customers, such as recent problems with not sufficient funds (NSF) checks, bankruptcies, accounts being sent to collection, and other financial difficulties, so the credit department can take quick action to tighten credit where necessary. This is also an excellent opportunity for networking, so credit personnel across the industry can more easily exchange information.

The National Association of Credit Management (NACM, *www.nacm.org*) maintains a listing of national credit management groups, including the following:

National agricultural credit conference

National Christian suppliers

National coated paper and film manufacturing

National electronics and communications

National fundraising manufacturers

National garage door and operating devices

National home centers credit group

National housewares / consumer products manufacturers

National lawn and garden suppliers

National leisure living manufacturers

National metal building and components

National metal producers

National musical instrument

National paper packaging credit group

National professional apparel manufacturers

National seed distributors

National steel mill

National suppliers to window manufacturers credit group

National tool and accessories

National truck, trailer, and equipment credit group

National vinyl fence credit group

National water products manufacturers

National waterway carriers / suppliers

The NACM lists meeting intervals and contact information for each group's administrator.

Cost: *Installation time:* 🕐 🕐

3.9 Access the SEC Filings of Public Customers

It can be difficult to obtain financial statements for many customers. If a company is privately held, it may be nearly impossible to obtain information once the customer has completed the initial credit application. If the credit manager insists on receiving the latest financial information, a testy customer may take its business elsewhere.

Although there is no easy solution to the problem of obtaining up-to-date financial information for private companies, this is not at all the case for public ones. By going to the Securities and Exchange Commission (SEC) Web site, *www.sec.gov*, one can easily call up all of the most recent financial filings submitted by a publicly held customer. The best source of information is the 10-Q report, which details and discusses a company's quarterly results. Although this report is shorter than the annual 10-K report, it contains much more current information, and so is of more use to the credit department.

Accessing public filing should be integrated into the daily activities of the credit department. For the greatest degree of consistency, add a quarterly 10-Q review task to the monthly departmental calendar of activities. Also, although the time required to review financial statements is modest, limit this quarterly review to only the largest customers. From the perspective of credit risk, it should be sufficient to review the financial statements of smaller public customers annually.

Cost: *Installation time:* 🕑

3.10 Refer a Potential Customer to a Distributor

After reviewing a customer's credit application, the credit department may conclude that it has no interest in providing any type of credit to a prospective customer. If the customer is not willing to provide either cash in advance or some form of security, there may be no further avenue for the company to make a sale.

Even if the company cannot grant credit, it is possible that a distributor will have a looser credit policy. If the company has a distribution network, refer the customer to a distributor. This approach can indirectly result in a sale for the company, although of a lesser size than it would have experienced with a direct sale (because of the distributor commission or markup). Nonetheless, if the credit department considers a customer to have significant credit risk, this alternative may be viable.

Cost: 　　　　　　Installation time: ⏰

3.11 Require Salesperson Collection Assistance in Advance

A common occurrence is for a salesperson to arrive in the credit department with a customer order in hand and beg for a sufficiently large credit level to cover the amount of the order. With the juicy prospect of a guaranteed order, the sales manager will apply a great deal of pressure on the credit manager to make the deal happen, even if a credit review reveals that the customer will likely represent a difficult collection problem.

One solution is to turn the tables on the salesperson and require him to assist in collection of the account if the customer proves to be a difficult one. The salesperson will have a hard time arguing against this request, because he is the one forcing the sale. The salesperson can also be of great assistance in making a collection, because he has the best customer contact. The main problem with this best practice is getting the sales staff to remember this commitment at the time of collection. The best approach is to document the agreement with the salesperson, send him a copy of the agreement, and store the original in the customer file for ready access.

Cost: 💵　　　　　　Installation time: ⏰

3.12 Require Partial Cash-In-Advance Payments

The primary goal of the credit department is to find a way to make sales happen. This is a particular problem when customers have a poor credit record and their owners have so few funds that a personal guarantee would be of minimal use. The common solution is to require cash on delivery (COD), which does not go over well with cash-strapped customers.

A solution is to require cash in advance only on the company's cost embedded in a product. By doing so, the company has covered its cost and only has the incremental product margin at risk. This is especially attractive for high-margin products for which the customer may be required to pay only half the price in advance and the rest under standard payment terms. Customers may be glad to take these terms when they cannot find anything better than 100% cash-in-advance (CIA) terms from other suppliers.

A significant problem with this approach is ensuring that the credit staff knows product costs, so they can match payment terms to product margins. One approach is to recalculate margins by product family on a periodic basis and have the credit staff use this smaller number of margins for credit extensions. Margins by product tend to be more consistent within a product family, so using an average margin across all products in a family is a simple way to address the proportion of initial cash payment to be made on an order.

Cost: *Installation time:*

3.13 Use COD Terms Sparingly

A common threat used by a company's credit and collection personnel is to switch a customer over to COD terms. Although this approach may work with ongoing customers who have nowhere else to turn for some goods, a canny recipient can issue a stop payment on a check or not fund its checking account, deliberately letting the check bounce. In the meantime, the customer will have already received the goods and perhaps sold them, so the company is once again in a receivable situation. Furthermore, a rejected COD means that the company must pay for freight in both directions and also runs the risk that the goods may be damaged in transit, either outbound or inbound.

Although one should not eliminate COD terms entirely, consider using them sparingly. It is a good tool for ongoing customers who cannot afford to have future deliveries stopped by the company. However, for the reasons just noted, cash in advance is a better payment approach to use for customers with whom the company has no prior credit history or who are not likely to do business with the company again.

Cost: *Installation time:*

3.14 Combine COD Terms With a Surcharge

Customers may be unable to pay off existing receivables in anywhere near the established time interval because of financial problems. However, the company may be the only supplier of a key product, so the customer cannot go elsewhere for its purchases. The company's credit department may be extremely unwilling to extend additional credit, so what can the two parties do to make the relationship beneficial for both?

If the customer is in a position where it can pay a small amount each month toward the existing receivable balance, the credit department can consider offering either COD or CIA terms, coupled with a surcharge designed to gradually pay off the existing balance. By doing so, the company can record additional sales while avoiding the incurrence of a bad debt on the existing receivables. Furthermore, the customer is much more likely to pay off the existing balance, because it needs the company's continuing product sales.

If there is a choice between offering COD or CIA terms with a surcharge, always go with the CIA terms, because a check issued at the time of delivery can always bounce or be cancelled by the customer.

Cost: Installation time: 🕐

3.15 Offer a Lease-Purchase Option to Customers

The collections staff may have a difficult time collecting on large sales, simply because the cash outflow for the customer is so large. Even if the customer is capable of paying on time, the company is at more collection risk because of the sheer size of the sale. Very large sales tend to take somewhat longer to collect, just because of the presence of additional customer controls, such as extra approval paperwork and multiple signatures on the payment check.

One way to improve the odds and speed of receipt on large sales is to offer a leasing option to the customer, thereby allowing the customer to make a series of smaller payments over time. Although the company could offer this service itself and earn extra interest income on the sale, this still leaves the risk of collection with the company. An alternative is to engage the services of an outside leasing firm, so the company receives payment from the lessor as soon as the payment is authorized by the customer, thereby eliminating the collection risk in the shortest possible time frame. A company can also earn a small interest percentage on the lease as part of its outsourcing agreement with the leasing company, usually in the range of 1/2% to 1%.

This approach is most effective when the company and the leasing agency have come to a joint leasing agreement well in advance of a customer sale, so the sales staff can present the leasing option to the customer as part of the initial sale presentation. This frequently gives the company a distinct advantage in making the sale. Of course, a lease is a viable alternative only when the company is selling a fixed asset that the customer intends to retain.

Cost: *Installation time:* 🕐 🕐

3.16 Install a Financing Program for Marginal Customers

The goal of the credit department should be to find a way to assist the sales department in making a sale while still ensuring payment. This can be an exceptionally difficult goal for marginal accounts, who deserve CIA terms, but who don't have the money to pay in this manner. The typical result is no sale.

If there is a significant customer base falling into the marginal credit category and management is determined to achieve sales in this niche, consider creating a financing program. This can be an internal program funded by the company or one outsourced to a third party. Interest rates charged are likely to be extremely high in order to offset the very high bad debt risk. However, bad debts will arise in this area, and a smartly managed financing program that takes risk into account can achieve significant additional sales for a company.

If a company chooses to use a captive financing program for this best practice, it should be keenly aware of the risks involved and monitor the program's bad debt losses closely. Also, it should regularly track usury laws in every state to ensure that the company does not run afoul of them.

Cost: 💵 💵 *Installation time:* 🕐 🕐

3.17 Perfect a Security Interest in Personal Property Sold to a Customer

When a company sells goods to a customer on credit terms but the customer's financial situation is marginal, the credit department may approve only a small credit limit or require some portion of the delivery to be paid in advance. This can be restrictive for the customer and may result in a lost sale.

An alternative is to advance the full amount of credit requested, but only on the condition that the company obtains a perfected security interest in the goods sold until such time as the customer pays for the full amount of the order. To do this, the customer must sign a security agreement in which the goods are listed (typically an appendix to a Uniform Commercial Code 1 (UCC-1) financing statement), and then the company files the UCC-1 form and attachments in the jurisdiction where the goods reside. If other liens have been filed in advance of this form, then the company has a junior position in regard to its security interest, although still higher than that of general creditors.

The company must meet several criteria in order to perfect a security interest. It must have given some form of consideration (e.g., value) to the customer in exchange, the company must have an established right to the assets in question, and the customer must have signed a security agreement containing the asset's description.

The establishment of a security interest is not as good as a purchase money security interest (see the Obtain a Purchase Money Security Interest in Goods Shipped (3.18) best practice), which is more senior than any other security interests, even if they were correctly filed before the date of the purchase money security interest. Also, the UCC-1 will lapse after five years (which is generally sufficient for a receivable claim); if a company needs a longer period in which to have a security interest, it can file a UCC-3 continuation statement to extend its interest for another five years.

 Cost: Installation time: 🕐 🕐

3.18 Obtain a Purchase Money Security Interest in Goods Shipped

A company may find that it has filed a UCC-1 financing statement after any number of other creditors and is secured only to the extent that funds are left after the debts of all other secured creditors have first been paid off in full, which is to say, the company is nearly in the same position as an unsecured creditor.

A solution is the purchase money security interest (PMSI). Under this approach, a company obtains a secured position ahead of all other secured creditors, although only in regard to repossessing company products sold to the customer or proceeds the customer has obtained from those sales. To ensure that a PMSI is properly filed, one must first send a notice to all other secured parties, telling them about this arrangement; this can be done through a UCC search to see who else has filed a UCC-1 form pertaining to the customer. Then file a UCC-1 Financing Statement and the PMSI statement with the Secretary of State's office in the state where the company's primary office is situated. Be sure to have the customer sign the PMSI statement, because this clearly shows that the customer is aware of the security arrangement and further protects the company's rights. The company only has to go through this elaborate procedure once, after which all subsequent purchases by the debtor are covered without additional paperwork.

This approach only works if the company's products are readily identifiable from those of other suppliers to the customer. A unique approach to ensure that this is the case is to label the inventory with company-specific bar code or radio frequency identification tags, so the company's products can be easily separated from otherwise identical products.

Cost: Installation time: 🕐 🕐

3.19 Enter into a Consignment Arrangement with a Customer

There will be cases when a customer could be a potential sales outlet for a substantial amount of company products, but its financial situation is tenuous, and the customer is probably not in a position to repay the company until such time as it can sell the products to a third party. A conservative approach is to require advance payment of at least the company's cost basis in the ordered goods, but this will likely result in no sale at all.

A solution is to set up a consignment arrangement in which the company retains title in the goods, even though they are positioned at the customer location, and will be paid when the customer sells them. In the event of a nonsale, the company also has the right to take back the goods. A collateralization agreement calls for the completion of a detailed consignment agreement in which the parties establish who will pay for insurance coverage, how the agreement shall be terminated, the number of days the customer has in which to pay the company following purchase of the goods, specifies that the customer is responsible for any inventory shrinkage on its premises, and what procedure the company must follow to reclaim its goods. The agreement should also give the company the right to periodically inspect and verify its remaining inventory at the customer location. One must also follow the standard procedure to establish a PMSI in the inventory, including the filing of a UCC-1 financing statement in the jurisdiction where the customer is located and notification of all lien holders that the financing statement has been filed; this notification must also describe the goods under consignment. Unlike a PMSI, one can file the UCC-1 statement without the customer's signature, as long as the customer has signed the associated consignment agreement.

Substantially more work is required to establish a consignment arrangement, so the credit department should use this approach only when evidence exists of both a substantial and ongoing commitment by the customer to purchase inventory. Also, the company is not protected by the consignment agreement in the event of the customer's bankruptcy unless a UCC-1 financing statement is filed and other lien holders are notified. Otherwise, the bankruptcy trustee can sell the consigned goods for the benefit of other creditors who have perfected their security interests, while the company's claim is relegated to the ranks of other nonsecured general creditors. However, if the company's interest in the consigned goods has been properly perfected, the bankruptcy court can either require the customer to return the goods to the company or at least give the company a preferred position when creditor claims are eventually settled.

Also, if the company maintains any facilities in the state where the consigned inventory is located, such as a warehouse or sales office, it may be liable for sales taxes on goods sold by the customer.

Cost: Installation time: 🕑 🕑

3.20 Require Senior Lien Holders to Subordinate Their Liens Below the Company's Lien

Even when a company succeeds in establishing a lien against a customer's assets, it may find that another entity has already established a lien that is now senior to the company's lien. This is most common when a bank has been granted a lien against all customer assets in exchange for a loan. In such cases, a customer bankruptcy may result in no funds being available for payment to the company, once the senior lien holder's claim has been settled.

A solution in a minority of cases is to not ship goods to the customer unless the senior lien holder agrees to subordinate its lien below the company's lien. This approach is rarely palatable to senior lien holders unless the company's goods or services are so vital to the customer that it cannot stay in business without them.

Subordination agreements are customized for specific lien situations, so only have a qualified attorney write one on the company's behalf. Also, reference the agreement in the customer file and retain a signed copy in a locked, fireproof location.

Cost: Installation time:

3.21 Require Personal Guarantees

The key goal of the credit department is to find ways to assist the sales department in making a sale. This can be a difficult goal to achieve when so many prospective sales brought to the credit manager by the sales staff are clearly high risk. The credit manager must frequently turn down credit applications unless customers are willing to pay cash in advance, resulting in ill will from the sales department and lost sales.

A possible solution is having someone with personal assets guarantee payment. The simple act of signing a personal guarantee almost always makes collection easier, because the signer knows that he or she is on the hook for the amount of the receivable and will make sure that this invoice is paid before other unsecured invoices. In some cases when a customer has entered bankruptcy and clear evidence exists that the owners have siphoned off funds to their personal accounts, it is possible (although difficult) to pursue payment from the owners even without the presence of a personal guarantee; discuss this option with legal counsel before proceeding, to see if the odds of success are sufficiently high to make further action cost effective. As a negotiating position, it is best to demand a blanket lien on all of the customer's personal property and to mutually negotiate down to a lien on a subset of these assets, if necessary.

Some states require that a personal guarantee include limitations on the amount guaranteed, and sometimes also a date after which the guarantee terminates. If these provisions are not included in the legal document, it may be rendered void. Consequently, be sure to consult with an attorney regarding these local issues.

If possible, obtain a joint guarantee from the individual and his or her spouse. By doing so, the company can get around some state-level community property laws requiring collection only if the spouse also agrees to a guarantee. A personal guarantee is a legal document that should not be stuffed into a customer's billing file, where the risk of loss or misfiling is high. Instead, store it in a locking file cabinet and make prominent note of the guarantee's existence in the customer collection file.

The intent is not to legally pursue a guarantor unless other options have first been exhausted, because it is most unlikely that such customers would be willing to do business with the company again after this action. Nonetheless, if other options have been pursued with no result, the credit manager can still choose to take legal action against the guarantor. This option can be expensive and time-consuming, but it at least presents an increased probability of payment over time.

Cost: Installation time:

3.22 Require Intercorporate Guarantees

A credit manager is sometimes confronted with a situation where a customer does not have a good credit record and its managers are hired staff who have no intention of adding their personal guarantees to an order. Is there a way to still grant credit to this customer?

It is possible that the company is a subsidiary of another corporate entity. If so, request that the parent company issue a guarantee making the parent liable for the subsidiary's debt. If the company chooses to exercise this guarantee, it is customary to warn the customer that the company intends to contact the guaranteeing entity, not only as a courtesy, but also because this makes the customer more likely to pay.

This approach calls for the examination of the parent's credit in place of the subsidiary, so an additional credit review must be conducted. Also, this type of guarantee may be unenforceable if no obvious consideration is given to the guaranteeing entity in exchange for its guarantee. If this may be a problem, clearly specify the form of consideration given within the guarantee document. Furthermore, review the guaranteeing company's board minutes, articles of incorporation, or bylaws to see if it is authorized to grant a guarantee; if not, the guarantee is unenforceable.

If the guarantee is granted, be sure to store it in a locked file for safekeeping, and make note of the existence of the guarantee in the customer file.

Cost: 💸   *Installation time:* ⏰

3.23 Obtain a Letter Of Credit

Granting credit for an international sale is especially risky. In the event of default, it is far more difficult to obtain a legal judgment against a customer. For this reason, many smaller companies either accept a high level of credit risk when offering open credit to an international customer or avoid the international market entirely.

A common alternative for handling international credit is for the customer to issue a letter of credit (LOC). There are several varieties of LOC, but the basic concept is for the customer to apply for an LOC from its bank; the bank reviews the creditworthiness of the customer and then issues a guarantee (LOC) to pay the company on behalf of the customer once certain conditions related to the sale transaction have been completed. Once the company ships goods to the customer and fulfills all other requirements of the LOC, it can apply to the bank for payment (or to a local bank that corresponds with the customer's bank). The application involves sending to the bank all paperwork related to the shipment of goods, as well as any other requirements noted in the LOC. This approach can also be used for domestic sales, but its primary application is in the international market.

The overriding problem with an LOC is that "the devil is in the details." Credit managers typically do not enjoy using an LOC, because they must track the due dates of all LOC requirements, which can be quite involved, and ensure that all paperwork has been properly organized and forwarded to the bank for approval and payment. Banks tend to be extremely picky about making payment only if all requirements have been fulfilled in painstaking detail. If repeated attempts to garner bank approval are not completed by the LOC termination date, the bank does not have to make any payment at all, which greatly increases a company's credit risk. Thus, although using an LOC can reduce credit risk, it is both a time-consuming and annoying approach requiring constant attention.

Cost: 💵   Installation time: ⏰ ⏰

3.24 Obtain Credit Insurance

Letters of credit take time to set up, are difficult to monitor, and must be followed to the letter in order to be paid. This process makes smaller companies less than willing to enter into international sales. Also, companies of any size may be unwilling to grant large lines of credit or even smaller ones if customers have some risk of nonpayment. In both instances, a prudent credit manager may recommend dropping a potential sale.

An increasingly common solution to this dilemma is the use of credit insurance. This is essentially a guarantee against customer nonpayment. It is faster to set up than an LOC, can be used for both domestic and international receivables, and allows a company to increase its credit lines to customers. Also, for those companies that are willing to take on some credit risk themselves, they can extend a larger credit line than the credit insurance company may allow, thereby giving the company the opportunity to earn additional revenue. Furthermore, a company using credit insurance can reduce the size of its bad debt reserve, as well as offer a higher-quality accounts receivable base as collateral for a line of credit. Credit insurance is available for domestic credit, export credit, and coverage of custom products before delivery, in case customers cancel orders.

If a credit insurance policy stipulates a maximum credit limit per customer, the insurance company must make the decision to increase the credit limit, or the company can take on the uninsured risk of granting extra credit. If the policy contains no maximum limit at all, the insurance company has control over the credit limit granted to each customer. If a customer is considered by the insurance agency to be high risk, it will likely grant no insurance at all. Also, goods being exported to countries with a high perceived level of political risk will not be granted credit insurance.

The cost of credit insurance can exceed 1/2% of the invoiced amount, with higher costs for riskier customers and substantially lower rates for customers who are considered to be in excellent financial condition. The company does not have to absorb this cost; where possible, consider rebilling it to the customer, who may be willing to pay it in order to obtain a larger line of credit than would otherwise be the case.

Cost: 💵💵   Installation time: ⏰

3.25 Obtain an Export Credit Guarantee

Sometimes a company cannot obtain an LOC from a foreign customer, nor any credit insurance from a commercial provider, resulting in the painful decision to either extend credit in a risky situation or to walk away from a potential sale.

The Export-Import Bank of the United States (*www.exim.gov*) offers an export credit guarantee to anyone shipping domestic goods to a foreign customer. This approach allows a company to offer credit to foreign customers while avoiding the use of time-consuming letters of credit. Also, because the company's foreign receivables are now guaranteed by the U.S. government, the company will have a much better chance to obtain debt that is collateralized by its receivables. Furthermore, the bank's Multi-Buyer Policy guarantees payment on *all* qualifying international sales on open account terms. Other policies are available for short- and medium-term sales to individual buyers. It is also possible to obtain preshipment coverage, so a company will not have to worry about an order cancellation for a custom order requiring a long time period to prepare for shipment.

To obtain a guarantee, the exporting company must submit an application containing information about the customer, such as a credit report (containing a Dun & Bradstreet Paydex score of at least 50, which represents average payments no more than 30 days slow) and trade references; larger shipments also require the customer's financial statements (audited for several years, if the proposed guarantee exceeds $1 million). Also, the customer must have been in the same general line of business for at least three years. Finally, for large transactions, operating and net profit, current ratio, and total liabilities/net worth standards must be met. If accepted, the exporting company must pay the full amount of the coverage premium in advance. Premiums will vary by the amount of coverage, evaluation of the customer, and the country in which the customer is based. The minimum premium for any transaction is $500. However, this guarantee is only for a portion of the net contract value on domestic goods (of up to 90%, depending on the guarantee), so the company must still incur some of the risk of nonpayment. Also, this guarantee is not available for military sales, nor to countries that have not been approved by the government.

Cost: 💸 💸   Installation time: ⏰ ⏰

3.26 Obtain a Surety Bond

When a company contracts out work on a construction project, it has no way of knowing if the prime contractor on the job is paying the wages and other expenses of its subcontractors. If it does not do so, the subcontractors can file mechanic's liens against the construction project, meaning that the company must pay the subcontractors.

One can transfer this risk to an insurance company by requiring the prime contractor to purchase a surety bond, usually from an insurance company. The insurance company will pay any subcontractor claims and will have the right to sue the prime contractor for reimbursement of these funds. The company has no liability once the surety bond has been acquired.

The prime contractor may absorb the cost of a surety bond, but it usually passes some portion or all of its cost through to the company. This cost may be considerable if the prospective project is a large one in comparison to the prime contractor's financial size and ability to complete it, prompting the insurance company to perceive a high level of risk that calls for a high price for the bond.

Cost: 💸 💸   Installation time: ⏰

3.27 Shorten the Terms of Sale

There may be cases where a customer wants to place a large number of small orders with a company, cumulatively resulting in a large credit line before the company's typical terms period has expired. For example, it may plan to place ten orders for $3,000 each within the company's standard 30-day terms period, resulting in a required credit line of $30,000. However, the customer's financial condition may not warrant this level of credit risk by the company.

A solution is to shorten the terms of sale. In the previous scenario, reducing payment terms to 15 days would mean that the customer should be able to purchase the same quantity of goods from the company on a credit line of just $15,000.

This approach only works if a customer is placing many small orders rather than one large one, the orders are evenly spaced out, and the customer's own cash receipts cycle allows it to pay on such short terms. Thus, this best practice only applies to a minority of situations.

Cost: Installation time: 🕐

3.28 Review the Credit Levels of the Top 20 Percent of Customers Each Year

Conducting a careful review of the credit levels of all customers can require a massive investment of time by the credit staff. This can include requesting and reviewing customer financial statements, pulling Dun & Bradstreet credit reports, visiting customer sites, reviewing payment histories, and having customers revise existing credit applications. With the burden of processing new credit applications tacked onto this considerable chore, the typical credit department will be completely buried in work. Although the resulting credit-level revisions may yield a better level of credit protection to the company, the effort required can exceed the benefit of doing so.

A simple solution is to stratify the customer list by order volume over the past year and only review the credit of that 20% of the list comprising 80% of the order volume. This approach drastically reduces the amount of credit analysis work while still ensuring a high level of review on those accounts that could have a serious bad debt impact on the company.

This approach can be further refined to exclude obviously creditworthy government entities, such as the federal government. Conversely, it may be necessary to set up an additional system for reviewing the credit of customers with smaller order histories whose orders are increasing in size, even if they fall outside the 20% review threshold. For example, if an existing customer increases its orders from $1,000 per month to $10,000 per month, this sudden jump may be sufficient cause for a credit review. However, these exceptions should not noticeably alter the credit review workload.

Cost: 💵   Installation time: 🕐 🕐

3.29 Review the Credit Levels of All Customers Issuing Multiple NSF Checks

A company may have granted a credit line to a customer who repeatedly issues checks that are returned because of NSF in their bank account. Not only does the accounting department have to spend time resubmitting these checks for payment, but when they are eventually paid, the payments are substantially late. Because many companies only review the credit levels of their largest customers on a regular basis, this problem can persist for some time.

The accounting department should summarize NSF checks by customer and track this information on a trend line. If a customer issues more than a single NSF check within a predetermined time period, the controller should request that the credit department review that customer's credit level, which is clearly higher than the customer can support.

This best practice requires the use of NSF tracking by customer. To make this process easier, consider recording each NSF check returned by the bank in a separate general ledger account, with each journal entry clearly identifying the customer. One can then summarize this account to see which customers are repeat offenders.

Cost: Installation time: 🕐 🕐

3.30 Review the Credit Levels of All Customers Who Skip Payments

When a customer gets into financial difficulty, a common ploy is to pay the smallest invoice first, or to ignore the largest invoice in a group of invoices that are all payable at the same time. By doing so, a company will at least receive *something* on the due date, which may keep it from pursuing collection of the unpaid invoices quite so aggressively as would normally be the case.

Skipping payments is a clear sign that a customer is experiencing cash flow difficulty. As soon as the cash application staff sees this happening, they should notify the credit manager, who in turn should schedule the customer for an immediate credit review. This review cannot be delayed, because the financial condition of some customers may rapidly spiral down into bankruptcy.

There is not normally a linkage between the cash application and credit staffs. Those who apply cash tend to focus on applying payments to open receivables as fast and accurately as possible, without spending any time examining the completeness of the payments being applied. Thus, it may represent a shift in mindset for them to examine what they are applying in sufficient detail to recognize a skipped payment.

Cost: 💵   *Installation time:* 🕐

3.31 Review the Credit Levels of All Customers Who Stop Taking Cash Discounts

When a customer stops taking cash discounts, it may only mean that a new payables person is not aware of the discount and just needs a reminder from the company in order to start doing so once again. However, a more likely scenario is that the customer's financial condition has declined to the point where it no longer has the cash to make an early payment.

Not taking early-payment discounts is an excellent early warning of a decline in a customer's financial condition. If the cash application staff notices this change, they should notify the credit manager at once, who can reevaluate the customer's credit limit.

The real problem with this best practice is noticing when cash discounts stop. Unless a customer's payments are so large that their absence is clearly noticeable, there is not usually an automated way to note their absence. Instead, it may be necessary for a manager to regularly compare a list of customers who usually take discounts to the accounts receivable aging. This manual approach can be time consuming, but it can save the company from incurring a bad debt loss. This review should be conducted by a credit or collections person, on the grounds that this person has the largest vested interest in spotting this problem as early as possible.

Cost: 💵   *Installation time:* 🕐

4

Invoice Creation

This chapter contains 20 best practices related to the creation of invoices. The first seven fall into the general category of invoice simplification, with the objective of making invoices as easy to read as possible. The best invoice should present only the minimum amount of key information required for customers to make a payment and not confuse them with additional data. These best practices are summarized in Exhibit 4.1.

Customers will not pay for an invoice that is in error, so the next group of eight best practices presented address a variety of techniques for reducing the number of errors, including staff training, discovering changed customer addresses, address verification, and proofreading the invoices. These best practices are summarized in Exhibit 4.2.

There are also ways to reduce the amount of labor required to create an invoice. The final block of best practices describes some of these techniques. They are summarized in Exhibit 4.3.

Exhibit 4.1 *Summary of Invoice Simplification Best Practices*

4.1 Add contact information to the invoice

4.2 Add credit card contact information to the invoice

4.3 Clearly state the payment due date on the invoice

4.4 Clearly state the discount amount on the invoice

4.5 Remove unnecessary information from invoices

4.6 Add a receipt signature to the invoice

4.7 Add carrier route codes to billing addresses

Exhibit 4.2 *Summary of Invoice Error Reduction Best Practices*

4.8   Train the billing staff in the invoicing process

4.9   Mark all envelopes as "Address Correction Requested"

4.10   Immediately update the customer file with address changes

4.11   Have the sales staff review contact information for recurring invoices

4.12   Automatically check errors during invoice data entry

4.13   Computerize the shipping log

4.14   Track exceptions between the shipping log and invoice register

4.15   Proofread the invoices

Exhibit 4.3 *Summary of Invoice Efficiency Improvement Best Practices*

4.16   Reduce the number of parts in multipart invoices

4.17   Eliminate month-end statements

4.18   Replace intercompany invoicing with operating transactions

4.19   Use automated bank account deductions

4.20   Use fingerprint verification for credit card and check payments

---

As is usually the case with best practices, companies should not attempt to install all of the ideas presented here. Not all invoice creation best practices are applicable in all situations. For example, it makes no sense to take the extra time to include an image of a receipt signature on an invoice unless there have been receiving problems in the past or this is required by the customer. Instead, browse through these best practices and compare them to existing billing systems to see where they might profitably be included. As company systems change over time, occasionally return to the list and scan through it to see if additional best practices might apply.

4.1 Add Contact Information to the Invoice

When a customer receives an invoice and has a question about it, who does he call? The invoice usually only includes the company's mailing address and may only show a post office box where the corporate lockbox is located. The person having a question must instead contact the purchasing department to obtain contact information. Even then, the purchasing staff usually only knows the names of their counterparts in the company's sales department, so the inquiring person must go through the salesperson to finally locate the person who issued the invoice. This roundabout set of steps can be so frustrating that the customer just lets the invoice sit until the company's collections staff calls to determine why it is overdue for payment. Thus, a lack of contact information can result in a great deal of customer frustration, possibly extending into nonpayment.

The solution is to clearly state contact information on the invoice. This should be delineated by a box and possibly noted in bold or colored print. If the billing staff is large, it may not be practical to put a specific contact name on the invoice, but at least list a central contact phone number. If a company has chosen to assign specific customers to individuals in the collections department, it may be possible to list the name of the assigned collections person in the computer file of the customers for whom they are responsible, so the names of assigned people appear on invoices.

The main difficulty with this best practice is ensuring that the billing or collections staff returns customer phone calls. It is all too common for customers to leave messages in voice mailboxes that are never returned. This issue can be resolved by tying bonus pay to the speed of responses, setting up a daily procedure to review the voice message box, or sending out customer surveys.

Cost: *Installation time:* 🕰

4.2 Add Credit Card Contact Information to the Invoice

Some customers prefer to pay for invoices with a credit card, rather than a check. If so, they call the general number for the company, ask to be routed to the accounting department, and leave credit card information with the first "live" person they contact. This person is frequently not trained in the types of credit card information to collect (writing down the name on the credit card, card number, expiration date, billing address, and need for a receipt can be overwhelming for some), so inadequate information is eventually forwarded to the person who is trained in processing credit card payments. This person must call back the customer (who may not have left a return phone number!) to obtain the required information. Thus, a great deal of delay is built into the credit card payment process.

A solution is to list the credit card contact number on the invoice. A refinement of the concept is to list on the invoice the types of credit cards accepted by the company, which may prevent customers from making unnecessary calls if they do not have the right types of cards. If this approach is used, be sure to have phone calls roll over to a backup person, because customers rarely like to leave credit card information in a voice mailbox.

Cost: Installation time:

4.3 Clearly State the Payment Due Date on the Invoice

The standard invoice presentation shows the invoice date in one of the upper corners, and the payment terms (such as "Net 30") somewhere in the header bar, just above the detailed billing information. For the customer to calculate the proper payment date, she must locate the invoice date, add to it the payment terms, and enter this payment date into her computer system. The reality is more complex. The typical accounting computer system automatically defaults the invoice date to the current date (invariably later than the invoice date), and adds to it a default payment terms date that is stored in the customer file. Thus, there are two ways for a customer to delay payment: be lazy and accept the current date as the invoice date, and always use the preset payment terms. Even when a company carefully renegotiates new payment terms and lists this information on its invoices, the customer usually ignores it because of the presence of preset payment terms in the customer's computer system. The result is chronically late payments.

The solution is to take the payment date calculation chore away from the customer and clearly state the invoice payment date on the invoice, preferably in bold and located in a box. To make matters as simple as possible, it may make sense to even eliminate all mention of payment terms, so the customer does not try to second-guess the company on the proper payment date.

Cost: Installation time:

4.4 Clearly State the Discount Amount on the Invoice

Those companies offering early-payment discounts inevitably deal with the frustration of having customers either miscalculate the amount of their deductions or the dates by which discounts must be taken. Some have a difficult time interpreting such common discount terms as 2%/10, Net 30 (take a 2% discount if paid within 10 days or pay the full amount in 30 days). Admittedly, some accounting software packages jam these terms into the smallest possible space on the invoice, so the terms look more like "2/10 N30," which can be somewhat more confusing. Furthermore, customers have trouble determining the date by which they must pay a discount, frequently using their invoice receipt date rather than the invoice date. The result of these problems is incorrect discounts taken and usually later than the specified dates.

The solution is to state on the invoice the exact amount of the cash discount a customer can take, and the date by which payment must be made in order to earn the discount. This information should be stated clearly on the invoice, preferably in bold, and outlined by a box.

This can be a difficult best practice to implement, because few commercially available accounting software packages provide for including this information on invoices. Instead, one must customize the system to automatically calculate the information and include it on the invoice form. An alternative manual approach is to create a stamp on which this information can be printed, and use the stamp to manually calculate and enter the information on the invoices of just the largest customers or those customers who have a history of discounting problems.

 Cost: *Installation time:*

4.5 Remove Unnecessary Information from Invoices

Much of this chapter involves recommendations to add information to invoices. However, if there is too much clutter, customers will still have a difficult time locating key information. This is a particular problem if information is presented twice. For example, discount terms may be presented in their traditional location in the header bar, as well as the more clear presentation recommended in best practice 4.4, "Clearly State the Discount Amount on the Invoice." Also, other information sometimes used by the accounting staff but not by the customer is included in the header bar, such as the initials of the customer's salesperson (usually for commission calculation purposes) and the job number. At a particularly high level of obscurity, some accounting systems label the invoice number as something else, such as the document number. The end result is more time spent by the customer wading through an invoice to find the relevant information, and a greater risk that the wrong or incorrect information will be transferred from the invoice to the customer's accounts payable system.

The solution is a careful review of one's information format to strip out unnecessary information or clarify the labeling of needed items. For example, one can eliminate salesperson initials and job numbers from the invoice (which will usually still be available to the accounting staff through the accounting computer system). Other improvements are clarifying the labels of various types of information, as well as revising the invoice layout into a logical and readable format. All but the most primitive accounting computer systems contain report writers that should allow one to make these changes to the invoice template.

Cost: 🖿   Installation time: 🕐

4.6 Add a Receipt Signature to the Invoice

Some customers may demand proof of their receipt of a delivery from the company before they will pay its invoice. Normally, this proof is generated internally by the customer through the use of a receiving log or the forwarding of bill of lading information to the accounting department. However, there may be a paperwork disconnect between the customer's accounting and receiving functions, so that some company invoices are not paid for long periods, while the customer scrambles to find evidence of receipt.

This problem can be reduced by using either Federal Express (FedEx) or United Parcel Service (UPS) to make deliveries, both of which post receipt signatures on their Web sites. One can then copy the signature images out of the Web sites and paste them directly into an invoice, thereby providing proof of receipt to the customer on the invoice. If necessary, the billing staff can also add the delivery reference number used by either UPS or FedEx to the invoice. Either the customer or the company can then go straight to the Web sites of either package delivery company to obtain further evidence of the time and place of delivery of the package in question. This approach has the distinct advantage of consolidating both the billing and receiving information for a delivery on one piece of paper. The downside is that the invoice cannot be issued until the delivery has been received by the customer, rather than being sent when the package leaves the company's premises. Also, one must always use either of these package delivery companies in order to have access to the signature information, and less expensive shipping options may be available.

Cost: 💵   Installation time: ⏰

4.7 Add Carrier Route Codes to Billing Addresses

For those organizations that issue large quantities of small-dollar invoices, the cost of mailing is a substantial portion of the total cost of doing business. For these organizations, a lower-cost approach to mailing an invoice must be found. One alternative is to include a carrier route code in the address field for each customer. This information is used by the postal service to more easily sort incoming mail pieces by carrier route. In exchange for this information, the postal service allows a small reduction in the cost of each item mailed. At the time of this writing, the difference between the standard price for an automated letter-size mailing and one that includes the carrier route code is about three cents (for the most recent rates, go to *www.usps.com*). This difference is sufficiently large that a billing manager who processes thousands of invoices per year should certainly consider it as a potential way to save costs.

To implement this best practice, one must obtain the route codes from the postal service on either a monthly or bimonthly basis. Route code information is available on tape, CD-ROM, cartridge, or hard copy. The company's customer address files must be updated with the latest carrier route information, as specified in the postal service's Domestic Mail Manual. To determine the exact format of the file, one can download a sample file from the postal service's Web site. These steps obviously require some continual effort, so one must carefully determine the cost-benefit associated with this best practice before implementing it. Realistically, only a very large mailing operation will save money through this approach.

Cost: 💵 💵   Installation time: ⏰ ⏰

4.8 Train the Billing Staff in the Invoicing Process

The invoicing process is an area into which new staff tend to be dropped with minimal training. Those in the accounting department who are most experienced with this function do not think much expertise is required to complete it, and so they tend to give minimal training to new staff. The result is a higher transaction error rate, incorrectly filed invoice copies, the wrong invoice copy being sent to customers, and invoices sent to the wrong people at the wrong customers. The time required to correct these problems can be substantial.

The solution is a training program. In a smaller company, this may be as simple as having the most senior invoicing person certify new staff in the invoicing process. However, if the senior staff person is a poor trainer or too busy on other projects, the training task will not be accomplished or be given too little time. An approach yielding more consistent results is to write a detailed procedure for the invoicing function that the new staff person can refer to both during and after training, and require the trainer to walk through this document with the trainee, step by step, to ensure that all key invoicing steps are covered. The best approach is to have all training conducted by a corporate trainer, but this alternative is not available to smaller companies that cannot afford the trainer position.

The main problem with this best practice is the time required to create a training document, which typically requires the assistance of a senior staff person, whose other tasks may keep him or her from participating in the project.

Cost: Installation time: 🕑 🕑

4.9 Mark All Envelopes as "Address Correction Requested"

Customers move to new locations all the time and sometimes do not notify their suppliers of this change. When this happens, the collection process can be significantly delayed while the collections team tracks down new addresses and resends invoices.

A simple best practice to circumvent this problem is to mark the words "Address Correction Requested" on each envelope mailed. If the customer has moved and filed a forwarding address with the U.S. Postal Service, the Postal Service will forward the mail to the new address and also notify the company of the new address, which can then be updated in the customer address file at once. The Postal Service will charge a small fee for this notification service.

If for some reason the company does not want its mail to be forwarded, it can instead mark envelopes with the words "Address Correction Requested—Do Not Forward." This will result in not only the return of the mail but also a notice of the forwarding address.

Cost: *Installation time:* 🕐

4.10 Immediately Update the Customer File with Address Changes

Invoices will inevitably be sent to the wrong address sometimes. This can happen despite the best prescreening of invoices by the sales staff, who generally have the best knowledge of customer address changes. This can seriously slow down the speed of cash receipts, because it can easily take two weeks for the Postal Service to return an invoice to the company for retransmittal.

The solution is to put a procedure in place whereby the company's mailroom staff walks returned mail directly to the accounting department. The accounting staff should give this mail the highest priority in researching the correct address, entering changes into the accounting database, and reissuing the invoice. In cases where the invoice is large, one should consider either resending the invoice by overnight mail or converting it into an electronic format and sending it to the customer by e-mail, thereby hopefully accelerating the customer's payment speed.

Cost: *Installation time:* 🕐

4.11 Have the Sales Staff Review Contact Information for Recurring Invoices

Many companies issue invoices in the same amounts to the same customers at the same addresses for years. These situations typically arise for maintenance or subscription products. Through the natural attrition of customer employees and changes in customer locations, it is inevitable that the contact information that was correct the month or year before for the last billing is no longer correct. This results in returned mail and delays while the accounting or sales departments determine to whom the invoice should now be sent.

A good solution is to print out the list of invoices to be sent in the near future and have the sales staff review the list for errors before printing the invoices. The sales staff typically has the most current contact information, and so they are most likely to spot outdated information.

The primary difficulty with this best practice is the unwillingness of the sales staff to assist in the invoice review process. One can meet with the sales staff to personally impress on them the importance of this task. An alternative is to only verify with the sales staff the contact information for the largest invoices, thereby keeping the allocation of their valuable time to this task to a minimum. A better approach is to grant the sales staff a small commission based on the cash collected from recurring invoices. By doing so, they will see a more immediate need to ensure the accuracy of all contact information.

Cost: *Installation time:*

4.12 Automatically Check Errors During Invoice Data Entry

Errors created during the data entry phase of creating an invoice can result in a variety of downstream problems. For example, an incorrect billing address on an invoice means that the customer will never receive it, which means that the collections staff must send a new invoice copy. Also, if the quantity, product description, or price is entered incorrectly, the customer may have a good reason for not paying the bill. If this happens, the collections staff will have to get involved to work out the reason for nonpayment and negotiate extra payments (if possible) by customers. All of these problems are exceptions and require large amounts of time to research and fix.

A useful best practice is to prevent as many data entry problems in advance as possible by using computerized data checking methods. For example, a field for zip codes can only accept five-digit or nine-digit numbers, which prevents the entry of numbers of an unusual length. The field can also be tied to a file of all cities and states, so that entering a zip code automatically fills in the city and state fields. Also, prices of unusual length can be automatically rejected, or prices can be automatically called up from a file that is linked to a unique product number. Similarly, product descriptions can be automatically entered if the product number is entered. An example of a "smart" data entry system is one that flags part numbers being entered for an existing customer for the first time. The computer can check the part number entered against a file of items previously ordered by a customer and verify whether the part being ordered might not be the correct one. There can also be required fields that must have a valid entry or else the invoice cannot be processed; a good example is the customer purchase order number field, which is required by many customers or else they will not pay an invoice. By including these automatic error checking and expert systems into the data entry software, it is possible to reduce the number of data entry errors.

The main problem with creating automatic error checking is that it can be a significant programming project. There may be a dozen different error checking protocols linked to the invoice data entry screen, and each one is a separate programming project. Also, if a company purchased its software from a third party, it is common for the supplier to periodically install software updates issued by the supplier, which would wipe out any programming changes made in the interim. Accordingly, it is best to apply these error checking routines only to custom-programmed accounting systems. An alternative is to use error checking as a criterion for the purchase of new packaged software, if a company is in the market for a new accounting system. In either of these two cases, having automatic error checking is a worthy addition to an accounting system.

Cost: 💵💵   *Installation time:* ⏰ ⏰ ⏰

4.13 Computerize the Shipping Log

For a company with no computer linkage to the shipping dock, the typical sequence of events leading up to invoice creation is that copies of the packing slip and the initial customer order form are manually delivered to the accounting department from the shipping dock; then the accounting staff uses this information to create an invoice. Unfortunately, this manual transfer of information can sometimes lead to missing documents, which means that the accounting department does not create an invoice and sales are lost. In addition, this system can be a slow one; if the shipping department is a long way away from the accounting department, perhaps in a different city, it may be several days before the invoice can be created, which increases the time period before a customer will receive the invoice and pay it. Finally, there is a problem with data entry, because the accounting staff must manually reenter some or all of the customer information before creating an invoice (depending on the amount of data already entered into the computer system by the order entry department). Any additional data entry brings up the risk of incorrect information being entered on an invoice, which may result in collection problems, especially if the data entry error is related to an incorrect shipment quantity.

The solution to this problem is to provide for the direct entry of shipping information by the shipping staff at the shipping location. By doing so, time delays in issuing invoices are eliminated, as is the risk that the accounting staff will incorrectly enter shipping information into an invoice. The shipping staff may still incorrectly enter information, but this is less likely, because they are the ones who shipped the product and are most familiar with shipping quantities and other related information. For this system to function properly, a computer terminal that is directly linked to the accounting database must be located in the shipping area. In addition, the shipping staff must be properly trained in how to enter a shipment into the computer. There should also be a continuing internal audit review of the accuracy of the data entered at this location, to ensure that the procedure is continuing to be handled correctly.

Finally, the accounting software should have a data input screen allowing the shipping staff to enter shipping information. These problems tend to be minor at most companies, because a computer terminal is usually available in or near the shipping area, and most accounting packages are already set up to handle the direct entry of shipping information; some packages even do so automatically as soon as the shipping staff creates a bill of lading or packing slip through the computer system. In short, unless antiquated systems are being used or the shipping staff is poorly trained or unreliable, it is not normally a difficult issue to have the shipping employees directly enter shipping information into the accounting system, which can then be used to immediately create and issue invoices.

Cost: 💸💸   *Installation time:* ⏰ ⏰

4.14 Track Exceptions between the Shipping Log and Invoice Register

If a company relies on the manual transfer of shipping information from the shipping dock to the accounting department, it is likely that some shipments are never billed, resulting in a permanent loss of revenue. This situation arises because information can be lost on its way from the shipping dock; it can be mixed with other paperwork, put into the wrong bin, given to the wrong person, or any number of other variations. In even the best-run companies, there is a strong chance that, from time to time, a shipment will not be invoiced. If the shipment in question is a high-dollar one, the cost of the missing transaction can be considerable and may make it worthwhile to take steps to remedy the situation.

Fortunately, the solution is not an expensive one. To avoid any missing invoices, one must continually compare the shipping log maintained by the shipping department with the invoice register that is maintained by the accounting department. Any shipment that is listed on the shipping log, but that has not been invoiced, must be investigated at once. There may be good reasons for a shipment that is not invoiced, such as the delivery of a free sample, but the investigation must still be completed in order to ensure that there are no problems. If a problem is uncovered, it is not enough to just issue the missing invoice. One must also determine the reason why the paperwork for the shipment never reached the accounting department and fix the underlying problem. Only by taking this extra step can a company keep from having a continual problem with its invoicing. Any company using a manual transfer of information between these two departments should always track exceptions between the shipping log and invoice register.

It is also possible to avoid the entire problem by having the shipping department record all shipments directly into the accounting database, as described in best practice 4.13, "Computerize the Shipping Log." By using this approach, there is no manual transfer of information, so there is no exception tracking to perform. It is also possible to have the shipping department not only enter shipments into the computer, but also print out invoices in the shipping department for delivery with the shipments. However, if the shipping area staff does not have the level of computerization or training to use either of these more advanced best practices, a periodic comparison of the shipping log to the invoice register is mandatory, in order to avoid not billing customers for shipments made to them.

Cost: 📼   *Installation time:* 🕐 🕐

4.15 Proofread the Invoices

Some invoices are so complex, involving the entry of purchase order numbers, many line items, price discounts and other credits, that it is difficult to create a perfect invoice. This is a particular problem when employee expenses are sent to customers for reimbursement and the submitted expenses are incomplete or inaccurate. When sent to the customers, they end up being the proofreader, and they reject the invoice until the company goes through more delays and eventually issues an accurate invoice. The time delay can be substantial.

The solution is to assign a second person to be the invoice proofreader. This person does not create the invoice, and so has an independent view of the situation and can provide a more objective view of invoice accuracy. Because this best practice can introduce some delay into the invoice creation process, proofreading can be limited to only the larger invoices or to invoices that are sent to customers who are most apt to comb through invoices looking for mistakes.

Cost: Installation time: 🕐 🕐

4.16 Reduce the Number of Parts in Multipart Invoices

Some invoices have the thickness of a small magazine when they are printed because they have so many parts. The top copy (or even the top two copies) usually goes to the customer, and another copy goes into a file that is sorted alphabetically; another copy goes into a file for invoices that is sorted by invoice number, and yet another copy may go to a different department, such as customer service, so they will have an additional copy on hand in case a customer calls with a question. This plethora of invoice copies causes several problems. One is that the printer is much more likely to jam if the number of invoice copies running through it is too thick. Another much more serious problem is that each of those copies must be filed away. The alphabetical copy is probably the necessary one, because all of the shipping documentation is attached to it, but there is no excuse for filing invoices in numerical order; they can be found just as easily by calling them up in the computer system. A final problem is that multipart forms are more expensive.

A solution is to reduce the number of invoice copies. Only one copy should go to the customer, and one copy should be retained. That is two copies, not the four or five that some companies use. By reducing the number of invoice copies, there is much less chance that the printer will jam, and the cost of the invoices can be substantially reduced. The biggest cost saving, however, is of the filing time that has been eliminated, which can be many hours per month, depending on the volume of invoices created.

The biggest objection to reducing the number of invoice copies is from those parts of the company that are accustomed to using the extra invoice copies. This group is rarely the accounting department, which must do the work of filing the extra copies, but rather other departments that have an occasional need to look at the invoices. The best way to overcome these objections is to educate the dissenters in advance regarding the required filing time needed to keep extra copies, so they understand that the cost of additional filing does not match the benefit of their occasional need for the invoices. Another option is to give these people read-only access to invoices in the accounting computer system, so they can view invoice information on their computers rather than looking for it manually in an invoice binder. The combination of these two approaches usually eliminates any opposition to reducing the number of invoice copies, allowing the accounting staff to achieve extra efficiencies with this best practice.

Cost: *Installation time:*

4.17 Eliminate Month-End Statements

Those employees in charge of printing and issuing invoices each day have another document that they print and issue each month: the month-end statement. This is a listing of all open invoices that customers have not yet paid. Although it seems like a good idea to tell customers what they still owe, the reality of the situation is that most customers throw away their statements without reading them. The reason is that the person receiving a statement, the accounts payable clerk, does not have time to research strange invoices that appear on a supplier's statement, nor is this person likely to call the supplier to request a copy of the missing invoice. Instead, it is easier to wait for a contact from the supplier, asking about a specific invoice. By waiting, the onus of doing some work falls on the supplier instead of the accounts payable person, which is a preferable shifting of the workload from the latter person to the former.

The simple approach to eliminating this problem is to stop printing statements. By doing so, one can avoid not only the time and effort of printing the statements, but also eliminate the cost of the special form used to print the statements, as well as the cost of stuffing them in envelopes and mailing them.

Although it is possible that the collections staff may complain that this collection tool is being taken away from them, it is at best a poor method for bringing in errant accounts receivable and does little to reduce the workload of the collections personnel. Thus, eliminating the periodic issuance of statements to customers is an easy way to shift the accounting staff away from a non-value-added activity, giving them time to pursue other more meaningful activities.

Cost: *Installation time:* 🕰️

4.18 Replace Intercompany Invoicing with Operating Transactions

Those companies with subsidiaries will have some difficulty at the end of the fiscal year, because they must back out all sales between subsidiaries, which are not, according to accounting rules, true sales. The most common way to record product shipments between locations is to issue an invoice to another subsidiary, which pays the invoice as though it is from an independently owned organization. At the end of the year, the accounting staff must then determine the margin on all sales to subsidiaries (which can be a lengthy undertaking) and create a journal entry to reverse out the margin. This is clearly not a value-added activity, and reducing it to the minimum gives the accounting staff more time to deal with other, more productive issues.

A best practice that multiple-subsidiary companies can use is to avoid using invoices when shipping between company-owned facilities. Instead, there are two ways to record the transactions. The first and easiest approach is to record any inventory transfers as a simple movement of inventory between warehouse locations in the computer system. This approach is only possible if a company uses a single enterprise-wide database to control activities in all company locations. If such a system is in place, a shipping clerk can simply record a delivery as being moved from one warehouse to another, or as being in transit to another warehouse, where it will be recorded as having been received as soon as it arrives at that location.

The other possibility is to accumulate all material transfers in a log and create a journal entry at the end of each reporting period (or sooner, such as daily) to record inventory as having been shifted to a different company location. This second approach requires more manual labor and is more subject to error than the first approach, but it can be used even if no enterprise-wide computer system exists for all locations. In either case, there is no need to create an invoice, nor does the accounting staff have to worry about backing out the profit on sales to company subsidiaries.

Cost: 💵   *Installation time:* ⏰ ⏰

4.19 Use Automated Bank Account Deductions

In some industries, the invoices sent to customers are exactly the same every month. This is common in service industries, where there are standard contracts for providing the same services for the same price, month after month. Examples of such cases are parking lots or health clubs, both of which put their customers on long-term contracts to pay fixed monthly amounts. In these cases, a company issues invoices for the same amount every month to all of its customers.

When the same amount is due every month, a company can use automatic deductions from customer bank accounts. This approach eliminates the need to run any invoices, because customers do not need them to make a payment. There are also no collection problems, because payments are made automatically. Thus, this approach can completely eliminate the invoicing and collection steps from the accounting department.

Before implementing automatic deductions, one must first review the obstacles to a successful project. One issue is that some invoices will still be needed if a company elects to "grandfather" its existing customers so they do not have to pay through bank deductions. Another problem is that invoices are also required for the first month or two of business with a new customer, because it usually takes some time before the automatic deduction is set up and operating smoothly. A regular invoice may also be necessary for a new customer because the first month of service may be for only part of the month (e.g., if the customer starts service in the middle of the month rather than at the beginning), which is easier to bill through an invoice than a deduction. Another issue is if the customer's bank account is cancelled. Although these issues appear to be significant, they are still a small minority of the total number of transactions processed. Generally speaking, if a company has a large base of customers for whom there are consistent and identical billings, this is an effective best practice.

Cost: 💵   *Installation time:* ⏰

4.20 Use Fingerprint Verification for Credit Card and Check Payments

Those businesses accepting a large number of credit card or check payments notice several problems with these methods of payment. First, it takes longer to process a payment transaction, which can cause substantial queues of customers who are waiting to pay. Also, credit card companies take a fee that is generally in the range of 2% to 3% for each transaction processed. Furthermore, a bounced check can be charged back to the company, with all attendant costs. One can avoid all of these problems through the use of a new fingerprint image reader that is positioned next to an existing point-of-sale terminal.

This product, which is sold by Indivos, is a combination fingerprint scanner and keypad. Customers must first be set up in the system, which requires them to present two forms of identification, fill out a short form, have a fingerprint scanned, and enter a seven-digit search code (which allows Indivos to later conduct more rapid searches through its database for the fingerprint image). They can also enter a variety of payment methods at this time, such as Mastercard, Visa, American Express, or checking accounts. Then, when they decide to make a purchase, they place a finger on the scanner and select a payment method on the terminal. Once the system verifies their scan, the payment is processed through the usual financial networks in the same manner as a regular credit card or check payment.

Customers like the system because there is no risk of having their financial information stolen, they no longer have to carry credit cards or checks with them, and they can pay for items faster than with more traditional payment systems. Also, once they are set up in the system, they can use this payment method in any business that carries the same scanning terminals. The benefits for businesses include a reduction in fraud costs, faster customer checkouts, and reduced service fees. The reduction in service fees is a substantial issue to consider; because customers can select immediate payment withdrawals directly from their checking accounts through this method, companies can give them incentives to do so, thereby substituting a few cents charge for an ACH transaction for a 2% to 3% credit card fee.This savings can be substantial over a large number of transactions. Also, if one credit card company's fee is substantially lower than that of other companies, a business can offer a discount or other incentive to shoppers who use the Indivos system to select from a range of payment choices.

Cost: 　　　　　Installation time:

5

Invoice Delivery

This chapter contains ten best practices related solely to the delivery of invoices. Some are concerned with the timing of invoice creation, whereas others address the speed of transmission to the customer. The main underlying point is that the invoice needs to reach the customer as soon as possible.

Several of these best practices are mutually exclusive. For example, one recommends issuing invoices every day, whereas another describes the issuance of a single, summarized invoice per accounting period. In this instance, large-dollar invoices should be sent every day, whereas billings for small amounts may be more easily summarized and billed at long intervals. A company's specific circumstances will indicate which approach works best. Exhibit 5.1 itemizes all of the best practices found in this chapter.

Exhibit 5.1 *Summary of Invoice Delivery Best Practices*

5.1   Submit early billing of recurring invoices

5.2   Print invoices every day

5.3   Print separate invoices for each line item

5.4   Issue single, summarized invoices each period

5.5   Issue invoices to coincide with customer payment dates

5.6   Have delivery person create the invoice

5.7   Have delivery person deliver the invoice

5.8   E-mail invoices in Acrobat format

5.9   Issue electronic invoices through the Internet

5.10 Transmit transactions via electronic data interchange

5.1 Submit Early Billing of Recurring Invoices

There are many situations in which a company knows the exact amount of a customer billing, well before the date on which the invoice is to be sent. For example, a subscription is for the preset amount, as is a contractual obligation, such as a rent payment. In these cases, it makes sense to create the invoice and deliver it to the customer one or two weeks in advance of the date when it is actually due. By doing so, the invoice has more time to be routed through the receiving organization, passing through the mailroom, accounting staff, authorized signatory, and back to the accounts payable staff for payment. This process makes it much more likely that the invoice will be paid on time, which improves cash flow and reduces a company's investment in accounts receivable.

The main difficulty with advance billings is that the date of the invoice should be shifted forward to the accounting period in which the invoice is supposed to be billed. Otherwise, the revenue will be recognized too early, which distorts the financial statements. Shifting the accounting period forward is not difficult for most accounting software systems, but the controller must remember to shift back to the current period after the invoice processing has been completed; otherwise, all other current transactions that are subsequently entered will be recorded in the *next* accounting period, rather than the current one.

Cost: Installation time:

5.2 Print Invoices Every Day

The accounting departments of smaller companies do not like to issue invoices every day, because some setup time is typically involved in the process, rendering it inefficient. They prefer to let shipment information pile up for a few days and then periodically create invoice batches. Although this approach may be the most efficient, it delays the receipt of cash by several days, which not only results in lost interest income, but may also have serious funding repercussions for those businesses operating on minimal levels of working capital.

A possible solution is to force the accounting department to print invoices every day. There will be complaints about inefficiency, but this system will improve the speed with which cash is collected. It also encourages the accounting department to find the most efficient way to set up the invoicing process. This is akin to the use of rapid setup times in the manufacturing area so that production runs of a single unit become economical.

A variation on this approach for those companies providing labor-related services is to bill on a weekly basis instead of monthly. This requires one to accumulate staff timesheets more frequently, and of course quadruples the amount of billing time required to create four times the number of invoices. The timesheet accumulation problem can be reduced by having employees use the Internet to log into a central timekeeping system, so the billing staff can easily see who has not entered their time and can issue reminders in a timely manner.

This best practice is not a good one in all situations. For example, if only a few shipments comprising a tiny dollar value are the only ones to be issued, it is entirely reasonable to wait a few days until the dollar volume of prospective invoices makes it worthwhile to conduct a print run.

Cost: 🖟   Installation time: 🕰

5.3 Print Separate Invoices for Each Line Item

When an accounting department issues an invoice containing a large number of line items, it is more likely that the recipient will have an issue with one or more of the line items and will hold payment on the entire invoice while those line items are resolved. Although this may not be a significant issue when an invoice is relatively small, it is a large issue when the invoice has a large dollar total, and the customer holding the entire invoice will have a serious impact on the amount of accounts receivable outstanding for the company.

One way to avoid this problem is to split large invoices into separate ones, with each invoice containing just one line item. By doing so, it is more likely that some invoices will be paid at once, whereas other ones with issues will be delayed. This best practice can have a significant positive impact on a company's investment in accounts receivable.

The only complaint arising from this approach is that customers can be buried under a large pile of invoices. This can be ameliorated by clustering all of the invoices in a single envelope, rather than separately mailing a dozen invoices on the same day. Also, it may be prudent to cluster small-dollar line items on the same invoice, which will cut down on the number of invoices issued, while not having a significant impact on the overall receivable balance if these invoices are put on hold.

Cost: *Installation time:*

5.4   Issue Single, Summarized Invoices Each Period

Some companies make a business out of selling small quantities of products in small batches, which necessitates a large quantity of invoices. For example, a company that sells nails in batches of an ounce per sale will issue 16 more invoices than one selling nails in batches of one pound. If the cost of issuing an invoice is as little as $1 (and it is usually much more), then the price at which the nails were sold will probably be far less than the cost of issuing the associated invoices. Clearly, companies that must issue enormous numbers of invoices in this manner will find that their administrative costs are excessive.

A way out of this dilemma is to group all sales for a specified time period, such as a month, and then issue a single invoice covering all sales during that period. This approach is similar to the invoicing method used by credit card companies, which congregate all sales for a full month and then issue a single billing. By using this best practice, a company can eliminate a large proportion of its total invoice volume.

There are some issues to consider before using this best practice, however. One is that this approach is obviously most suitable for companies issuing large quantities of low-dollar invoices. Conversely, it is *not* a reasonable approach if invoice volume is low and dollar volumes are high. If a billing is for a large amount of money, it makes little sense to wait until the end of the month to issue an invoice, because this only delays the time period before the customer will pay for it. Another issue is that the existing accounting software may not support this feature. If not, a company must go through the added expense of custom programming to group a series of shipments or sales into a single invoice.

Another problem may be customers: they are accustomed to receiving a single invoice for each shipment, with a separate purchase order authorizing each invoice, and they will not know what to do when a single, summary-level invoice arrives in the mail. The best way to resolve this problem is to make it an option for customers to accept summary-level invoices, rather than unexpectedly springing this change on them with no warning and requiring them to use it. By taking the time to explain the reason for the single invoice and how it can benefit customers, too (with less paperwork for them to sort through), the customer acceptance rate should be high.

The final problem with this method is that it takes longer to bring cash in to pay for shipped goods, because some shipments may be sent out at the beginning of a month but not billed until the end of the month. To avoid this problem, a company can impose a shorter due date in which customers must pay, although customers rarely receive this requirement well. Instead, it is best to carefully analyze the interest cost of invoicing; if there is a clear benefit despite the added cost, then this best practice should be implemented. For many billing departments, it should be implemented sooner rather than later.

In short, issuing a single invoice to customers each period makes a great deal of sense for those companies shipping many small-dollar orders. Companies dealing with large-dollar orders should probably leave this best practice alone, because an added working capital cost is associated with its use.

Cost: 💵 💵   *Installation time:* 🕐 🕐

5.5 Issue Invoices to Coincide with Customer Payment Dates

Some customers with extremely large payment volumes create payments only on certain days of the month in order to yield the greatest level of efficiency in processing what may be thousands of checks. If a company does not send an invoice early enough to be included in the next check processing run, it may have to wait several additional weeks before the next check run occurs, resulting in a late payment.

The solution is to ask customers when they process checks, and make sure that the company issues invoices well in advance of these dates in order to be paid as early as possible. This best practice is not worth the effort if customers pay as frequently as once a week, but payment dates are well worth knowing if a customer pays only once or twice a month.

To save time, only contact customers about payment cycles if the company has a significant volume of business with them. If customers are unwilling to divulge this information (after all, they are trying to avoid paying early), one can probably guess at the check printing dates after a few months by tracking the dates when payments are received. If only a few customers pay infrequently, the database of payment dates can be an informal written list.

Cost: *Installation time:* 🕭

5.6 Have Delivery Person Create the Invoice

Many companies have difficulty with their customers when the company bills for the quantity that it believes it shipped to the customer, but the customer argues that it received a different quantity and only pays for the amount it believes it has received. This problem results in the invoicing staff having to issue credits after the fact in order to reconcile the amount of cash received from customers to the amounts billed to them. The amount of work required in these cases to match the amounts billed to the amounts paid is usually greatly in excess of the dollar amounts involved and has a profound impact on the efficiency of the billing staff.

New technology makes it possible for some companies to completely bypass this problem. If a company has its own delivery staff, it can equip them with portable computers and printers and have them issue invoices at the point of receipt, using the quantities counted by the customer as the appropriate amount to invoice. A flowchart of the procedure is shown in Exhibit 5.2. To begin, the shipping staff determines the amount to be shipped to a customer and enters this amount into the main accounting database. The amount in a specific truckload is downloaded into the portable computer of the delivery person, who then brings the truckload of goods to the customer. The customer counts the amount received. The delivery person calls up the amount of the delivery on the portable computer's screen, enters the quantities that the customer agrees has been delivered, and prints out an invoice for the customer (which may be on a diskette or CD if the customer prefers an electronic copy).

The delivery person then returns to the company and uploads all invoicing information from the portable computer to the main accounting database, which records the invoices and notes any variances between the amounts shipped and the amounts received by customers (which will be investigated if the variances are significant). It is also possible to upload information at the customer site, either by dialing up the accounting database through a local phone connection or with cellular phone access. This process is capable of eliminating problems

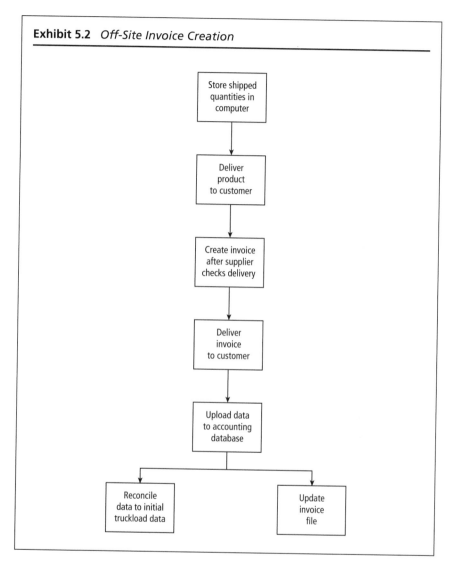

Exhibit 5.2 *Off-Site Invoice Creation*

caused by customer disputes over delivered quantities, resulting in less work for the accounting staff.

Although a technologically elegant solution, this best practice applies only to a small number of companies meeting specific criteria. First, a company must make deliveries with its own staff; a third-party delivery service will not perform the on-site invoicing function. Next, this solution requires a good knowledge of computer systems to implement. There must be not only a qualified and knowledgeable in-house computer systems department, but also one with the budget to create such a system. Also, this solution is expensive to implement (if only because every driver must be furnished with a computer and printer), so there must be a clear trade-off between the implementation and capital cost of the system and benefits from reduced accounting staff labor. These criteria tend to point toward only larger companies making frequent deliveries to many customers.

Cost: 💵 💵 💵   *Installation time:* ⏰ ⏰ ⏰

5.7 Have Delivery Person Deliver the Invoice

It may be possible to have the delivery person hand-carry the invoice at the time of delivery to the customer's accounts payable department. By doing so, a company can compress the mail time that would otherwise be required to get an invoice to a customer and ensure that the invoice is delivered directly into the hands of the person who is responsible for paying it. Thus, direct delivery of an invoice carries with it the advantages of reducing the total transaction time, while also ensuring that the invoice is not lost in transit.

Having the delivery person deliver the invoice works only in a small number of situations, however. The key element is that a company must make deliveries with its own personnel; if not, a third-party delivery person will not hand-carry an invoice, which makes this best practice impossible to implement. Also, the accounting department and the shipping dock must be closely linked, so that invoices are prepared slightly in advance of shipment and sent to the delivery person at the time of shipment. In addition, a customer may not allow delivery personnel to have access to the accounting department, resulting in the delivery of the invoice to the customer's front desk, which may result in a delayed or incorrect delivery to the accounting department. Finally, there may be a problem with creating invoices slightly in advance of shipment: what if the invoice is created but the shipment never leaves the dock? The invoice must then be credited out of the computer system, which adds an unneeded step to the invoicing process. Consequently, given the number of problems with this best practice, it is best used in only a few situations, where a company has its own delivery staff and the accounting department can efficiently produce accurate invoices either in advance of, or at the time of, shipment.

Although there seem to be many obstacles to this best practice, it can work well in one scenario: If the shipping dock has a computer terminal and printer, it may be possible to create an invoice at the dock as soon as a delivery is ready for shipment. This alternative keeps the accounting staff from having to be involved in the invoicing process and keeps invoices from being produced by mistake when a delivery is not actually ready for shipment. This alternative requires a modification to the accounting system, so that invoices can be produced singly, rather than in batches, which is the customer mode of invoice creation. The shipping staff must also be given permission to create invoices in the computer system and must be thoroughly trained in how to do so. If these problems can be overcome, an incremental increase in the level of technology used at the shipping dock can make this best practice a viable alternative.

Cost: *Installation time:* 🕧

5.8 E-Mail Invoices in Acrobat Format

It can be extremely difficult to obtain payment for some invoices. This problem usually arises when the approval of a specific individual at a customer is required, and that person is either rarely available or so disorganized that the paperwork invariably disappears. Traditional approaches have been to attempt routing an invoice around the person in question, repeatedly mailing or faxing copies of the invoice, or e-mailing reminders at regular intervals. Despite the variety of possible actions, this situation can become a frustrating impasse that may take months to resolve.

Of the approaches just noted, the one that works best is a reminder e-mail to the approving party, because that person can simply forward the e-mail to the accounting department with a note asking to expedite the payment. However, the problem with e-mails is that a perfect copy of the invoice cannot be included with the e-mail message, which could otherwise be forwarded straight to the accounting department with an approval notation by the approving party. Another problem is that the approving party may not have seen the invoice, and so may claim that he or she cannot approve it.

Adobe's Acrobat software has eliminated these problems by creating a perfect copy of an invoice as printed by any accounting system into a portable document format (PDF) file that can be attached to an e-mail and forwarded straight to a customer's accounting department, where it can be opened, printed, and paid. By using this approach, one can create a completely electronic methodology for obtaining approval of invoices by customers.

Implementing the conversion of invoices into the Acrobat format is simple. First go to the Adobe Web site (*www.adobe.com*) to order the Acrobat software, and pay the fee to either download it or have a copy shipped to you on CD. Once the software is received and installed, go to your accounting software package and prepare to print an invoice. When the printing screen appears, change the assigned printer to the Acrobat Distiller, which will appear as one of the available printers. The software will ask you where to store the resulting file and what to name it. After a few seconds, the conversion of the invoice into a picture-perfect PDF file will be complete.

The resulting PDF file can be easily incorporated into an e-mail message as a file attachment. However, do not assume that the recipient of the message has Adobe's Acrobat Reader software available to open and view the invoice file. Instead, add a line in your e-mail message, noting where the recipient can download a free copy of the software. A sample message might read as follows:

> I have not yet received payment for our invoice number 4762 for $12,500, dated April 12. It is somewhat overdue for payment. For your convenience, I have attached a PDF version of the invoice, which you may review with Adobe's Acrobat Reader software. If you don't already have this software, you can download it for free at *www.adobe.com*. Please contact me if you have any questions. Thanks!

Converting invoices to the PDF format can accelerate the receipt of cash from customers, reduce the collection efforts of the accounting staff, and allow customers to approve invoices electronically. This is a significant, inexpensive, and operationally elegant way to accelerate cash flow.

Cost: *Installation time:*

5.9 Issue Electronic Invoices through the Internet

The traditional invoicing process is extraordinarily wasteful in terms of the effort and time that goes into creating and issuing an invoice. It must be created and inserted into an invoice-printing batch, which in turn requires the use of a customized invoice with prepositioned fields and logos, plus a review of the printed invoices, stuffing into envelopes, affixing postage, and mailing. Even then, the invoice can be lost in the mail, either because of a problem at the post office or because the recipient's address has changed. Furthermore, there are delays at the receiving company, while the mailroom sorts through the mail and delivers it internally (sometimes to the wrong person).

Some of these problems can be avoided through the use of e-mailed billings that are delivered through the Internet. There are several ways to complete this task. The least recommended approach is to post the invoices on a company's own Web site. This means that customers can access the company's credit card payment system at the same time they access their invoices, which results in accounts receivable that are collected with inordinate speed. However, this approach requires customers to access the company's Web site in order to find their invoices, which they are not likely to do (especially because this will result in their immediate use of funds to pay for the invoice). In addition, this approach requires an interface between the accounting database and the Web site, so that invoices are posted regularly to the Web site. Furthermore, there may be a need to create user identification numbers and passwords, so that customers can access their invoices (otherwise they would be viewable by *all* visitors to the Web site). Also, if customers forget their access codes, there must be an internal customer service function that can assist them with this information, and this involves additional personnel costs to maintain.

A better approach is to "push" electronic invoices to customers by e-mail. This requires the collection of an e-mail address from each customer at the time an order is taken (or verification of an existing one when a reorder occurs). This address is then attached to an electronic invoice form that is generated instead of a paper-based invoice and issued to the customer over the Internet. This invoice is then available to the customer a few moments later, allowing for immediate payment (possibly) or at least a quick perusal of the invoice and a return of information to the company regarding any problems discovered by the customer. This approach greatly reduces the time required to get invoicing information to the customer.

Internet invoicing has several problems, however. First, some customers change their e-mail addresses regularly, so invoices may be sent to an old address, and therefore never accessed. Also, customers may accidentally erase an incoming electronic invoice without reviewing it. Furthermore, this approach leaves no paper record of the invoice at the company, just a computer record; this is a problem in those organizations where the collections effort is primarily based on paper files, rather than ready access to the accounting database.

Another issue is creating the software that will in turn create an invoice (either text-based or using the industry-standard PDF promulgated by Adobe) and then send it to an e-mail address. This programming effort can be significant if done internally and runs the additional risk of being wiped out if the attached packaged accounting software is upgraded, which may destroy or alter some of the software linkages to which the custom software is attached. Fortunately, several accounting software providers are now adding this feature to their accounting systems, so that internal programming can be avoided.

Some of the problems with e-mailed invoices can be addressed through the careful analysis of which customers reliably pay their invoices by this means and (more important) which do not. If there is a consistent problem with payment by some customers, they can be flagged in the accounting database, and a traditional paper-based invoice can be created for them. Alternately, the same invoices can be continually reissued every week or two by e-mail. This is a zero-cost option, because no mailing or printing costs are incurred. When using this approach, the entire file of unpaid invoices can be reissued electronically to customers. To avoid multiple payments for the same invoices, however, it may be useful to alter the format of these secondary issuances, so that they are clearly labeled as reminder invoices. An alternative format is to cluster all unpaid invoices for each customer into an electronic statement of unpaid invoices, which can be issued at regular intervals.

The use of direct e-mails to customers is particularly enticing, not from an accounting perspective, but from a marketing view. A complete list of customer e-mail addresses allows one to send sales, marketing, and customer service information to a company's entire mailing list at the touch of a button and with no associated distribution cost whatsoever.

A final variation on the use of electronic invoices through the Internet is the use of a consolidator. This entity maintains a Web site that allows a company's customers to access not only its billings, but those of their other customers, too. This approach has the distinct advantage of allowing customers to pay several different bills at the same time, without switching to different Web sites in order to do so. Examples of these consolidators are Checkfree, Transpoint, Speedpay, Derivion, and Microvault.

A company that wishes to have its invoices posted on a consolidator's Web site must create a data file that reformats the invoice information into the format needed by the consolidator, and then send this file (over the Internet) to the consolidator, which then posts the information. Customers then access their invoices in a summary format, which are clustered together for all of their suppliers, and either accept or reject them for payment; if there is a problem, customers can access greater levels of detail for each invoice, and usually access an e-mail account that will be sent to the company's customer service department.

The cost of this service varies considerably by consolidator, with some charging the customer, some the company, and some charging both. It is best to refer to the fee schedule of each one to determine the precise amounts. The fees charged to a company are not excessive and should not limit adoption of this option.

The main problem with using a consolidator is that not all customers will want to use the one that the company prefers to send its invoicing information to, because they may have already set up payment plans with many of their other suppliers through different consolidators. Accordingly, a company may have to issue invoice files to a large number of consolidators, which presents additional work for the person reformatting the invoice file.

The most common of these electronic invoicing options is bill posting on a company's own Web site, because it is the simplest. However, with the growing use of invoice consolidators by customers, the issuance of invoices through this medium, in addition to their posting on a company-owned Web site, is a reasonable alternative. These are not mutually exclusive options.

Cost: 🏷️🏷️   Installation time: ⏰ ⏰

5.10 Transmit Transactions Via Electronic Data Interchange

Sending an invoice to a customer requires some labor, cost, and time, but does not guarantee that the invoice will be paid. For example, someone must print an invoice, separate the copy going to the customer, stuff it into an envelope, and mail it, which may then take several days to reach the customer, be routed through its mailroom, reach the accounts payable department, and be entered into the customer's computer system (where the data may be scrambled as a result of keypunching errors). The invoice may even be lost at the customer site and never entered into the computer system for payment at all.

To avoid all of these issues, a company can use electronic data interchange (EDI). Under this approach, a company's computer system automatically issues an electronic invoice that is set up in a standard format (as defined by an international standard-setting organization) and transmits it to a third-party mainframe computer, where it is left in an electronic mailbox. The customer's computer automatically polls this mailbox several times a day and extracts the electronic invoice information. Once received, the format is automatically translated into the invoice format used by the recipient's computer and stored in the accounting system's database for payment. At no time does anyone have to manually handle the data, which eliminates the risk of lost or erroneous invoicing data. This approach is excellent for those companies that can afford to invest in setting up EDI with their customers, because it fully automates several invoicing steps, resulting in a high degree of efficiency and reliability.

There are several problems with EDI that keep most smaller companies from using it, however, especially if they have many low-volume customer accounts. The main problem is that it takes time and persuasion to get a customer to agree to use EDI as the basis for receiving invoices. This may take several trips to each customer, including time to send trial transmissions to the customer's computer to ensure that the system works properly. To do this with a large number of low-volume customers is not cost-effective, so the practice is generally confined to companies with high-volume customers, involving a great many invoices, so the investment by both parties pays off fairly quickly.

The other problem is that the most efficient EDI systems require some automation. A standard EDI system requires one to manually enter all transactions, as well as manually extract them from the EDI mailbox and keypunch them into the receiving computer. To fully automate the system, a company must have its software engineers program an interface between the accounting computer system and the EDI system, which can be an expensive undertaking. Without the interface, an EDI system is really nothing more than an expensive fax machine. Thus, installing a fully operational EDI system is usually limited to transactions with high-volume customers and requires a considerable programming expense to achieve full automation.

Cost: 💸 💸 💸   *Installation time:* ⏰ ⏰ ⏰

6

Cash Collection and Application

This chapter contains 11 best practices related to cash collection and application. The first two involve the personal approach to collection—going to the customer location and personally picking up the check. The next four best practices dwell on lockboxes—their general use, periodically reviewing their locations, and accessing information from them. We then shift to several miscellaneous methods to retrieve customer payments as soon as possible—either with overnight deliveries, credit card payments, or via payments over the Internet. Finally, we look at cash application—both the process and the danger of cashing checks containing restrictive endorsements. These best practices are summarized in Exhibit 6.1.

Exhibit 6.1 *Summary of Cash Simplification and Application Best Practices*

6.1 Have a salesperson pick up the check in person

6.2 Send a messenger to pick up the check

6.3 Institute lockbox collections

6.4 Install a lockbox truncation system

6.5 Periodically review lockbox locations

6.6 Access online check images from a lockbox

6.7 Issue the corporate overnight delivery account number to customers

6.8 Accept credit card payments

6.9 Offer customers secure Internet payment options

6.10 Conduct immediate review of unapplied cash

6.11 Review restrictive endorsements before cashing checks

6.1 Have a Salesperson Pick Up the Check in Person

Some companies have a large and active staff of salespeople who constantly visit customers, perhaps as much as on a weekly basis. They usually have a relationship only with their purchasing counterparts and have little interaction with the customer's accounts payable staff. As a result, the collections staff must try to collect long-distance even though the company has a personal representative on-site at regular intervals.

A solution that is helpful in limited situations is for the salesperson to pick up the check in person. This approach can reduce the payment interval somewhat, but the main point is the psychological impact on the customer, who realizes that the company, personified by the salesperson, is going to walk into his or her office regularly and ask to be paid. Such a direct approach is sufficiently rare to make a customer want to pay right on time.

This best practice works only if the sales staff visits customers regularly, so picking up a check does not take them out of their way; their primary function is to sell, not move paper from Point A to Point B. To make this approach more effective, consider e-mailing the accounts receivable aging report to each salesperson, so they know when invoices are coming due for payment. Furthermore, send the sales staff the name of the accounts payable clerk who normally cuts checks, so they will be more comfortable navigating through the accounting department to the correct person. Also, the sales staff does not have to physically carry payments back to the company's accounting department; dropping it into a mailbox and letting the collections staff know the payment is in the mail will be sufficient.

Cost: Installation time: 🕑

6.2 Send a Messenger to Pick Up the Check

Customers who are trying to delay a payment will try every trick to keep from putting a check in the mail. This is most frustrating for the collections staff, which is never entirely certain when a payment will arrive, if ever. A solution is to tell the customer that a messenger will be there today to pick up the check in person. This approach is sometimes worth it just to hear that moment of silence while the customer realizes that the bluff has been called!

There is a downside, however—cost. Messenger services are available in every major city, but their fees can be substantial if they must send someone a fair distance outside the local metropolitan area to make a pickup. Consequently, a company should call up a customer's location on an Internet search engine such as Mapquest or Yahoo to verify the location before engaging the services of a messenger. Also, the customer may attempt a last-minute delay and keep the messenger waiting on-site for a long time, which will increase the messenger service's fee to the company.

Cost: *Installation time:* 🕰

6.3 Institute Lockbox Collections

Customers sometimes have difficulty in sending their payments to the correct address; they send them to the attention of someone they know at a company, such as a salesperson, or they send it to the wrong company location. Even if customers do send a payment to the correct company location, sometimes the mailroom personnel mistakenly direct it to the wrong department, where it languishes for a few days until it is rerouted to the correct person. Finally, even if the payment goes to the correct person in the correct department, that person may not be available for a few days, perhaps because of sickness or vacation. In all of these instances, there is a delay in cashing checks and, more important from a collections standpoint, there is a delay in applying checks to open accounts receivable. When this delay occurs, the collections staff may make unnecessary phone calls to customers who have already paid, which is a waste of time. How can one eliminate this problem?

The easiest method for consolidating all incoming payments is to have them sent to a lockbox, which is a mailbox maintained by the company's bank. The bank opens all incoming envelopes, cashes all checks contained therein, and forwards copies of the checks to a single individual at the company. The advantage of this approach is that if all customers are properly notified of the address, all checks will unerringly go to one location, where they are consolidated into a single packet and forwarded to the cash application person at the company. By sending a single packet of each day's receipts to a single person, it is much easier to ensure that the packet is routed to the correct person for immediate application.

There are two disadvantages to be considered. One is the one-day delay in routing checks through a lockbox, which translates into a one-day delay in applying the cash. The other problem is that all customers must be notified of the change to the lockbox address, which usually requires several follow-up contacts with a few customers who continue to send their payments to the wrong address. Despite these restrictions, a collections staff suffering from mislaid check payments should seriously consider switching to a lockbox solution.

Cost: *Installation time:* 🕐 🕐

6.4 Install a Lockbox Truncation System

What if checks come directly to a company, despite all efforts to have customers send them to a lockbox? Customers sometimes ignore lockbox instructions because they know there is some additional float time while the checks wend their way through the company and from there to the local bank. Also, depending on the check processing speed of the local bank, several additional days may be added to the float time. This can add up to substantial dollars of lost interest expense as well as reduced cash flow.

A solution is to use lockbox truncation. This is the process of converting a paper check into an electronic deposit. The basic process is to scan a check into a check reader, which scans the magnetic ink characters on the check into a vendor-supplied software package. The software sends this information to a third-party Automated Clearing House (ACH) Network processor, which typically clears payment in one or two days. The system has the additional benefit of eliminating deposit slips and the per-transaction deposit fees usually charged by banks. Also, not sufficient funds (NSF) fees are lower than if a regular check payment had been made, while NSFs can be redeposited at once. An additional benefit of lockbox truncation is the handling of NSF checks. If such a check is returned by the bank, one can scan that check into the truncation system as well for processing through the ACH system.

A third use of lockbox truncation is to enter into the system check information given to the company over the phone or fax by a customer. Rather than use the check scanner, one can manually punch in the information. This approach avoids the age-old "check is in the mail" excuse. This service is offered by several suppliers who charge a transaction fee for it. For more information, access *www.encorefinancial.com*, *www.acheftproviders.com*, and *www.bizcashflow.com*.

Cost: *Installation time:* 🕐

6.5 Periodically Review Lockbox Locations

Although having one or more lockboxes in place will eliminate some of the issues noted in the last best practice, the lockbox locations will become out of date as customer locations change. For example, if a company with its accounting headquarters in Kansas City sets up a lockbox on the West Coast to service the bulk of its customers, this does little good when a geographic expansion to the East Coast results in all of the East Coast checks being sent to the West Coast lockbox, thereby lengthening the mail float before the company receives its cash. The solution is a periodic review of lockbox locations. A company can conduct a simple lockbox review by comparing customer locations to the nearest lockbox locations. Banks also offer this service.

This best practice can result in several issues. One is that a company may be forced to switch from a local bank it may have been using for years to a larger bank with a greater geographic distribution, just to obtain access to a greater range of lockbox locations. One can set up lockboxes through a large number of small banks, but this adds a great deal of complexity to the consolidation of cash from the lockboxes. Another issue is setting up the accounting system to assign a different "remit to" address based on a customer's location. Low-end accounting systems do not always contain this feature, so the use of multiple lockboxes may call for the implementation of a more advanced accounting system. Finally, the periodic change of lockbox locations will require ongoing contacts with customers to inform them of the address changes, inevitably resulting in many repeat contacts before all customers are mailing payments to the new addresses. Given the effort required for this last item, it is unwise to change lockbox locations more than once a year.

Cost: 💵 *Installation time:* 🕐 🕐

6.6 Access Online Check Images from a Lockbox

The typical bank lockbox requires a wait of a few days, during which time the bank assembles all of the checks and related information it receives in the mail and sends the statement via the U.S. Postal Service to the company. The statement then arrives in the corporate mailroom and eventually wends its way through the company to the accounts receivable department, where the checks are applied against invoices in the accounting system. This delay of a few days is irritating for the collections staff, which may be contacting customers about allegedly overdue accounts receivable that have already been received at the lockbox but about which the company is not yet aware.

The answer is to only use lockboxes operated by banks that scan the incoming checks and post the images on secure Web sites. This approach allows the collections staff to access check images immediately after checks arrive at the lockbox. Alternately, the cash application staff accesses the images and records them in the accounting system as having been received, which the collections staff uses for receipt information instead. The only downside to this best practice is the substantially reduced number of lockbox locations available, because only the larger (usually nationwide) and most technologically advanced banks offer this service.

Cost: Installation time: 🕑

6.7 Issue the Corporate Overnight Delivery Account Number to Customers

Sometimes the collections staff identifies a late-paying customer, works with the customer to determine the problem causing the late payment, and gets the customer to agree to a payment—and waits for days while the check meanders through the postal system. If the payment is a large one, the company is losing valuable interest income for every additional day the check is in transit.

A solution is to give the customer the company's account number with an overnight delivery service. Although one might argue that it is the customer's fault that the check is late and so the customer should pay for overnight delivery, the main point is to move the funds to the company as soon as possible. Because overnight delivery by one of the major carriers (e.g., FedEx, Airborne, UPS) will likely cost about $10 to $15, the check must be sufficiently large to offset the delivery cost. For example, if the delivery service costs $15, the company's interest rate on funds invested is 4%, and payment would otherwise take an additional four days to arrive by regular mail. It is therefore cost effective to use this best practice when the check is $34,219 or higher (the calculation is $(($15/(4\% \times 4/365))$).

The only problem with this best practice is when customers continue to use it without authorization. This typically happens when someone inadvertently enters the overnight delivery instructions into the customer's accounting system so that all future payments are dealt with in the same manner. This is still cost effective if future checks are sufficiently large. However, the collections staff should call and ask the accounts payable staff to stop using overnight delivery when smaller checks continue to arrive in this manner.

Cost: Installation time:

6.8 Accept Credit Card Payments

For some companies, the process required to cut a check is so convoluted that many days can pass between the point when a late-payment issue has been cleared up and a check finally arrives in the mail. This problem is common when checks are cut only on a few scheduled days during a month. Even worse is a government entity, for which the payment systems appear to be set up in order to deter all payments.

An alternative is to accept credit card payments, preferably from every major credit card company. By doing so, one can frequently persuade the customer to place payment for smaller amounts on either a corporate or personal credit card and have the money appear in the corporate bank account in one or two business days. The maximum amount customers can charge will vary according to internal customer credit card policy, although somewhere in the range of $1,000 to $2,500 is common.

One downside is the credit card servicing fee charged by the bank, typically resulting in a deduction of 2% to 3%. However, consider this to be the same as offering an early-payment discount; it is equivalent to a 2% discount in exchange for nearly immediate cash. The other problem with accepting credit card payments is the time it can take to set up credit card accounts. Although one can complete the task much sooner if there are no hitches, be sure to allocate one to two months for the setup process.

Cost: *Installation time:* 🕐 🕐

6.9 Offer Customers Secure Internet Payment Options

Many prospective customers are not interested in shopping at a company's Internet store, because they are concerned that their credit card information will either be intercepted at the point when they transmit it to the store or that it will be kept on file by the company, where it may be illegally accessed at any time in the future. As long as credit cards are viewed as the primary form of payment on the Internet, these shoppers will find other channels for buying products and services. However, a company called IPin has created an alternate way to process payments that may attract these additional shoppers.

A company that wants to offer its customers the alternative of being able to pay without the transmission of credit card information can use IPin's service. This service (*www.ipin.com*) allows customers to store their credit card information in a highly secure environment at that Web site in exchange for an IPin identification number, which they can use as a form of payment at selected Web sites (which must set up operating agreements with IPin to use its software to process customer transactions). This approach has the advantage of keeping customer-specific credit card information off the Internet. Also, for those customers who are truly paranoid about leaving their credit card information in the hands of *anyone*, including IPin, it also offers the option of linking customer payments through their IPin identification numbers to the billing statements of selected Internet service providers or the monthly invoices of a customer's phone company or wireless phone company.

This last option also yields the unique benefit of allowing a company to charge its customers for micro-purchases (those purchases of just a few cents), which can be summarized and billed directly to customers. This avoids the use of credit cards, which charge minimum fees (usually 20 cents) for purchases, while also allowing companies access to a new form of revenue—perhaps fees for access to small amounts of data that were previously given away for free.

Cost: *Installation time:* 🕐

6.10 Conduct Immediate Review of Unapplied Cash

A collections person often calls a customer about an overdue account, only to be told that the check was already sent. Upon further investigation the collections staff finds that, for a variety of reasons, the errant check has been sitting in an accounting clerk's inbox for several weeks, waiting to be applied to an invoice in the accounts receivable aging. Common reasons for not performing this cash application include not having enough time, not understanding what the check is intended to pay, or because there are unexplained line items on the payment, such as credits, requiring further investigation before the check can be applied.

None of the reasons for not applying cash are valid, given the consequences of wasting the time of the collections staff. Only two solutions need to be installed to ensure that cash is applied at once. First, cash application is always the highest priority of whomever is responsible for cash applications, thereby avoiding all arguments regarding other items taking priority or not having enough time to complete the task. Second, all cash must be applied, even if it is only to an unapplied cash category in the accounts receivable register for those items that cannot be traced immediately to an open invoice. In these cases, simply having the total of unapplied cash for a customer clearly shown in the aged accounts receivable listing is a clear sign that the customer is correct: it has paid for an invoice and now the collections person knows how to apply the cash that was already received.

Ensuring that cash is applied on time is a key internal auditing task. Without periodic review by a designated auditor, the person in charge of cash applications may become lazy and delay some application work. To avoid this problem, audits must be regularly scheduled and should verify not only that all cash is applied in a timely manner, but also that the amount of cash received each day matches the amount applied. If these controls are rigidly followed, it becomes easy to enforce this most fundamental of best practices.

Cost: *Installation time:* 🕐

6.11 Review Restrictive Endorsements before Cashing Checks

When a customer sends in a check payment with a restrictive endorsement on it, cashing the check may mean that the company agrees with the endorsement, thereby limiting it from collecting additional funds. The most common restrictive endorsement is the words "paid in full," which may leave a company with no legal option to pursue additional payment if it cashes a check with this wording. The problem is compounded when a lockbox is used, because the bank operating the lockbox may have no instructions regarding restrictive endorsements and will automatically cash such checks.

The solution is to create a policy requiring all checks with restrictive endorsements to be pulled from the cash application process and sent to an attorney for an opinion regarding what to do. If checks go through a bank lockbox, send instructions to the bank to forward these checks to the company without cashing them. By doing so, the company has a clear idea of its rights before processing a check. Even if the attorney allows the company to cash a check, the collections staff should send the customer a letter, stating its concern that a restrictive endorsement was added to the check. Furthermore, this sort of behavior by a customer should automatically flag the customer for a credit review, probably resulting in restricted credit terms.

A company may find that certain restrictive endorsement phrases occur repeatedly over time; an attorney can create a standard action list for the company, describing how to process a check when these phrases appear. By doing so, the company can take immediate action on the most common restrictive endorsements, saving it the time and expense of having an attorney review them again.

Cost: 　　　　　　*Installation time:* 🕐

7

Managing the
Collection Department

This chapter contains 28 best practices related to the management of the collection department. There are ten best practices related to the general organization of the department, five concerning communications with either the sales department or customers, seven related to the improvement of departmental efficiencies, and six dealing with miscellaneous topics. These best practices are summarized in Exhibit 7.1.

Although not all of the best practices noted in this chapter will apply to every collection department, a few have nearly universal application. In particular, creating and training collection specialists, rather than assigning the collection task to accountants during their spare time, will vastly improve collection results. Similarly, consider assigning customers to specific collectors, contacting customers only during specific hours, building relationships with customer accounts payable managers, sending the accounts receivable aging to the sales staff, and conducting bad debt postmortem reviews. These changes result in immediate improvements to collection results.

7.1 Create an Integrated Customer Service Department

Several problems arise between the credit, order entry, and collections departments. Although they are all positioned along the process flow of granting and collecting customer credit, they are frequently managed by different functional areas, with credit falling under the Treasury Department, order entry under Sales, and collections under Accounting. Thus, any departmental rivalries are likely to

Exhibit 7.1 *Summary of Collection Management Best Practices*

7.1	Create an integrated customer service department
7.2	Hire a credit and collection manager
7.3	Create collections specialists
7.4	Train the collections staff in collection techniques
7.5	Assign new collectors to payment confirmation tasks
7.6	Assign the best collector to the worst customers
7.7	Clearly define account ownership
7.8	Utilize collection call stratification
7.9	Periodically assign collectors to different territories
7.10	Structure the collections work day around prime calling hours
7.11	Join the sales staff on customer visits
7.12	Maintain an ongoing relationship with customers' payables managers
7.13	Schedule a regular accounts review with key managers
7.14	Meet with the sales staff regularly
7.15	E-mail the accounts receivable aging to the sales staff
7.16	Write off small balances with no approval
7.17	Access customer payment information over the Internet
7.18	Simplify the pricing structure
7.19	Grant percentage discounts for early payment
7.20	Periodically reevaluate the discount percentage offered
7.21	Only pay commissions from cash received
7.22	Route cash-in-advance orders straight to the collections staff
7.23	Conduct bad debt postmortems
7.24	Review confirming purchase orders
7.25	Offer bonuses to the collections staff
7.26	Offer bonuses to the sales staff
7.27	Report on bad debts by salesperson
7.28	Post collection results by collector

be reflected at this level. Also, the simple existence of separate departments calls for paperwork or process flow hand-offs between the departments, which builds in the prospect of longer work queues and translation errors between systems.

An increasingly common solution is to combine all three functions into an integrated customer service department (the exact department name is subject to debate). By moving all three functions under a common management structure, it is far more likely that a single integrated computer system will be used, workflows can be simplified, and problems can be resolved with a minimum of fuss. Furthermore, responses to customer queries will be much faster. It is also common to see multiple functions from all three areas given to individual employees, so they have responsibility for a customer order all the way from initial credit approval to final collection, thereby streamlining systems immensely. Also, addressing dunning letters as being from the "customer service department" (at least initially) may be less threatening than having them sent by the collections department.

The chief difficulty with this approach is politics. Only one department manager will gain by running the entire function, whereas two managers will lose all control over this area. Gaining the acceptance of senior management to the concept is therefore critical to its implementation. Also, there will be a question regarding which department gains control over this new group. The less-likely choice is the sales manager, because this person has a conflict of interest in managing both sales and credit. A better alternative is either the controller or CFO, because these individuals are experienced in systems management and are more likely to have an objective view of the credit granting process.

Cost: *Installation time:* 🕑 🕑 🕑

7.2 Hire a Credit and Collection Manager

Even with people specializing in nothing but credit and collections, the controller or treasurer rarely has time to allocate work among them, determine and enforce credit policies, or handle daily relations with the sales staff. This last point is the most important, because the sales staff will determine which person is the easiest on credit and collection terms and come to that person with their requests, thereby creating a looser credit environment than management may have intended.

The solution is to hire a credit and collection manager. If this person is solely responsible for the credit function, then key job tasks will be creating a credit policy, obtaining its approval by management, and enforcing its use consistently, as well as conducting standard management of the function. If responsibilities extend to collections, then a great deal can be done to standardize the manner of customer contact, determining the timing of enhanced collection activities, selecting when to turn over accounts to collection agencies, and when to initiate legal proceedings. The job description of a credit and collection manager should include the following tasks:

- Creates, updates, and enforces credit policies and procedures
- Trains the staff in departmental procedures
- Creates and updates a credit scoring model for granting credit
- Approves credit levels for the largest customers
- Reviews staff performance
- Communicates regularly with counterparts in the sales, accounting, and customer service departments
- Selects and manages relations with collection agencies and attorneys
- Approves and monitors the installation of various departmental best practices
- Monitors the use of collection techniques on customers

This position may be filled from the ranks of the collections staff, but it is best to find someone with specific management training, as well as the force of personality to deal with other department managers; this person needs to be comfortable with both making and defending difficult decisions on a daily basis. Clearly, a small company probably cannot afford such a position. If so, do not leave the management tasks with one of the clerical staff. Instead, make sure that someone with sufficient management skill, such as an assistant controller, takes on the position until further company growth warrants the hiring of a full-time credit and collection manager.

 Cost:　　　　　　Installation time:

7.3 Create Collections Specialists

In smaller companies, the problem with late payments on receivables is not necessarily the customers. The cause of many late payments is that customers never received invoices, they are waiting for responses on issues, or they made an incorrect payment and have no idea that an outstanding balance exists. Even when the problem lies with the customer, frequently no organized attempt is made to collect funds. Instead, collection contacts are made only when someone has a few spare moments of free time. Also, because the collections task is sometimes considered to be menial or uncomfortable labor, the accounting staff tends to shirk this work.

The solution is to create specialized collection positions. By doing so, there is no question about who is supposed to contact customers to resolve issues. Also, a focused collections person can readily follow up on hanging issues that would likely be dropped entirely if no one were responsible for collections. In small companies that cannot afford a separate collections person, the solution is to allocate a portion of every day (typically early in the morning, so there is no avoiding the task) to collections, and preferably have the same person do the work every day, so there is continuity in the function. Also, assign a high performance score to the successful completion of collections tasks, so those employees tasked with collections will know that a significant part of their performance will be based on collections. One can also consider paying small bonuses for personnel who bring in exceptionally large or old invoices, so there is an added incentive to complete collections work.

This may seem like an obvious best practice, but the author has repeatedly found that the single most important reason for old receivable balances is that no one is consistently contacting customers.

Cost: *Installation time:*

7.4 Train the Collections Staff in Collection Techniques

The collections department suffers from one of the highest turnover levels in any company. A key underlying cause of turnover is that new employees are thrust into the position with minimal training and are expected to achieve a respectable rate of cash recovery right away. If they do not, they are fired for lack of performance or become so frustrated that they quit. A select few will learn collection techniques on their own and become good collectors, but the department will churn through an extraordinary number of new employees to find these few keepers.

A solution is to require all new employees to attend a collections training class. This can be an in-house program or one taught by a third party. If the resources are available, an intensive in-house program is best, because the trainer can cover those collection techniques that have worked best with the company's customers. The trainer can also discuss the company's most common invoicing errors requiring resolution by the collection team, the types of products sold, and even identify in advance those customers who are most liable to pay late and their stated reasons for doing so. An outside training class cannot offer all of these specialized tidbits of knowledge and so is of less use. Nonetheless, if no other training is available, sending new staff to a generalized collections class is still of considerable help. Also consider refresher training, especially for those employees who are not performing well over time.

Of all the billing, credit, and collections functions noted in this book, training in the collections area is by far the most important one to address.

Cost: 💵 💵   *Installation time:* ⏰ ⏰

7.5 Assign New Collectors to Payment Confirmation Tasks

Breaking in new collectors in such a manner as to keep them from quitting is a difficult process. If immediately handed a block of customers to manage, new collectors may initially have difficulty making collections without any personal knowledge of customers, how customers process payments, or what problems lead to late payments. Although intensive training and role-playing can reduce this initial level of tension, being thrown into the collections fray can still be quite a shock.

An alternative is to break the collections process into two pieces: (1) initial contacts before the invoice due date and (2) more intensive collection efforts after that date. New collectors can spend their first few weeks or months doing nothing but making initial customer contacts to confirm that invoices have been received and asking what other information customers may need for payment. This serves the triple function of putting new collectors in a stress-free initial contact mode, allowing them time to talk to their future customer contacts, and familiarizing them with customer payment systems. Furthermore, it makes the collection job easier for the more experienced collectors who make a second contact once payments become overdue.

Cost: 💵   *Installation time:*

7.6 Assign the Best Collector to the Worst Customers

The typical assignment of overdue customer accounts to the collections staff is basic: Customer names beginning with A through D go to collector Smith, E through H to collector Jones, and so on. Although this approach to handing off work may seem fair and equitable, what if the most difficult customers are all lumped into one cluster of collection assignments? When the distribution of difficult customers does not match the method of job assignment or (more commonly) the skill level of collectors does not match the customers to whom they are assigned, a company will find that its collections are not overly efficient.

One solution is to measure the collection staff's performance to determine which ones are the top performers, and then assign them the most difficult customers. By doing so, the company orients its collection resources in the most targeted manner to achieve the highest possible collection percentage. This best practice works best when the collections manager periodically reviews the open accounts receivable list to determine which customers have risen into the corporate equivalent of the Ten Most Wanted. This list is likely to experience a great deal of turnover, because good collectors focus on the underlying problems causing collection difficulties and can sometimes eliminate collection problems entirely.

This approach does not work well if a bonus system is in place for rewarding high collection rates, however, because the best collectors will not respond well to being assigned customers for which the collections task is likely to be a considerable chore. An alternative approach is to create some degree of esprit de corps by giving higher base pay to the top collectors and celebrating their entry into the top cadre of collection staff.

Cost: Installation time: 🕑

7.7 Clearly Define Account Ownership

The sales staff is frequently unwilling to make collection calls on behalf of the accounting staff, because this task takes away from their time in making new sales. However, the best contact with the customer is the salesperson, who has probably met with the customer multiple times and has built up a firm relationship, thereby making the salesperson the most effective collections person a company has available.

To improve the collections process, a company should clearly define who "owns" each customer account and assign collection responsibility to the salesperson who has been given account ownership. "Ownership" means that the salesperson's name or sales region number should be included in the accounting database for each customer name. This does not mean that the bulk of the sales staff's job is now collections, but rather that the accounting department's collections staff can now call on specific individuals in the sales department when they feel that payment on an invoice will not otherwise be collected. To enhance the cooperation of the sales staff in the enforcement of collections, the compensation of the sales department manager should be tied to the proportion of cash collected from customers, which will entice this person to force the cooperation of his or her staff with the accounting department.

This concept should also be extended to the collections staff. Specific customer issues are usually associated with nonpayment of an invoice, which must be repetitively researched if a collection problem is circulated throughout the collection staff. A better approach is to assign customer accounts to specific collections personnel. By doing so, they gain an understanding of each customer's particular issues and have a chance to build relationships with their accounts payable counterparts at the customers' offices, which frequently results in faster resolution of issues and therefore quicker payment by customers.

Cost: 💰   *Installation time:* 🕐

7.8 Utilize Collection Call Stratification

The typical list of overdue invoices is so long that the existing collections staff cannot possibly contact all customers about all invoices on a sufficiently frequent basis. This problem results in many invoices not being collected for an inordinately long time. Additional problems requiring time-consuming research include incorrect product prices, missing shipping documentation, or a claim that the quantity billed is incorrect. Consequently, correction problems linger longer than they should, resulting in slow collections and substandard cash flow.

A good approach for improving the speed of cash collection is to utilize collection call stratification. The concept behind this approach is to split up, or stratify, all of the overdue receivables and concentrate the bulk of the collection staff's time on the largest invoices. By doing so, a company can realize improved cash flow by collecting the largest dollar amounts sooner. The downside of this method is that smaller invoices will receive less attention and therefore take longer to collect, but this shortcoming is reasonable if the overall cash flow from using stratified collections is improved. To implement it, one should perform a Pareto analysis of a typical accounts receivable listing and determine the cutoff point above which 20% of all invoices will constitute 80% of the total revenue. For example, a cut-off point of $1,000 means that any invoice of more than $1,000 is in the group of invoices representing the bulk of a company's revenue. When it is necessary to contact customers about collection issues, a much higher number of customer contacts can be assigned for the invoices over $1,000. For example, a collections staff member can be required to contact customers about all high-dollar invoices once every three days, whereas low-dollar contacts can be limited to once every two weeks. By allocating the time of the collections staff in this manner, it is possible to collect overdue invoices more rapidly.

The stratification approach can also be expanded to include other members of a company. If an extremely large invoice must be collected at once, the collections staff can be authorized to request the services of other departments, such as the sales staff, in making the collection. This approach needs to be limited to large-dollar invoices, because the sales staff does not want to make collection calls all day. However, using the stratification approach, it is reasonable to request their assistance in collecting the largest invoices. This approach is effective for accelerating the collection of large overdue accounts.

Cost: *Installation time:* 🕐

7.9 Periodically Assign Collectors to Different Territories

Collections personnel can become too familiar with a long-standing set of customers. They may have met the customers, talked to them for years, and thus identified themselves so well with customer problems that they gradually allow the customers more slack in making payments. The result is a trade-off between improved customer relations and a larger outstanding accounts receivable balance.

A possible solution is to periodically assign collectors to different territories. Not only does this approach allow collectors to more firmly identify themselves with the company instead of customers, but the collections manager can also mandate new collection terms whenever the change is made. For example, a new collector can be told that only three days' grace period will be allowed before collection activity begins, whereas the former collector may have been allowed seven days. Thus, a changing of the guard allows a company to also modify its collection techniques.

The main problem with reassigning collectors is the resulting loss of experience with customers. However, by physically positioning the new and old collectors near each other, they can still swap information about the characteristics of each customer. Alternately, if a collections database is used, collectors can enter key customer information and tips into it for their replacements to see.

Cost: Installation time:

7.10 Structure the Collections Work Day around Prime Calling Hours

The prime calling hours for most business customers are in the early to midmorning, before they have been called away for meetings or other activities. If customers are concentrated in a single time zone, this can mean that the time period available for calls is extremely short and is a particular problem if the collections staff is not prepared to call customers during that time period. Also, if the customer base spans multiple time zones, a collections staff based in one time zone may be making calls to customers that are outside the customers' prime calling hours, resulting in few completed calls.

Awareness of prime calling hours for individual customers is key. The collections manager should avoid attending any meetings during prime calling hours, instead focusing on having the collections staff fully prepared to make calls, with all required information close at hand. Furthermore, the rest of the organization should be made aware of this time block and be asked to avoid contact with the collections department during that period. In addition, the collections manager should require a collections work day that is built around prime calling hours. For example, if the collections staff is based on the West Coast but most of its customer contacts are on the East Coast, its work day should begin very early to make up for the three-hour time difference.

The collections staff should be aware of the time zone they are calling before making the call, so they do not inadvertently place calls outside a customer's prime calling hours. To be even more precise, it may be useful to record the exact time when a customer answers the phone, thereby establishing when that person may be available again for future calls.

Most of these recommendations are simple, requiring only changes to the collection staff's schedule. The use of a computer system to track times when customers answer the phone, or to set up a calling queue based on customer time zones, can be substantially more expensive, but this process can begin with simple paper-based systems.

Cost: 　　　　　　　*Installation time:* 🕐

7.11 Join the Sales Staff on Customer Visits

A wily customer can play off the sales staff against the credit and collections department, knowing the conflicting goals of these two functional areas. This game typically involves hanging a large order in front of a salesperson, if only the salesperson could intercede on behalf of the customer with the credit department, which may not grant credit for such a large order. This approach works well for multitudes of customers, resulting in far more bad debts or delayed payment situations than would normally be the case.

A solution is to occasionally have the credit manager or senior credit staff join salespeople in visiting customers. By doing so, the company presents a united front to customers, who realize there will be few ways to get around two departments that obviously have excellent lines of communication. This best practice can significantly reduce collection problems. In addition, the credit manager, salesperson, and customer can jointly develop imaginative ways for the company to still accept large orders while keeping credit risk within a tolerable range. Because these discussions are face-to-face, the interchange of information tends to go faster, resulting in quick resolution of credit issues that might otherwise take days to complete.

In order to present a united front to a customer, be sure to discuss in advance with the salesperson the nature of your meeting objectives and settle any differences before going into the meeting. Otherwise, the salesperson may begin defending the customer during the meeting.

This best practice may require considerable travel, so the credit manager should restrict visits to major customers or those requesting unusually large amounts of credit. Also, do not send junior credit personnel on these visits without accompanying senior credit employees because junior personnel probably do not have sufficient experience to effectively bargain on the company's behalf in creating credit terms.

Cost: 💵 💵   *Installation time:* ⏰ ⏰

7.12 Maintain an Ongoing Relationship with Customers' Payables Managers

Customer contact is usually only initiated by an overdue invoice. The collections staff calls with the usual request for payment and must deal with an accounts payable clerk who hears the same request all the time. The result? The payment request is relegated to the payables clerk's inbox, where it may remain for some time.

A better approach for some situations is to develop a continual relationship with the customer's accounts payable manager. If the customer is located nearby, this can involve a meeting or a phone call for more distant customers. Almost any excuse can be used to arrange a meeting—discussion of payment terms, a new invoicing format, or a change in company address. The main point to is build a friendly relationship that one can occasionally use to ensure intervention on the company's behalf by the payables manager, resulting in more rapid payment.

If the company has many customers, it is not cost effective to build up relations with all of these payables managers. Instead, limit relation-building to the largest customers. Also, do not call on these contacts all the time, because continual requests for assistance will wear out one's welcome. Instead, make contact only when significant collection issues are involved.

Cost: 💵   *Installation time:* ⏰ ⏰

7.13 Schedule a Regular Accounts Review with Key Managers

The collections department is usually squirreled away in a far corner of the accounting or credit department and is rarely heard from. They quietly collect overdue receivables and only make a noise when they require assistance in this task. Unfortunately, this also means that other parts of the company have no insight into the creditworthiness of their customers and may continue marketing and selling to customers from whom funds are collected only with the greatest difficulty.

The good solution is for the collections manager to regularly schedule a meeting with the managers of other departments who need first-hand knowledge about the ability of customers to pay. This group should include either the controller or CFO, the sales manager, and the marketing manager. If the credit department is separate from collections, then the credit manager should attend, too. The topic of this meeting should be collection problems encountered since the last meeting, ongoing trends in collection issues, and upcoming problems of which the other departments should be aware. Given the type of information imparted, a monthly meeting for an hour or less should be sufficient.

An interesting improvement on this concept is to have the cost accounting staff prepare a cost analysis by customer, factoring in collection costs, so the other departments can see which customers are the most profitable (or not) and structure their sales, credit, and marketing activities accordingly.

Cost: Installation time: 🕐

7.14 Meet with the Sales Staff Regularly

The sales staff and credit and collection employees must sometimes wonder if they work for the same company. The sales staff sees itself as trying to bring in new orders to bolster company revenues and market share, while the credit and collections people do not like the burden of having to collect on overdue invoices from some of the less creditworthy customers brought in by the sales staff. Thus, it is not uncommon to see a considerable amount of bad feeling between these groups.

Although some tension is always likely to exist between the sales and credit organizations, one can at least try to make the two groups see each others' viewpoints by fostering regular communications, which can take a variety of forms. One option is to have representatives of each department present to or at least attend the regular meetings of their counterparts. Another option, which is especially useful for wide-ranging sales forces, is to include the credit staff in periodic conference calls with the sales staff. Any of these approaches is especially useful when the company has a change in credit policy, so the staff will be aware of its impact on them as soon as possible. Other potential topics of conversation include descriptions of the credit and collection procedures used, whom to contact within each department about a variety of issues, and having open discussions about prospective changes within each department that may affect the other group. Although these extra communication efforts will take some time out of everyone's busy schedules, the pay-off in improved communications between the departments is well worth the effort.

Cost: Installation time:

7.15 E-Mail the Accounts Receivable Aging to the Sales Staff

The sales staff rarely has any idea of the payment status of their customers. Instead, the collections staff only calls on salespeople after they have already spent a considerable amount of time on collection efforts. Although this approach keeps the sales staff occupied with making new sales, the company incurs the interest cost associated with late payments.

A better approach is to e-mail the accounts receivable aging report directly to the sales staff, so they can quickly ascertain the payment status of their customers. This is easily done in most commercially available accounting software packages by converting the aging report to Microsoft Excel, sorting the report by salesperson, and issuing the file as an e-mail attachment. Because most salespeople have Excel on their computers, they can easily call up the report, spot impending late-payment situations, and take action before accounts become so old that collection becomes problematic. This best practice is also an excellent communications tool that gives the accounting staff an opportunity to share information with the sales staff.

The main problem with this best practice is ensuring that the sales staff has computers on which to access the information, as well as network or Internet access over which they can download the information. Even if some salespeople have no computers, rolling out this best practice to those salespeople who do should have a noticeable impact on the timeliness of cash collections.

Cost: Installation time:

7.16 Write Off Small Balances with No Approval

The typical procedure for writing off a bad debt is for a collections person to write up a bad debt approval form, including an explanation of why an account receivable is not collectible, which the controller must then review and sign. The form is filed away, possibly for future review by auditors. This can be a time-consuming process, but it is a necessary one if the amount of the bad debt is large. However, some bad debts are so small that the cost of completing the associated paperwork exceeds the bad debt.

The obvious solution is to eliminate approvals for small overdue amounts. A company can determine the appropriate amount for the upper limit of items that can be written off; an easy way to make this determination is to calculate the cost of the collection staff's time, as well as that of incidental costs, such as phone calls. Any account receivable that is equal to or less than this cost can be written off with no approval. The timing of the write-off, once again, depends on the particular circumstances of each company. Some may feel that it is best to wait until the end of the year before writing off an invoice, whereas others promptly clear these bad debts out of the accounts receivable aging as soon as they are 90 days old. Whatever the exact criteria may be, it is important for management to stay out of the process once the underlying guidelines have been set. By not interfering, management is telling the collections staff that it trusts employees to make these decisions on their own, while also giving managers more time to deal with other issues. If managers feel that they must review the write-offs, they can let an internal audit team review the situation periodically.

Cost: *Installation time:* 🕐

7.17 Access Customer Payment Information over the Internet

The collection process does not normally begin until at least five days after the payment date specified on an invoice. At that point, the collections staff usually sends an overdue notification and may not call the customer for another ten days or so. Resolution may require several more days, so final payment is in the vicinity of 20 to 30 days late.

If the customer is a large one, it may have created an Internet-based linkage to its accounts payable database for its suppliers to review; this system keeps suppliers from calling the accounts payable staff. By having this information available, the collections staff can access the database well in advance of the payment due date and see if the payment has been posted for payment. If not, it can contact the company *before* the due date to ascertain the problem and resolve it. The result is payment on or near the original due date.

Each customer Web site will probably require the collections staff to enter a vendor code and perhaps a password in order to access payment information, so the collections staff needs to centralize this information for all customers. Also, to make the accessing process easier, consider bookmarking all customer payables Web sites and storing the bookmarks in a network subdirectory for easy access. If there are many bookmarks, it may make sense to back them up or at least print out the Web links occasionally, so they can be recovered without much trouble in the event of a computer failure.

Cost: 💰   *Installation time:* ⏰

7.18 Simplify the Pricing Structure

A common problem for the collections staff is when it tries to collect on an invoice containing a pricing error. This problem most commonly arises when the order entry staff has a complicated set of rules to follow when deriving product pricing. For example, rather than using a single price for each product, a different price may be used for various volume levels of customer orders—perhaps $1 per unit if 1,000 units are ordered and $2 if only 500 units are ordered. The situation can become even more complicated if special deals are in place, such as an extra 10% discount if an order is placed within a special time period, such as the last week of the month. When all of these variations are included in the pricing structure (and some companies have even more complicated systems), it is a wonder that the order entry staff ever manages to issue a correct product price!

A special circumstance under which pricing becomes nearly impossible to calculate is when the order entry department of an acquired company is merged with that of the buying company, leaving the order entry people with the pricing systems of both the purchased company and their own. This situation can quickly result in bedlam. The inevitable result is that customers disagree with invoiced pricing and will not pay invoices without a long period of dissension regarding the correct price. Alternately, they will pay the price they think is the correct one, resulting in arguments over the remainder. In either case, the collections staff must become involved.

One can resolve this situation by simplifying the pricing structure. The easiest pricing structure to target is one allowing only one price to any customer for each product, with no special discounts of any kind. By using this system, not only does the collections staff have a much easier time, but so does the order entry staff; there is no need for them to make complicated calculations to arrive at a product price.

There are two main implementation barriers to this approach: the sales staff and customers. The sales staff may be used to offering a blizzard of promotional discounts to move product and may also have a long tradition of using volume discounts as a tool for shipping greater volume. Similarly, customers may be used to the same situation, especially those benefiting from the current tangle of pricing deals. To work through these barriers, the collections manager must clearly communicate to senior management the reasons why a complicated pricing structure causes problems for the collections and order entry staffs. The end result is usually a political tug-of-war between the sales manager and the collections manager; whoever wins is the one with the most political muscle in the company.

 Cost: Installation time: 🕐 🕐 🕐

7.19 Grant Percentage Discounts for Early Payment

Some companies have large customers that pay late all the time. These customers are important to the company, and the customers abuse the one-sidedness of the relationship by stretching out their payments. In these cases, a company has little leverage, because it will lose a significant volume of sales if it cuts off the errant customers or cuts back on their credit limits.

A company may have no choice other than to grant an early-payment discount to customers in order to bring in cash sooner. This approach is especially effective if a company is in immediate need of cash. Also, accounts receivable that are outstanding for a long time period will require several collection actions, whereas one that is paid immediately will not require any; thus, the use of an early-payment discount reduces the cost of collections. Also, if a customer does not use the offered discount, consider contacting someone at the customer who cares about discounts—the treasurer or CFO. This person is usually in a position to require the customer's accounts payable staff to take all available early-payment discounts that make economic sense.

The collections staff should also disallow any cash discounts taken on checks that are later returned because of not sufficient funds. This policy should be included in the company's credit manual.

The discount is an easy one to implement. A company usually prints the discount on its invoices so customers will see the discount the next time an invoice is mailed to them. However, most customers already have payment terms included in their payment databases, and a sudden change in terms may not be noticed. Accordingly, it may be necessary to call the customers' accounts payable staffs to notify them of the change. An alternative approach is to offer the discounts to only a few key customers representing a high volume of sales or who are constant late payers. By reducing the number of customers who take discounts, a company can use this tool more selectively.

There are three problems with using an early-payment discount. One is the cost. To entice a customer into an early payment, the discount rate must be fairly high. A common discount rate is 2%, which translates into a significant expense if used by all customers. Another problem is a slight increase in the difficulty of applying cash receipts against accounts payable when a discount is involved. Depending on the facility of the accounting software, an accounting clerk may have to go to the extreme of manually calculating the discount amount taken and charging off the difference to a special discounts account. Finally, a discount offer can be abused by customers. If a customer is already stretching its payments, it may take the discount rate without shrinking its payment interval to the prescribed number of days. This can lead to endless arguments over whether the discount should be taken, which the customer will win if it makes up a large enough percentage of a company's sales. The collections staff should show no leniency in pursuing customers who take unearned early-payment discounts.

Cost: 💸 💸   *Installation time:* ⏰

7.20 Periodically Reevaluate the Discount Percentage Offered

When a company elects to offer early-payment discount terms to its customers, it frequently offers the standard 2% discount, because this rate is used so heavily throughout many industries. However, the full set of terms (2% if paid in 10 days, net to be paid in 30 days) works out to an annualized interest rate of 36% per year. This is a good deal for the customer in a seriously inflationary environment and an astonishing deal in today's more common single-digit inflation environment!

It pays in reduced interest costs to periodically reevaluate the discount percentage offered to customers, perhaps by setting up a review date on the annual calendar of department activities. One should compare the rate to the company's cost of money and the general level of inflation to see if the terms offered should be altered to keep the discount an attractive deal for customers while reducing its cost to the company. The formula for determining the cost of a discount is as follows:

(Discount rate offered × 365 days) / Number of days saved)

As the formula implies, one can alter not only the discount percentage offered, but also the number of days' difference between the date by which the discount can be paid and the net payment is due.

The primary difficulty with making frequent changes to the discount rate is getting customers to change the discount in their computer systems to the new deal. This discount is usually stored in the customer file, and someone must persuade a customer staff person to access and update this file. If the new deal offered is worse for the customer than the old deal, one may find customers to be lethargic in switching to the new terms. Thus, it is best to alter discount terms only at long intervals.

Cost: *Installation time:* 🕐

7.21 Only Pay Commissions from Cash Received

A major problem for the collections staff is salespeople who indiscriminately sell any amount of product or service to customers, regardless of those customers' ability to pay. When this happens, the salesperson is focusing only on the commission resulting from the sale and not on the excessive work required by the collections staff to bring in the payment, not to mention the much higher bad debt allowance needed to offset uncollectible accounts.

The best practice that avoids this difficulty is to change the commission system so that salespeople are paid a commission only on the cash received from customers. This change will instantly turn the entire sales force into a secondary collection agency, because they will be motivated to help bring in cash on time. They will also be more concerned about the creditworthiness of their customers, because they will spend less time selling to customers who have little realistic chance of paying.

A few problems make this a tough best practice to adopt. First, because it requires salespeople to wait longer before they are paid a commission, they are markedly unwilling to change to this new system. Second, the amount they are paid will be somewhat smaller than what they are used to receiving, because inevitably a few accounts receivable will never be collected. Third, because of the first two issues, some of the sales staff will feel slighted and will probably leave the company to find another organization with a more favorable commission arrangement. Accordingly, the sales manager may not support a change to this type of commission structure.

A tougher variation is to not pay commissions at all if invoices go over 90 days old, on the grounds that the commission system should push the sales staff to collect as soon as possible. This variation is least effective when commissions are small in comparison to the base pay of the sales staff and most effective when commissions make up a large proportion of a salesperson's pay.

A problem directly related to the accounting systems (and not the intransigence of the sales department!) is that because commissions are now paid based on cash received, a cash report must show the amounts of cash collected from each customer in a given time period, in order to calculate commissions from this information. Most accounting systems already contain this report; if not, it must be programmed into the system.

Cost: *Installation time:* 🕰 🕰 🕰

7.22 Route Cash-In-Advance Orders Straight to the Collections Staff

If a customer has been granted no credit, a manual order entry system is not likely to flag this fact, and instead will route the order to the warehouse for fulfillment. The problem arises when the credit database is not linked to the order entry database. In many companies, no computer database is used for credit information, so the credit department must issue reports that the order entry staff must remember to consult before they finish entering an order. The result is orders shipped for which little likelihood of payment exists.

A solution is to route all cash-in-advance orders straight to the collections staff, which must collect the funds before it releases the order for shipment. If systems are manual, the order entry staff must still review credit status and hand over the order to the collections department, so an order can be mishandled in several ways. The manual approach works better if the credit, order entry, and collections staffs are combined into one department (see the Create an Integrated Customer Service Department best practice (7-1)). If an integrated computer system is installed, such as an enterprise resource planning (ERP) system, this process flow is much easier to achieve. Simpler computer systems without a workflow capability are not usually able to route orders to the collections department.

Cost: *Installation time:*

7.23 Conduct Bad Debt Postmortems

Bad debts will occur despite a company's best efforts. When receivables are written off, small ones tend to be ignored, whereas really large ones may result in a tense meeting between the credit and sales managers and a senior company officer, with an impressive amount of fingerpointing taking place. After the smoke clears, the company goes back to its normal operations until the next large bad debt comes along.

Those who ignore history are doomed to repeat it. The solution is to conduct regularly scheduled postmortems of bad debts. The meetings should include the credit and sales managers, as well as those salespeople whose accounts caused the bad debts. This group should discuss the reasons for the bad debts, what systematic changes can be implemented to reduce the likelihood of their reoccurrence, and assign responsibilities for follow-up. This creates an excellent feedback mechanism for reducing the problems leading to bad debts, while giving all involved personnel an education in why bad debts occur.

The primary difficulty with a regular postmortem is follow-up. No one wants to be saddled with the tasks arising from the meeting. To correct this problem, have someone take detailed meeting notes, distribute them to the participants, and have a company officer occasionally attend subsequent meetings, notes in hand, to discuss with everyone the progress on their assigned tasks. Once the committee members realize that upper management is serious about this process, the problems leading to bad debts are likely to decline rapidly.

Cost: *Installation time:*

7.24 Review Confirming Purchase Orders

Unscrupulous customers sometimes place a verbal purchase order and later send a confirming purchase order containing altered terms. Because this is the only written evidence authorizing the transaction, the written purchase order may very well stand up in court, thereby potentially giving a customer the ability to unilaterally alter the price, payment, or other terms of a delivery.

The solution is to *always* review the terms of confirming purchase orders in great detail, and verify them against the company's written record of any verbal orders placed by the customer. If there are many confirming orders to review, skip the ones for small-dollar amounts and focus on the few large ones for which terms changes could cause significant problems for the company. This task should fall on the order entry staff, because they already recorded the original verbal order. If this group has any question about the legal terms used on a confirming purchase order, it should call in the company's legal counsel for assistance. If the document contains a clearly unacceptable provision, cross it out, initial the change, and send a copy back to the customer by registered mail. An alternative approach is to accept no verbal orders at all, thereby eliminating the comparison task; this option may not be possible, however, in industries where verbal orders are common practice.

It is likely that only a few customers will alter purchase order terms in this manner. If so, flag all incoming written orders from these customers for review, or require cash-in-advance terms in order to avoid payment problems. For ethical reasons, company management should strongly consider cutting off all business with these customers, or at least informing the senior management of customers about the unacceptable behavior of their purchasing staff.

Cost: *Installation time:* 🕐

7.25 Offer Bonuses to the Collections Staff

Collecting payment on overdue invoices from customers is not a pleasant task. Although there are many ways to make the job more efficient and to bring more and better information directly to the collection staff's desk, the simple fact is that badgering people all day about money is not an enticing activity. A frequent result is a smaller number of collection calls than one would expect, a high rate of employee turnover, and little attention to tracking the status of customer contacts.

One solution is to set up a performance-based bonus plan for the collections staff, structured so they have a clear monetary incentive to retrieve overdue payments. This means that the bonus plan has to be sufficiently substantial to get their attention, while also aligning their activities with company goals. For example, the bonus plan should pay out a minimum of 20% of the collection staff's base pay for top performance, and preferably a great deal more for superior performance. Anything less will result in a collection plan that will not get the staff's attention. As another example, the bonus plan should provide incentives to collect the largest overdue amounts first, rather than the largest number of overdue invoices (which can orient the staff toward obtaining payment on a large number of small-dollar invoices). An unusual side effect of a bonus plan is demands by the collections staff for more support, so they can spend more time contacting customers and less time tracking down paperwork. This creates an excellent environment in which other efficiency improvements can be implemented with much more ease than would normally be the case.

A significant downside of a collections bonus plan is adverse changes in collections behavior. The staff may become excessively aggressive during customer contacts, resulting in lost customers. Thus, one should consider putting the collections staff through collection training classes, as well as monitoring phone calls for improper behavior.

Cost: Installation time:

7.26 Offer Bonuses to the Sales Staff

The sales staff is generally particularly unwilling to engage in collection activities. They usually feel that their time is best spent on acquiring new sales, not only from the perspective of finding new revenues, but also because they can earn more in commissions. Thus, they tend to be slow in responding to requests for help from the collections staff and overly protective of their customers.

One solution is to offer a small bonus to those salespeople who assist in collection activities. This is generally not a large bonus, because they already receive the bulk of their variable compensation through a commission plan. This can be a spot bonus granted at the request of the collections staff when a salesperson renders a particularly useful amount of assistance in a collection situation. An alternative is to grant collection bonuses to the collections staff (see the Offer Bonuses to the Collections Staff best practice (7-25)) and to include a provision for splitting the bonus with a salesperson if the collections person has requested assistance. Under this latter approach, the collections staff will only contact the sales staff if they really need the help, because they know they will receive only a share of the full bonus as a result. The problem with this approach is administration; tracking the bonus splits between the collections and sales staffs can be a difficult and error-prone manual process.

Cost: Installation time:

7.27 Report on Bad Debts by Salesperson

It is all too common for the sales staff to view themselves simply as the corporate hunter-gatherers—they go in quest of new sales, and the rest of the company supports their quest. While theoretically noble, this means they do not see the carnage that is sometimes wrought by landing the wrong sort of customer. Although the sales staff prefers to focus on the prime metric of gross dollars by salesperson, corporate managers prefer to see profits by customer or salesperson.

A good solution is for the accounting staff to periodically issue a report listing bad debts by salesperson. Because many sales should never have been made except at the insistence of the sales staff, and many collections are never made because of salespeoples' nonresponsiveness in assisting in the collection effort, this report serves as a report card.

The bad debt report must be issued with considerable caution, for it only shows the bad side of the sales staff. Despite the negative tone just used to introduce this best practice, the sales staff is in fact an exceedingly valuable part of the company. Thus, it is best not to issue the report at all if there are reasons for a bad debt other than salesperson-related issues (such as a customer getting into financial trouble after the sale was concluded). Furthermore, considering the potential level of conflict this report can engender, it is best to present it to the sales manager during a face-to-face meeting and not to spray it all over the company with an e-mail distribution.

Cost: Installation time:

7.28 Post Collection Results by Collector

The collections department is an extremely results-oriented group; cash must be collected or the department is not doing its job. Any form of monitoring system that does not focus on this effort is not targeting the correct issue.

A possible approach is to publicly post the collection results by collector within the department. This should be some sort of proportional measure, such as the percentage of total receivables past due, the percentage of receivables within different aging categories, or days sales outstanding. Reporting on total accounts receivable overdue can be misleading, because one collector may have been assigned a larger dollar volume of accounts receivable than his or her associates.

Calculating this measurement is impossible if collectors are constantly switched among accounts, so some long-term consistency in account responsibilities is necessary. Also, the collections staff may not initially enjoy having their performance posted for all to see, so consider turning the issue into a competition, with small bonus payments based on the best performance.

Cost: *Installation time:*

8

Collection Systems

This chapter contains 20 best practices related to the policies, procedures, training, and supporting systems required to collect overdue funds in an efficient manner. After describing two best practices covering the use of policies and procedures, we address nine databases of various kinds, all relating to the collection function. The next three best practices involve the use of faxed or online systems to collect or disseminate collection information, and the following two best practices address the use of system flags. The chapter concludes with a discussion of variations in the standard mode of communications with customers and of doing everything possible in advance of a payment due date to ensure that customers will pay on time. These best practices are summarized in Exhibit 8.1.

For a basic collections system, the most important best practices are using a collection call database, maintaining a list of customer emergency contacts, and ensuring that all customer billing requirements are met. More comprehensive collection systems focused on large numbers of customers will require a higher level of collection efficiency, and so should consider maximizing the use of a comprehensive collections software package and online document management system. Of particular importance for the long-term reduction of collection problems is the use of a payment deduction investigation system, so management can address the root internal problems causing customers to delay payments.

8.1 Create a Collection Policies and Procedures Manual

Many tasks are involved in the collections process, ranging from how to file a shortage claim with a freight carrier to the process used to issue dunning letters or turn over an invoice to a collection agency. This body of knowledge can be lost

---

Exhibit 8.1 *Summary of Collection Systems Best Practices*

8.1   Create a collection policies and procedures manual

8.2   Train the sales staff in credit policies and procedures

8.3   Use a collection call database

8.4   Link to a comprehensive collections software package

8.5   Create an online document management system for credit information

8.6   Maintain a database of customer emergency contacts

8.7   Maintain a database of personal information about contacts

8.8   Maintain a customer orders database

8.9   Compile a customer assets database

8.10   Install a payment deduction investigation system

8.11   Implement a customer order exception tracking system

8.12   Set up automatic fax of overdue invoices

8.13   Issue dunning letters automatically

8.14   Trace individuals through an online tracking service

8.15   Lock access to the credit hold flag

8.16   Flag slow-paying customers for early contact

8.17   Periodically alter the mode of communication with customers

8.18   Periodically alter dunning letters and issuance intervals

8.19   Issue a notification letter before the due date for large invoices

8.20   Do everything required by customers' payables systems

---

if a considerable amount of turnover occurs within the collections department, resulting in gradual changes in how procedures are completed. Eventually, the alterations can result in less efficient or incorrect activities within the department.

The solution is to capture the correct way to process transactions in a policies and procedures manual. This document can then become an excellent training manual and ongoing reference, so departmental staff can be relied on to consistently follow the same approach to every transaction, every time. Examples of policies and procedures to include in the manual are as follows:

- Accessing the accounting system to research check receipts
- Accessing the online lockbox database to research check receipts
- Authorization for imposing credit holds
- Authorization for writing off outstanding balances
- Authorization levels for granting credits
- Criteria for contacting the sales department for collection assistance
- Criteria for evaluating collection agencies
- Criteria for stratifying collection calls
- Criteria for turning over accounts to collection agencies
- Criteria for giving the corporate overnight delivery account number to customers
- Flagging customer orders for nonshipment
- Handling partial payments
- Issuing dunning letters
- Itemization of all standard forms and how to complete them
- Maintenance of a customer file
- Management of subsidiary credit and collection departments
- Perfecting security interests
- Processing shortage claims
- Pursuing personal guarantees for payment
- Use of a credit scoring model
- Use of credit agencies to obtain credit reports
- Use of the collection call database

The best way to complete a policies and procedures manual is to assign each procedure to the most knowledgeable person for completion, and then run the document through a rigorous review process to ensure that all errors are weeded out. This review can also be an opportunity to add controls and best practices to the procedures, thereby incorporating improvements into the source document used by the entire department. The collections manager should make a note in the department calendar to revise the manual at least once a year in order to reflect any changes in operations.

Cost: *Installation time:* 🕐 🕐

8.2 Train the Sales Staff in Credit Policies and Procedures

A great deal of the conflict between the sales and credit and collection departments arises because of the uncertainty regarding what level of credit is to be granted, when credit holds are imposed, when accounts are referred to a collection agency, and what procedures are required to change a credit limit. In far too many companies, these issues are based on a rough guess regarding what customers are capable of paying. Although some senior credit and collection managers with multiyear industry experience may be able to get away with this judgmental approach, it is extremely difficult for the sales staff to determine what sorts of decisions will be reached in regard to their customers. Even if the credit and collection department is highly organized, with an excellent written credit policy, this will still do little good if the sales staff is not aware of the policy.

A fine solution is to have an initial training session with all sales staff, handing out a copy of the corporate credit and collection policy and then reviewing several scenarios in which the sales staff is educated in exactly what sort of response they are likely to receive, given different situations. Also, because a company may change its credit and collection policy over time for a variety of reasons, be sure to hold follow-up training sessions with all of the sales staff to discuss the changes. Furthermore, it is useful to have brief presentations of these issues at sales meetings, even if there are no policy changes, just to have an opportunity to meet with the sales department and open a line of communication. In addition, if the sales staff has an opinion about the credit and collection policy, this is an excellent time for them to make their point, so their view can be considered in the next policy revision.

This approach will require significant time to create training materials and make presentations, but the value of having both departments be fully aware of the credit and collection policy will pay off tremendously by avoiding ongoing debates over it.

Cost: *Installation time:* 🕐

8.3 Use a Collection Call Database

A poorly organized collections group is one that does not know which customers to call, what customers said during previous calls, and how frequently contacts should be made in the future. The result of this level of disorganization is overdue payments being ignored for long periods, other customers being contacted so frequently that they become annoyed, and continually duplicated efforts. These problems can largely be overcome by using a collection call database.

A typical collection call database is a simple one recorded on paper, or a complex one that is integrated into a company's accounting software package. In either case, the basic concept is the same—keep a record of all contacts with the customer, as well as when to contact the customer next and what other actions to take. The first part of the database, the key contact list, should contain the following information:

- Customer name
- Key contact name
- Secondary contact name
- Internal salesperson's name with account responsibility
- Phone numbers of all contacts
- Fax numbers of all contacts
- E-mail addresses of all contacts

The contact log comprises the second part of the database and should contain the following:

- Date of contact
- Name of person contacted
- Topics discussed
- Action items

The information noted is easily kept in a notebook if there is a single collections person, but may require a more complex, centralized database if there are many collections personnel. In the latter case, a supervisor may need to monitor collections activities for all employees, and he or she can do this more easily if the data is stored in a single location. However, a notebook-based database can be set up in a few hours with minimal effort, whereas a computerized database, especially one closely linked to the accounting records for each account receivable, may be a major undertaking. The reason for the added effort (and expense) is that it may be necessary to custom-program extra text fields into the accounting software so that notations can be kept alongside the record for each invoice; this endeavor is surprisingly difficult, given the number of changes that must be made to the underlying database. The most difficult situation of all is if a company uses a software package that is regularly updated by a software supplier. Any changes made to the software (such as adding text fields) will be destroyed as soon as the next upgrade is installed, because the upgrade will wipe out all changes made in the interim.

A good midway approach for avoiding these difficulties with a computerized database is to use a separate tracking system that is not linked to the accounting software. Such software packages are commonly used by the sales department to track contacts with customers and can be easily modified to work for a collections department. They can also be modified for use by multiple employees, resulting in a central database of contact information that can be easily perused by a collections manager. An example of such a software package is Act! The only problem with this approach is that the customer contact information contained in the accounting software (e.g., names and addresses) and the same information in the tracking software are not linked to each other. This contact information must be reloaded manually from the accounting software into the tracking software. Likewise, any change to the contact information in the tracking software must be manually updated in the accounting system. Despite its limitations, maintaining a separate computerized tracking system is an inexpensive way to maintain a centralized contact database.

Cost: 💵💵   *Installation time:* 🕐 🕐 🕐

8.4 Link to a Comprehensive Collections Software Package

Many of the other system-related best practices noted in this chapter are based on the assumption that a company wants to incrementally create separate applications that are directly linked to an existing accounting computer system. If so, a fair amount of programming work will be required to arrive at a complete in-house solution. This process can be both expensive and time-consuming. For those who prefer to install a complete solution on a more rapid time schedule, it is also possible to purchase a software package that incorporates many of the system-related best practices for collections.

An example of this new breed of software is GetPAID (*www.getpaid.com*). This product is linked to a company's legacy accounting system (specifically, the open accounts receivable and customer files) by customized interfaces, so there is either a continual or batched flow of information into it. A key feature it offers is the assignment of each customer to a specific collections person, so that each person can call up a subset of the overdue invoices for which he or she is responsible. Within this subset, the software will also categorize accounts in different sort sequences, such as placing at the top those customers who have missed their promised payment dates. Also, the software will present on a single screen all of the contact information related to each customer, including the promises made by customers, open issues, and contact information. The system will also allow the user to enter information for a fax and then route it directly to the recipient without out requiring the collections person to ever leave his or her chair. It can also be linked to an auto-dialer, so the collections staff spends less time attempting to establish connections with overdue customers. To further increase the efficiency of the collections staff, the software will even determine the time zone in which each customer is located and prioritize the recommended list of calls, so that only those customers in time zones that are currently in the midst of standard business operating hours will be called.

The GetPAID system does not just store collections data; it can also export it to other systems, where it can be altered for other uses or reformatted for management reporting purposes (although the package contains its own reporting features as well). Some of the standard reports include a time-series report on performance of individual collection personnel, as well as the same information for each customer. It can also create reports that are tailored by recipient (e.g., all of the collection problems for a specific salesperson's customers can be lumped into one report and sent to that salesperson for remedial action). The software can also export data files into Microsoft Excel or Access.

Several cost issues should be considered when installing this type of software—not only of the software, but also for staff training time, installation by consultants, and ongoing maintenance costs. Offsetting these problems is a much shorter time period before a company will have an advanced collections software system fully operational. The record time period for a GetPAID installation is just five days, although a more typical installation speed is 60 days. For those companies with a serious collections problem, and that need help right away, a comprehensive collections software package may be the answer.

Cost: 💵 💵 💵   Installation time: ⏰ ⏰

8.5 Create an Online Document Management System for Credit Information

When a company obtains crucial information about customers, such as credit reports, completed credit applications, and personal guarantees, the usual home for this information is a folder in a storage cabinet. If many credit or collections personnel need access to this information, they must waste time retrieving and returning files, and that paperwork under review could be lost or misfiled. Worse, if employees are lazy or overworked, they will not spend the time necessary to review stored documents at all and will acquire no knowledge of available information. This is a particular problem if the staff becomes ignorant of the existence of a customer's personal credit guarantee. The staff may also order a new credit report on a customer when a fairly recent one is already on file, thereby incurring a needless expense.

For all of these reasons, it may make sense to acquire a document management system, so that electronic document images can be retrieved from employee workstations. The basic system involves a document scanner, a computer on which the scanned documents are assigned a unique index number, and a server on which the images are stored for immediate retrieval. Many software packages are available for managing documents, produced by such companies as FileNet, LaserFiche, and OnBase. With such a system in place, employees have instant access to needed customer information, and multiple employees can review images of the same document at the same time. There is also no risk of document misfiling, because there is no need to touch original documents again.

Such a system can also be used to incorporate document images into letters sent to customers. For example, a scanned image of a customer's not sufficient funds (NSF) check can be pasted into a collection letter, which points out to the customer with great immediacy (and no possibility of argument) that it needs to pay the company.

Depending on the system in use, it may also be possible to convert scanned images into a portable document format (PDF) file and e-mail it directly to customers for their review. By using the electronic transmission of scanned documents, one can move key documents directly to the customer's computer for immediate review, thereby resolving collection issues sooner and shrinking the collection cycle by several days.

The main problem with document imaging is its cost. This solution is not cost-effective for smaller companies with only a few hundred customers. It is best for massive customer bases, especially when companies have multiple credit and collection centers that need to access the same information. Although simple document management systems can be created for about $20,000 for a small number of users, it is common to see multimillion-dollar installations at larger companies.

Cost: 💵💵   *Installation time:* ⏰ ⏰

8.6 Maintain a Database of Customer Emergency Contacts

As can be the case in a long marriage, a company's collections staff and a customer's accounts payable department can grow tired of each other, resulting in the same old collection procedures that the customer gradually begins to ignore. This can also happen when a jaded or overworked person is in a customer's accounts payable department. In either case, the collections department may find that it cannot work with its counterpart in effectively keeping actual payments within terms.

One solution is to maintain a special database of emergency customer contacts. This list should never include an accounts payable person, focusing instead on someone a level or more higher in the customer's organization. There should be a personal connection with any person on the list, such as a prior meeting with a salesperson or a counterpart within the company, so the individual will be more likely to assist the collections staff with an occasional request. Alternately, the emergency contact may be someone who is familiar with the original terms of the company's credit agreement with the customer, such as an assistant controller or controller.

The database may take considerable time to accumulate, because information may come from all over the company. Once created, do not use it too much. People outside of the accounts payable area do not enjoy being pestered and will not appreciate a flood of requests. Instead, call emergency contacts only when an overdue receivable is large or collection cannot be obtained through normal channels.

Cost: 💵   *Installation time:* ⏰ ⏰ ⏰

8.7 Maintain a Database of Personal Information about Contacts

A customer's accounts payable staff deals with collection people all the time, and they are sick of the contacts. Every one of them calls and demands money.

Period. A payables clerk tends to think of them as a horde of aggravating people, and so treats all of them with disdain—and certainly does not go out of his way to pay their invoices.

The trick is to stand out from the crowd—not through being more aggressive than the other collection people, but by the reverse. Be willing to spend a few extra moments on the phone with payables personnel and listen to them. It is surprising what you can discover; perhaps they are avid skiers, golfers, have a child in college, a birthday coming up, or a pending surgery. Write down all of this personal information in a database and call up each person's record before making a call. Then, when you make a solicitous inquiry about some nonbusiness issue, the payables staff are much more likely to relax and think of you as a pleasant caller and not just another collector.

A collector with a small number of customers can get by with a written log about customer contacts, but a larger company will need a computerized database in which to store this information. No matter which approach is used, creating this database will require a long time, because a collector will only garner small snippets of information during each call and will require a long series of customer contacts to build up a really useful database. Also, a greater degree of security should be imposed on this database than on other systems, because some information stored in it could be injurious to a customer if it were made public.

Cost: 🖐💵   *Installation time:* ⏰ ⏰ ⏰

8.8 Maintain a Customer Orders Database

If a customer has a large open order with a company, it is likely that the customer will respond to pressure to pay for open invoices when those orders are put on hold. Consequently, an excellent best practice to implement is to give the collections staff current knowledge of all open orders.

Implementation of this practice is easy for most companies; just give password access to the collections staff to the existing customer orders database. This access can be read-only, so there is no danger of a staff person inadvertently changing or deleting key information in a customer order. An additional issue is that someone must be responsible for flagging customers as "do not ship" in the customer orders database. This step is necessary because orders will inadvertently pass through the system if there is not a solid block in the computer on shipments to a delinquent customer. However, many companies are uncomfortable with allowing the collections staff to have free access to altering the shipment status of customers, because they may use this ability so much that customers become irritated. Consequently, it may be better to allow this access only to a supervisor, such as an assistant controller, who can review a proposed order-hold request with the sales staff to see what the impact will be on customer relations before actually imposing a hold on a customer order.

In summary, giving the collections staff access to the open orders database for customers results in better leverage over delinquent customers by threatening to freeze existing orders unless payment is made. The use of this database should be tempered by a consideration for long-term customer relations; it should only be used if a collections problem cannot be resolved in some other way.

Cost: 　　　　　*Installation time:*

8.9 Compile a Customer Assets Database

If a collections person finds that a customer will not pay, the usual recourse is to reduce or eliminate the customer's credit limit and to use threats—dunning letters and phone calls. These instruments are frequently not sufficient to force a customer to pay. However, what a collections person does not always realize is that the company may have some other customer assets on the premises that it can refuse to ship back to the customer until payment is made. When these assets are grouped into a database of customer assets, the collections staff has a much better chance of collecting on accounts receivable.

A customer assets database lists several items the customer owns but that are located on the company premises. One common customer asset is consigned inventory. This is stock the customer has sent to the company either for resale or for inclusion in a finished product the company is making for a customer. Another customer asset is an engineering drawing or related set of product specifications. Yet another is a mold, which the customer has paid for and which a company uses in the plastics industry to create a product for the customer. All of these items are valuable customer assets that a company can hold hostage until all accounts receivable are paid.

The best way to keep this customer asset information in one place is to store it in the inventory database, which is already set up in most accounting systems and includes location codes, so it is easy to use the database to determine each asset's location. Most important in using this database is that a collections person can designate a customer in the accounting system as one to which nothing can be shipped (with a shipping hold flag of some kind), which effectively keeps the shipping department from sending the asset to the customer—it cannot print out shipping documentation or remove the asset from the inventory database. This is an extremely effective way to keep customer assets in-house, rather than inadvertently being sent back to a customer who refuses to pay its bills.

The only problem with this best practice is making sure that customer assets are recorded in the assets database when they initially arrive at the company. Otherwise, there is no record of their existence, making it impossible to use them as leverage for the collections staff. The best answer to this problem is to force all receipts through the receiving department, whose responsibility is to record the receipts in the inventory database. The internal auditing staff can review the receiving log to verify that this action has been completed. The only customer asset that may not be recorded in this manner is a set of engineering drawings, which enters the company site through the engineering department rather than the receiving dock. The only way to record this information is by fostering close cooperation with the engineering manager, who must realize the need for tracking all customer assets. These steps will result in tight control over customer assets and a better chance of collecting overdue accounts receivable.

Cost: *Installation time:*

8.10   Install a Payment Deduction Investigation System

Customers usually deduct payment amounts from invoices they owe because of problems caused by the originating company. Examples of these problems are product returns caused by faulty products or incorrect order processing, product damage caused by incorrect shipment packaging, incorrect sales deals issued by sales personnel, and promotional or advertising deductions taken for deals that were not clearly specified by the marketing staff. Unfortunately, none of these areas in which the problems originated are likely to hear about the resulting collection problems, because the collection task is placed in the hands of a clerk in either the accounting or treasury departments who is thoroughly overworked, and who certainly has neither the tools nor the authority to drive corrective changes back through the organization.

The solution is to give this person the tools to do so, which can then be accessed by a high enough level of management to ensure that corrective actions are taken. A properly functioning deduction investigation system requires workflow software in which one can route information about the problem to the appropriate party. The software must be able to shift the action routing to different parties if action is not taken by predetermined dates, thereby ensuring that action is taken to correct deduction-related problems. The system must also allow one to review the linked electronic images of related documentation associated with the specific problem, which calls for a document digitizing system. Furthermore, the system must periodically summarize the various issues causing deductions to be taken and route this information to the senior management team, which can spot emerging problems and ensure that they are resolved.

Finally, an implementing company must have a central database for its various functional areas, such as is provided by an enterprise resource planning (ERP) system, so that all parties can have ready access to the various stores of information throughout the company that may relate to the issue at hand. Clearly, these requirements are expensive, but they give one the opportunity to continually monitor the reasons for deductions and fix the underlying problems causing them. This capability is invaluable not only from the perspective of improving customer relations, but also because it reduces the ongoing cost of dealing with payment deductions.

Cost: 💵 💵 💵   *Installation time:* ⏰ ⏰ ⏰

8.11 Implement a Customer Order Exception Tracking System

Many of the problems resulting in collections work begin much earlier, from the time an order is entered into the system to the time it is produced, shipped, and invoiced. The collections staff has no direct control over this interval (unless the collections manager happens to run the entire company!), which means that problems upstream from the collections department will nonetheless have a direct and continuing impact on the quantity and type of problems that the collections staff must handle.

A good best practice for rooting out problems before they become collection issues is to set up a reporting system to track exceptions for customer orders as they move through all of a company's various processes. By keeping close tabs on these reports, the collections manager can tell when collection difficulties may occur. By determining problems with specific customer orders in advance, the collections manager can work with the managers of other departments (mostly by suggestion) to correct problems before orders are shipped. A crucial factor in the success of this best practice is the interpersonal skills of the collections manager, who must bring customer order exceptions to the attention of other managers in such a way that they will not react negatively, but rather work with the presented information to make prompt corrections to their systems.

Another use of these reports is to recognize which orders are likely to result in collection problems and to use this information to start making collection calls earlier than normal, so any customer problems can be discovered, addressed, and resolved before the associated accounts receivable become inordinately old. By using the exception reports to manage accounts receivable more closely, it is possible to maintain a high accounts receivable turnover ratio, which frees up working capital for other purposes.

The number of reports used to track customer order exceptions will vary dramatically, depending on the types of systems already in place, the services or products offered to customers, and the type of industry. This range of options makes a complete list of exception reports impossible to present, but the following list represents the types of information a collections manager should consider using as the foundation for a comprehensive order exception tracking system:

- Customer orders for which the delivery date has exceeded the requested date
- Customer orders for which the quantity on hand is less than the amount ordered
- Customer orders for which the scheduled production date is later than the requested delivery date
- Customer orders for which partial deliveries have been sent
- Customer orders requiring special-order parts
- Customer orders requiring a special form of transportation
- Customer orders requiring a special form of packaging
- Customer orders with nonstandard prices

All of these exception reports focus on nonstandard customer orders or orders for which some kind of shortfall exists. These reports are an effective tool for homing in on those orders for which there will probably be customer complaints.

The ability of a collections manager to create all of these reports will depend on the type of computer database used to collect data about customer orders. If the database does not cover all of the items noted in the previous list of reports, it will be difficult to create the reports, unless it is cost-effective to do so manually. Also, there should be a good report-writing tool or a willing programming staff to assist in the creation of these reports. If these factors are in place, a collections department can benefit greatly from an advance knowledge of which customer orders are likely to result in collection problems.

Cost: 💵 💵   *Installation time:* ⏰ ⏰

8.12 Set Up Automatic Fax of Overdue Invoices

The most common request that a collections person receives from a customer is to send an invoice copy that the customer cannot find. To do so, the collections person must either access the accounting computer system to print out a copy or go to the customer's file to find it. Then the collections person creates a cover letter and faxes everything to the customer. In addition, the fax may not go through, in which case the collections person must repeat this process after learning from the customer that the fax never arrived. This process is typically the longest of all collections tasks; a collection call may take only a few minutes, but faxing an invoice can take several times that amount.

The solution is to automatically extract an invoice record from the accounting database and fax it to the customer—all at the touch of a button. To do so, a company must link the invoice file in the accounting database to another file containing the name and fax number of the recipient, combine the two files to create a cover letter and invoice, and route the two records to a fax server for automatic transmission, one that will keep transmitting until the fax goes through, and then notify the sender of successful or failed transmissions. The advantages of this approach are obvious: immediate turnaround time, no need for the collections person to leave his or her desk to complete a fax, and automatic notification if a problem occurs in completing a fax. For a company with a large collections staff, this system represents a monumental improvement in efficiency.

The trouble with setting up this system is that one must put together several functions that are not normally combined. This almost certainly calls for customized programming, and the system may periodically fail, because of the complex interlinking of different systems. To give a picture of the complexity of this system, its front end must include an input screen for the collections person, allowing entry of the customer's contact name and fax number, as well as any accompanying text that should go on the cover letter to accompany the faxed invoice. On the same screen, one should be able to enter an invoice number so that the screen automatically searches the invoice file and selects the correct invoice. There may be an additional step at this point where the system presents a text image of the invoice so the collections person can verify that the correct invoice is about to be transmitted. Next, both the invoice text and the cover letter must be converted to a digital image for fax transmission. After that, the images are sent to a server that is a stand-alone fax transmission device. The server repeatedly faxes the images to the recipient for a fixed number of attempts. If the transmission is not successful, the fax server sends a notification e-mail to the sender (which requires a preexisting e-mail system); conversely, it should also send a message indicating a successful transmission.

Obviously, it is a difficult task to combine the accounting database with a fax server and e-mail system and expect everything to work properly at all times. Common problems are that information will not be successfully transmitted between the various components of the system, resulting in no fax transmission, or that the e-mail notification system does not work, resulting in no messages to the collections staff, who have no idea if their faxes are being sent or not. Consequently, smaller companies usually do not deem it worth the effort to attempt such an installation. Only the largest corporations, with correspondingly large collections staffs, attempt to install this best practice.

Cost: 🖢 🖢 🖢   Installation time: 🕐 🕐 🕐

8.13 Issue Dunning Letters Automatically

Some companies have so many small accounts to collect that they cannot possibly take the time to call all of them to resolve payment disputes. This is an especially common problem for very small accounts receivable, where the cost of a contact call may exceed the amount of revenue outstanding. In other cases, contacting customers by phone is difficult, usually because all collection calls are automatically routed to the voice mail of the accounts payable departments. In these cases, a different form of communication is needed.

The best way to contact either unresponsive customers or accounts with small overdue balances is the dunning letter. This letter lists the overdue amount, the invoice number and date, and requests payment. There are normally several degrees of severity in the tone of the dunning letter; the initial one has a respectful tone, assuming that some mistake has been made, resulting in nonpayment. The tone gradually increases in severity through several intermediate letters, with the final letter being the most threatening and requiring immediate payment by a specific date if the customer wishes to avoid legal action. Because it is impossible to craft a separate dunning letter for every customer situation (given the cost of doing so), a collections department must create a standard set of dunning letters that can be used for all customers. Although it is an informal way of communicating, a form letter still gets the point across to the customer. There is also a standard time interval between the issuance of each series of dunning letters—perhaps two weeks past the initial invoice due date before the first letter is sent, with additional letters being issued every two weeks thereafter. This use of a series of dunning letters, issued at standard intervals, is an effective and low-cost way to communicate with customers for whom it is not cost effective or otherwise possible to communicate.

Various degrees of automation can be applied to the use of dunning letters. The easiest approach is to have a standard preprinted letter, which is easily copied and mailed to a customer. The next level of automation is to store standard letters in a computer network, where all collections personnel can access the letters and make small modifications to match the customers to whom the letters are being sent. Although simple, both of these approaches suffer from the same complaint: there is no way to automatically issue dunning letters at set intervals. Instead, one must rely on the collections staff to remember to send out the letters.

A more automated approach that takes into account the time interval since the last letter is merging the dunning letters into the accounting software. To do so, some custom programming is required. The program must automatically access a text file as soon as an invoice reaches a certain number of days past due and issue a dunning letter. A different text file must be accessed as soon as the number of days past due increases, because more strident letters must be sent as the invoices ages. The letters can then be printed and mailed out each day in a batch. Although this last method provides the tightest control over the standard issuance of the correct kinds of dunning letters, it is more complicated to set up, so it is generally best to calculate the programming cost of making such a significant enhancement before proceeding with this best practice.

The automatic issuance of dunning letters is a cost-effective method for establishing continual communication with customers regarding overdue invoices. It is particularly suitable to those situations where it is impossible to create personal relationships with customers through more expensive collection calls.

Cost: 💵 💵   *Installation time:* ⏰ ⏰

8.14 Trace Individuals through an Online Tracking Service

The collections staff has an especially difficult time tracking customers if they are individuals rather than businesses, because they are more difficult to trace. In many instances, the small size of amounts owed by individuals coupled with their propensity to change locations drives the collections staff to write off accounts much more readily than would be the case for business receivables.

One solution is to use the services of a third-party tracking service that accumulates and correlates address information for millions of consumers. Three major providers are TransUnion (*www.tudesktop.com*), Equifax (*www.equifax.com*), and Experian (*www.experian.com*). All of these services provide rapid access to information over the Internet. One can use their databases to search by name, social security number, address, or phone number to call up additional information about a customer's last-known whereabouts, additional phone numbers, and aliases, all of which can be useful in the collection effort.

Cost: 💵   *Installation time:*

8.15 Lock Access to the Credit Hold Flag

In many organizations, the staff has not learned to let the computer system drive operations. Instead, they have many manual systems built around a basic computer system (typically containing just accounting and inventory databases), and tend to consider the information in the computer as simply an aid to their activities, possibly containing inaccurate information that they must manually correct. In this environment, the introduction of a credit hold system through the computer can result in significant trouble, because the production or shipping staffs may consider a credit hold flag to be some sort of system error to be overridden. This problem is especially difficult when management is driving toward a sales goal and credit holds stand in their way. An approach that initially appears simple enough is to lock down access to the credit hold flag in the computer system. This means that only an authorized person can put a customer on or remove it from credit hold status.

The trouble is that a shipping department that is still relying on some manual systems can easily ignore the hold flag and ship products anyway, especially if the computer system does not automatically print pick lists or bills of lading. Furthermore, if the credit hold report is not regularly used or even made available to the shipping staff, or if it is not integrated into the shipping system, locking down the hold flag will serve no practical purpose. Thus, one must incorporate additional controls into a shipping system in order to make restricted access to the hold flag work as intended.

Cost: *Installation time:*

8.16 Flag Slow-Paying Customers for Early Contact

Some customers always pay late. Despite knowing this, the collections staff typically only begins contacting customers after a certain number of days have passed. These customers are well aware of the interval before contact begins and never send payment until at least the first contact has been made. Consequently, the regimentation of the collection department's calling system is allowing some customers to delay payment.

The solution is to flag certain customers for early contact. For smaller companies, this can be as simple as a regularly updated memo listing which customers to call early. In an environment with many customers, one can write a program in which the computer system automatically determines which customers pay slow and flags them in the corporate calling system for early contact. A solution between these two extremes is to manually determine which customers are to be designated as slow payers and manually set up a flag in the accounting database to highlight the outstanding invoices of these customers.

No matter which approach is used, early contact can mean a contact before the invoice date, both to make sure that all paperwork is in order and to put customers on notice that the company is closely monitoring their payments. Also, consider an unusual form of contact to get the customer's attention, such as an overnight delivery of the invoice with a cover letter.

This best practice will require additional upfront labor to make the extra customer contacts, so be sure to assign the "slow customer" designation to only the worst offenders, thereby concentrating collection effort where it is really needed. This approach will have the best cost-benefit trade-off.

Cost: *Installation time:*

8.17 Periodically Alter the Mode of Communication with Customers

Persistently late-paying customers become used to the same old method of warning them to pay—an initial letter after an invoice is a week overdue, another invoice a few weeks later, and then finally a phone call. By this time, the customer has accomplished its goal of being multiple weeks late in paying and finally pays the bill. Alternately, some sort of payment problem may exist at the customer site, but the warning letters are all sent to someone who is no longer with the company, so payment is not made until someone finally begins calling the customer. In both cases, the mode of communication is at fault.

A good solution is to send a variety of messages using different modes of communication. A sample sequence of events could be as follows:

- *Payment late by five days.* Send an e-mail to the invoice contact with a PDF version of the invoice, asking if the customer has received the invoice and pointing out that it is late.

- *Payment late by seven days.* Send a fax to the same person, issuing the same information.

- *Payment late by nine days.* Call the same person. If no one picks up the phone, keep calling around the customer location until someone picks up the phone, and ascertain the whereabouts of the invoice contact.

- *Payment late by 11 days.* Still no contact? Send an overnight mail delivery to a senior manager at the customer. Be sure to require a customer signature on the package. Alternately, use certified mail for the delivery.

■ *Payment late by 13 days.* Call the senior manager to whom the overnight delivery was sent.

The approach outlined in the preceding bullets uses e-mail, facsimile, telephones, and overnight delivery to communicate with customers. Also note how different people were contacted, just to make sure that the collections person is not trying to contact someone who may not be available. Also note the short intervals between contacts; once customers become overdue, they will be subjected to a barrage of contacts that only ends when they pay. Furthermore, note the absence of traditional letters, because it takes too long to send and receive anything through the U.S. Postal Service, especially in comparison to the other modes of communication available. Finally, consider mixing up the style of presentation by using different colors of paper and different font sizes to grab the recipient's attention.

Cost: *Installation time:*

8.18 Periodically Alter Dunning Letters and Issuance Intervals

A canny customer who is determined to stretch out payment days as long as possible will eventually figure out which dunning letters are sent at what intervals and will schedule payment as close as possible to the last dunning letter before being referred to a collection agency. Thus, a stale set of dunning letters is almost like a calendar of collection events for the customer to read, resulting in perpetual late payments.

Consider rewriting the dunning letters periodically, as well as varying the intervals at which they are issued. By doing so, customers will be more uncertain of which collection event will occur next and will be more likely to pay sooner. More sophisticated collection systems even allow for a separate set of especially strident dunning letters to be sent to the most difficult customers, with shorter mailing intervals. It is easy to forget to alter dunning letters and payment intervals. To avoid this problem, include a periodic dunning letter review in the annual schedule of collections activities.

Cost: *Installation time:*

8.19 Issue a Notification Letter before the Due Date for Large Invoices

The collections staff does not normally begin contacting customers until several days after the payment due date. This can be anywhere from 5 to 30 days after the due date. If the customer has lost the invoice or has no intention of paying it for a variety of reasons, this delay in initiating contact has cost the company a great deal of time in getting paid. Even if the collections staff is resolute in following up on customer issues, payment will still be delayed for a considerable period.

One solution is to issue a notification letter to customers just *before* an invoice's scheduled payment date. The letter can include the invoice as an attachment and ask if there are any issues with payment; if so, the customer can contact the person listed on the letter for assistance in resolving matters. This is a labor-intensive solution that also requires some mailing costs, and so it is more appropriate for large invoice amounts.

A consideration is that if reminder letters are mailed to the same address to which the original invoice was sent and the invoice address was wrong, the company will have wasted the reminder letter as well. To avoid this problem, consider sending reminders by some other means separate from the initial mailing address, such as a fax delivery.

An alternative that has a higher fixed cost but lower variable cost is to link the accounting system to an automated fax server that automatically faxes reminders for *all* invoices a few days before the payment date. An advance faxing system can reach a sophisticated level, incorporating a statement of all overdue invoices, the invoices themselves, proof of delivery, and an image of the customer's purchase order. For all elements of the system to work properly, it is helpful to have a document management system linked to the accounting system. This is an expensive system whose components can be difficult to assemble, so it is best applied to situations where there are large invoice volumes and/or a significant number of overdue invoices to potentially be reduced.

The main problem with this approach is its passivity: the customer must still contact the collections staff to resolve issues. If the customer is having cash flow difficulties, this contact is unlikely to occur.

Cost: *Installation time:* 🕐

8.20 Do Everything Required by Customers' Payables Systems

Some customers have convoluted payment systems requiring the routing of invoices to a specific company address, inclusion of an arcane account code on the invoice, entry of the invoice into a Web site, or approval by a large number of managers within the company. These special steps are not necessarily designed to slow down payment; the customers have simply adopted what they believe to be the most efficient payables systems for their special circumstances. However, from the company's point of view, payments arrive much later than would normally be the case.

The only solution is to alter the billing process to match the customer's payables system. If this means adding special information to an invoice or mailing it to six different locations, do it. The company must perform all extra steps to make sure it is paid, and it cannot assume that the customer will exert any extra effort to assist it. To aid in this process, consider sending a questionnaire to all customers, asking them where the company should mail invoices, to whom they should be addressed, who authorizes payments, the timing of payments, and whether the customer is exempt from sales taxes. Because many customers will not take the time to answer the questionnaire, consider having a salesperson meet with each customer and fill out the questionnaire at that time.

Fortunately, not many customers require such special coddling, because the extra time required to meet their needs can be substantial and greatly reduces the efficiency of the accounting department.

Cost: *Installation time:* 🕰 🕰

9

Collection Techniques

This chapter contains 33 best practices related to collection techniques. It begins with four preventive best practices to be used before invoices become overdue, followed by four ways to send warning letters to customers. The remaining best practices list increasing levels of collection severity, ranging from polite requests for payment of undisputed balances, through a variety of options for delayed payment, to the use of legal recourse to achieve a settlement. These best practices are summarized in Exhibit 9.1.

There is no subset of the most recommended collection techniques. There are simply a range of possible options from which one can choose, depending on the specific circumstances of each overdue customer invoice. Perhaps the best advice is noted in the last best practice of the chapter, Negotiate with the Customer (9.33)—be prepared to negotiate a different payment plan with every customer, which requires a great deal of flexibility in thinking through possible options.

9.1 Thank Customers Who Pay on Time

The relationship between the collections staff and customers is essentially negative—they only talk to each other when there is a problem, so this does not encourage a great deal of mutual camaraderie. As an alternative, consider calling those customers who either always pay on time or who have recently improved their payment performance, and thank them for doing so. This will certainly startle customers enough to make them remember the company, and may possibly influence them in making sure that the company is paid on time when the next payment becomes due. Furthermore, this is an excellent time to ask customers about the company's performance and to see if the company could be doing anything to

---

Exhibit 9.1 *Summary of Collection Techniques Best Practices*

9.1   Thank customers who pay on time

9.2   Set up customers with EFT agreements

9.3   Require a signed purchase agreement for all major sales

9.4   Eliminate grace periods

9.5   Use dunning letters only for small overdue balances

9.6   Issue dunning letters by e-mail

9.7   Issue dunning letters to management positions outside accounts payable

9.8   Issue attorney letters

9.9   Stamp a reminder notice on late invoices

9.10 Send invoices by certified mail to customers who repeatedly lose their invoices

9.11 Insist on payment of undisputed balances

9.12 Insist on a wire transfer when payments are repeatedly reported to be "in the mail"

9.13 Offset an overdue receivable against a payable to a customer

9.14 Send a letter confirming payment commitments

9.15 Set up a periodic payment schedule

9.16 Convert a receivable into a promissory note

9.17 Accept a merchandise return

9.18 Accept payment in kind

9.19 Add the overdue customer balance to cash-on-delivery shipments for crucial items

9.20 Notify the customer and salesperson of credit holds

9.21 Inform the sales staff when accounts are sent to a collection agency

9.22 Have both parties to a settlement sign a mutual release agreement

9.23 Send the customer a completed small claims court complaint form

9.24 Sue customers in small claims court

9.25 Prescreen customers before initiating legal action

9.26 Have a court issue a restraining notice

9.27 Retain lawyers who are experienced in money judgment collection

9.28 Reclaim goods from insolvent customers

9.29 File an involuntary bankruptcy petition for a customer

Exhibit 9.1 *(continued)*

9.30   Report a customer to the Internal Revenue Service

9.31   Use the collections department to collect loans to former employees

9.32   Contact customers regarding credit balances

9.33   Negotiate with the customer

---

better serve the customer. Because thanking the customer has likely put him or her in a good frame of mind, responses may be both lengthy and detailed.

This best practice does not require one to block out large amounts of time by the collections staff to make thank you calls. On the contrary, this sort of treatment wears out over time if done too much. Instead, consider filling spare time in the collections department with occasional calls.

Cost: *Installation time:*

9.2   Set Up Customers with EFT Agreements

The standard payment approach is by check in most credit situations. The use of checks is basically flawed, because customers can cut checks even when they have no cash in their bank accounts and can use a variety of methods to increase their float time. The end result is minimal cash in the company's hands for many days past the invoice due date.

An excellent alternative is an Automated Clearing House (ACH) Network debit program, whereby the company obtains authorization from its customers to make an electronic funds transfer (EFT) from their bank accounts on the invoice due date. By doing so, the company does not have to send the customer an invoice at all and can precisely match its invoice due dates to the cash receipt date, reducing its outstanding accounts receivable balance. This approach is especially useful in cases when invoices of approximately the same amount recur every month, because customers are less likely to protest the use of EFT for repetitive invoices.

The use of EFT can be a difficult sell to customers, because they frequently do not want anyone removing funds from their bank accounts, they prefer the float associated with check payments, and they do not receive an invoice when EFT payments are used. One can avoid complaints on the last count by mailing or (better yet) e-mailing an EFT notice to customers shortly before funds are withdrawn from their accounts, specifying the amount and timing of the withdrawal. It is also useful to personally visit customers to elaborate on the benefits of the EFT system. Better yet, one can require its use for new customers and have the sales staff include an EFT authorization form in the new customer credit application packet.

The use of EFT will be most applicable for low-dollar, repetitive billing situations and least applicable for high-dollar, infrequent billings. Thus, one's business model will dictate the applicability of this best practice.

Cost: 💵   Installation time: ⏰ ⏰

9.3 Require a Signed Purchase Agreement for All Major Sales

If a customer issues a verbal purchase order to obtain goods or services and the company performs in accordance with this order, it will have a difficult time proving its case in court if the customer refuses payment. The customer can claim that it never wanted the company's delivery and can challenge the company to show written proof to the contrary. At this point, the company has probably lost the value of its delivery.

The solution, however time consuming, is to require customers to sign a purchase order, sales order, or engagement letter before any services or goods are delivered. This gives the company written evidence of the customer's order. Be sure to file this document where it will not be lost, in case the delivery is later disputed.

If the customer does not issue purchase orders (which is common in smaller firms), create a sales order for the customer to sign instead. In order to speed up the signing process, fax the sales order to the customer and ask that it be faxed back. This keeps the ordering process from being unnecessarily delayed. If a customer refuses to provide a signed purchase agreement, even one helpfully provided by the company's sales staff, then consider this to be clear evidence that the person placing the order does not have the authority to do so, which increases the odds of incurring a bad debt.

Cost: 💵   Installation time: ⏰ ⏰

9.4 Eliminate Grace Periods

Most collection departments do not start contacting customers until a certain number of days after an invoice due date, either on the assumption that the U.S. Postal Service takes a long time to make deliveries or that a customer's payment process may be interfering with timely payment. Whatever the reason, customers with an interest in delaying payment have an almost guaranteed extra week before a collections person even begins to think about contacting them.

A best practice that is used surprisingly infrequently is to begin calling immediately after the invoice due date has passed. If the invoice is due in 30 days, this means contacting the customer after 31 days. Although some checks will be in the mail at this time, rendering some calls unnecessary, most calls made will be made to customers who have not paid their invoices. By taking this approach, the company instills in its customers the idea that payment terms are to be taken seriously, and the company absolutely expects payment on the stated date.

Initially, this approach will require extra time to make customer contacts, because some payments will be in transit. However, once customers learn about the lack of a grace period, payments will arrive sooner, resulting in less collections work.

Cost: 🖋️ *Installation time:* ⏰

9.5 Use Dunning Letters Only for Small Overdue Balances

Some companies will use all possible methods to collect every overdue account receivable, no matter how small it may be. This can include meeting with customers, calling them repeatedly, referring accounts to collection agencies, and issuing dunning letters. The trouble is that excessively active collection work costs more than the amount of the overdue invoice, so the company is losing money by trying too hard to make a collection. This is a particular problem when the collections manager has a mindset that no invoice will go uncollected, or when this person is judged based on his or her ability to collect the highest possible proportion of overdue invoices, rather than the highest proportion of overdue dollars.

The best way to collect small overdue balances is to restrict collection activities to the use of dunning letters. This is the least expensive way to contact customers and is preferred over more labor-intensive activities such as direct personal contact or phone calls. Although only one collection method is advised in this situation, one can certainly mix up the method and timing of delivery in order to gain the customer's attention. Instead of the traditional mailing, try sending the letter by fax or e-mail, and distribute it to different people within the customer's organization in hopes of jarring loose a response.

Cost: *Installation time:* 🕐

9.6 Issue Dunning Letters by E-Mail

Dunning letters include the cost of paper and postage, which can be considerable when large numbers of dunning letters are issued. A built-in time delay also occurs while letters are routed through the postal system, the customer's internal mail delivery service, and eventually to the recipient. Although dunning letters are a generally inexpensive approach to collection, both factors can make them a less than ideal collection technique for large volumes of receivables.

An easy technological twist to the problem is to send the same dunning letters by e-mail. Not only is transmission instantaneous, but recipients also tend to forward the messages straight to the party who is best able to handle payment. Furthermore, an e-mail response is likely to be generated for a high percentage of these issuances, especially when dunning messages are custom written. This approach works so well that one should consider it the primary initial collection contact method in many situations.

This approach works best if the letter is incorporated into the body of the e-mail text, rather than as an attachment, because the recipient may be understandably wary of opening a file attachment in this age of computer viruses and because the recipient may not have the right program needed to open the file. This type of message should also be sent individually rather than in bulk to many recipients, because corporate spam filters will probably block messages sent with many addressees listed in the e-mail header. Finally, make an effort to keep customer e-mail addresses up to date; this means requiring e-mail updates from customers whenever they place an order, as well as investigation of all bounced e-mail messages.

Cost: 💵   *Installation time:* 🕐 🕐

9.7 Issue Dunning Letters to Management Positions Outside Accounts Payable

The typical dunning letter is automatically generated by the accounting system and goes to the standard accounts payable contact person already listed in the accounting system as the person who receives invoices. In many cases, the contact name is just Accounts Payable Department. This person is all too familiar with dunning letters and generally lobs them into the closest wastebasket. The solution is to address dunning letters to someone else in the customer's organization, preferably at a management level outside the accounts payable department. This recipient is far less used to receiving such notices and is also in a much better position to enforce payment.

A problem occurs in compiling a database of management-level names. The salesperson on the account is generally the most knowledgeable about what names to use. As an alternative, one can try the sales engineer or customer service person assigned to the customer, or just call the customer's main phone number and ask for the name of a person in a particular position. Customer Web sites also frequently list the names of high-level managers.

Another issue is inserting these names into the automated dunning letter–generation system. At the most manual level, one can print out the letters as usual and then readdress the envelope to the manager's name. The only alternative is to alter the accounting system to use a different name for the dunning letter, which is not a commonly available option except in high-end accounting software packages.

Cost: Installation time: 🕐 🕐

9.8 Issue Attorney Letters

A series of dunning letters may not force a delinquent customer into paying an overdue invoice. At this point, the usual next step is for the company to refer an account to a collection agency, which means that a hefty collection fee will be deducted from any eventual collection. Is there an intermediate step that may jar loose the cash for a lesser expenditure?

A good alternative is to first issue an attorney letter. This is a letter issued on an attorney's letterhead and supposedly written by the attorney, threatening legal action if payment is not made. The implication is that the customer is now much closer to a lawsuit, which sometimes brings about a rapid settlement of the outstanding balance.

Attorney letters are expensive if they are custom written for each customer by the attorney. To reduce the cost, write the letter for the attorney and just ask him or her to print it on official letterhead. To further reduce costs, state in the letter that all customer responses be made back to the company, not the attorney. This approach has the double purpose of keeping the attorney from being buried by phone calls and keeping down billed hours. Attorneys usually accept this type of letter-writing arrangement, despite the lowering of their initial legal fees, if the company guarantees them some portion of the eventual legal work required to actually bring legal actions against customers.

Cost: *Installation time:* 🕐

9.9 Stamp a Reminder Notice on Late Invoices

When a small-dollar invoice becomes overdue for payment, the collections staff usually does not have the time to make a series of collection calls to determine the payment problem. Instead, these invoices wind up on the monthly statement of account, which accounts payable clerks rarely enjoy wading through and sometimes just dump into the trash. The result is a high rate of noncollection on small invoices.

A simple solution is to purchase a reminder notice stamp, using a large print size. Print a copy of each overdue invoice and, using red ink, stamp the notice on the face of each invoice. Then mail the invoices to the accounts payable staff as usual. This approach tends to elicit a much better response from the customer, because there is no wading through a large account statement—the invoice is in front of the payables clerk and it is clearly overdue. To make this approach even more effective, send the stamped invoice to an accounting supervisor or a manager outside of the accounting department. Because these people do not usually receive invoices, they are more likely to take action to fix the problem. The only trouble with this approach is spending the time to find the name of the addressee and changing the mailing address to match that person's name.

Cost: *Installation time:* 🕐

9.10 Send Invoices by Certified Mail to Customers Who Repeatedly Lose Their Invoices

Some customers have an annoying habit of repeatedly "losing" invoices through their internal approval processes. If so, there must be an enormous pile of invoices cluttering a back room somewhere! This situation is especially annoying when the same customers insist on paying only from original invoices, not faxed or e-mailed copies. By taking this approach, they are earning extra days of non-payment while a replacement invoice is mailed to them.

A possible solution is to use certified mail or an overnight delivery service with a signature requirement, so the collections staff absolutely knows that the invoice has been received and the name of the person who received it. This approach does not prevent the customer from subsequently losing the invoice again, but at least provides proof of receipt.

This approach requires one to pull out of the standard invoicing process the invoices for those customers who lose invoices and to mail them separately using a relatively expensive shipping option. Not only is it expensive, but it makes the billing process less efficient by adding a processing step to it. Consequently, use this best practice sparingly.

 Cost: *Installation time:*

9.11 Insist on Payment of Undisputed Balances

Customers do not normally like to pay for an invoice until all disputes related to it have been resolved, thereby allowing them to pay the full amount, staple the remittance advice to the complete packet of resolution documentation, and file it away. This approach is also used by customers who are not willing to pay at all; they create a dispute over a small item and refuse payment on the entire invoice, resulting in long waits for payment.

The solution is to insist on payment of undisputed balances right away. This is especially appropriate on multiline invoices for which only a few items are being debated. If a customer has a history of withholding payment based on a disputed item, act quickly and insist on immediate payment of the undisputed balance until the customer figures out that this ploy will no longer work. Given the amount of arguing required to make customers pay partial balances, it is easiest to follow this best practice only when the invoiced amount is substantial.

Cost: *Installation time:* 🕐

9.12 Insist on a Wire Transfer When Payments Are Repeatedly Reported to Be "In the Mail"

When the collections staff calls a customer about an overdue receivable, the most common response is that "the check is in the mail." After waiting a few days, the check does not arrive, and the collections staff is now informed that the check must have been delayed by the U.S. Postal Service and that the customer wants to wait another week or two to make sure the check does not arrive. After that interval, the customer supposedly cuts another check, which is in the mail for more days. This approach can easily double the collection period for an invoice. The most common way for collections personnel to halt this delaying technique is to ask for the check number, which at least puts the payables person on the spot to come up with a check number. However, if the check is lost in the mail, having a check number does little to assist in collecting the debt.

If the collections staff is fairly sure that the customer has not really mailed a check, it can request that the customer issue a stop payment on the check and initiate an immediate wire transfer instead. The company can even offer to cover the wire transfer cost for the customer. By doing so, the collections staff removes the mail float excuse and forces an immediate conclusion to the payment problem. It may also be necessary to offer to reimburse the customer for its check stop payment charge. However, the company should require a copy of the customer's bank statement on which the stop payment fee is shown before authorizing payment. Otherwise, the customer may never have issued a check and yet is being paid by the company for fees it never incurred.

Customers commonly resist this approach because they must go to the extra effort of contacting their banks and issuing wiring instructions. If they actually had a check in the mail, they must issue a stop payment as well (for which there is a bank charge). Thus, this approach works best when the collections staff is sufficiently fed up with a customer's delaying tactics to risk irritating the customer. If the customer refuses to initiate a wire transfer, then the next logical step to enforce the request is an immediate credit hold until the company receives payment.

Cost: 💵   Installation time: ⏰

9.13 Offset an Overdue Receivable Against a Payable to a Customer

On rare occasions, a company may not only sell goods to a customer but also purchase goods or services from it. In these cases, the company may be paying the customer on time but the customer is not paying the company, resulting in a net negative cash flow position for the company. The company can offset overdue accounts receivable against its accounts payable obligations, thereby eliminating its need to collect funds from the customer up to the amount of the offset.

Because many transactions may be moving between the company and the customer, it is best to document any offsets and send this information to the customer; otherwise, the accounting records of both parties may become hopelessly confused. Also, if there is a question of fact regarding the items being offset, taking this step can annoy the customer and interfere with the two entities' business relationship, so use it with care. Another problem is that the collections staff in a larger company may be completely separate from the accounts payable department, and so has no idea that there are any payables to offset. A regularly scheduled comparison of payables to receivables to determine the existence of such relationships will eliminate this problem.

Cost: 💵   Installation time: ⏰

9.14 Send a Letter Confirming Payment Commitments

Customers like to promise payment by a certain date, wait for the date to pass, and then dispute the details of their promise with the collections staff. Even if a collector has properly documented the last customer contact, the customer can get into the "he said, she said" game and claim that the collector did not write down the details correctly. Besides being frustrating, this game also delays payment.

The best solution is to write down the promised payment information in a letter and send it to the customer. This confirmation approach ensures that customers see the collector's version of the earlier conversation as soon as possible and have an opportunity to dispute it at that time. By the time the promised payment date arrives, the customer should have few excuses left for not paying. Be sure to retain a copy of the confirming letter, in case the customer wants to dispute any parts of it. Also, consider sending the letter by registered mail in case the customer has an unfortunate habit of losing letters.

If customers have agreed to a repetitive series of payments, use this approach to both thank them for the most recent payment and remind them of the amount and due date of the next payment. Although this may call for the issuance of quite a few letters, customers will be aware that the company is keeping a close eye on the arrival dates of their payments.

Cost: *Installation time:*

9.15 Set Up a Periodic Payment Schedule

A customer may have a short-term cash flow problem and promises to pay in a few months, once some unspecified amount of cash is received. This places the collector in the awkward position of essentially authorizing a short-term loan to the customer, for which there is still no guarantee of payment. Also, once the customer's cash flow improves, whatever goods or services were provided by the company will seem to be in the distant past, and so the associated payments are likely to be shunted aside in favor of newer and more immediately required payments.

One solution is to set up a periodic payment plan. By convincing the customer to make some payments in the near term, the company is gradually reducing the amount of what may otherwise be a long-term receivable. Also, this approach gets the customer into the mode of making payments on a set schedule, so the company can eventually be paid in full even if its expected cash inflows never occur.

Collectors may be tempted to use this approach too much, because they can show some receipts in the near term. However, because the company is also extending an interest-free loan through this best practice, the credit manager or controller should personally approve all periodic payments exceeding a predetermined limit.

Cost: *Installation time:*

9.16 Convert a Receivable into a Promissory Note

The collections personnel will occasionally be confronted by customers with the fact that they have insufficient money to pay for an outstanding receivable—period. If so, sending accounts to a collection agency will do little good, because the customers do not have sufficient funds to pay, no matter who is badgering them for payment.

An alternative to bringing in a collection agency is to create a promissory note. Under its terms, the customers agree to periodic payments and interest that will gradually eliminate the debt. As an inducement, consider offering the customers limited open account terms if they agree to the promissory note. This approach considerably improves one's chances of being paid, because it is easier to win a lawsuit over nonpayment of a promissory note than over nonpayment of a receivable, because it is harder for customers to prove why they should not pay the note (which the customers have agreed to by signing it). However, if the customers refuse to sign the promissory note, this is a sure sign that the company will not be paid, so the credit manager has a much easier decision to immediately turn over the receivables to a collection agency for more aggressive collection tactics.

If possible, try to secure the note with customer assets, because this greatly increases the odds of being paid and also puts the company in front of unsecured creditors in the event of the customers' bankruptcy. Absolutely have a lawyer review the terms of the proposed promissory note to ensure that there are no loopholes through which the customers can avoid payment. Also, consider leaving the receivable in the receivable aging report rather than shifting it into a notes receivable account; this makes it easier for the collections staff to monitor incoming payments, because the aging report is their primary source of information.

Cost: 💸   Installation time: ⏰ ⏰

9.17 Accept a Merchandise Return

Customers usually purchase goods for resale or incorporation into their own products for sale to their customers. In either case, the normal production and sale cycle ensures that the company's products can no longer be retrieved in the event of a late payment, especially if the payment delay has gone on for quite some time.

There are a few cases in which the collection staff can assume that some product is still on hand and untouched by the customer, making it possible to accept a merchandise return. This possibility exists in seasonal businesses, for which customers may not have been able to sell off all goods during the peak season and now have no way to clear out their inventories. Another possibility is to review the latest customer financial statements and see if inventory turnover is very slow; if so, the customer's overstocking practices may mean that the company's goods are still untouched in the customer's warehouse. Even if a customer has used up most of the company's goods, there may still be a few units on hand that can be sent back in partial settlement of the outstanding debt. Conversely, a customer who practices just-in-time inventory management will have so little inventory on hand that pursuing this option would not be worth the effort.

Cost: *Installation time:*

9.18 Accept Payment in Kind

Some customers are completely unable to pay for outstanding receivables—they simply have no money. In many situations, the collections staff only looks at the customer's ability to pay and promptly writes off the receivable to bad debt.

A more innovative approach is to take a hard look at the goods or services offered by the customer and see if a payment in kind can be arranged. For example, a customer's poor financial condition may be caused by a large investment in nonperforming inventory. If that inventory can somehow be used by the company, make arrangements to accept the inventory in exchange for cancellation of the debt. Although less likely, the same approach can apply to acquiring a customer's fixed assets. It may also be possible to obtain customer services, such as legal advice, medical assistance, grounds maintenance, and so on. The possibilities are substantial in this area, so do not let an excessive focus on a customer's monetary assets cloud one's view of other types of payment.

An approval process should be in place for what types of payments are acceptable. For example, the collections manager may have some difficulty explaining why several tons of apples were just delivered when the company has no conceivable way to use them all!

Cost: *Installation time:*

9.19 Add the Overdue Customer Balance to Cash-on-Delivery Shipments for Crucial Items

When a customer does not pay the balance of an overdue invoice, one option is to shift the customer over to cash-on-delivery (COD) payment terms. At that point, the customer has presumably milked the company for all the credit it will ever get and frequently moves its business to another company, with no intention of paying its outstanding balance.

There are limited cases in which the company can use COD terms to obtain payment of the outstanding balance. This is possible when the customer has no other source for goods or when the company is repairing its products. In either case, one should make the customer aware in advance that either the entire open balance or a portion of it will be tacked onto the COD amount, thereby enforcing payment if the customer ever wants to see its goods delivered.

The main problem is altering the corporate accounting systems to include the extra payment requirement in the COD. A COD shipment is typically arranged by the shipping department, which may not know about the additional receivable balance outstanding. Consequently, the collections staff must either create a change to the computer system to list this information on the sales order or manually convey the information to the shipping manager. The same problem arises with the repairs department, which sometimes issues its own invoices for repaired goods. If this best practice applies to only a small number of cases, then it is more cost-effective to create a manual solution to the problem than to spend programmer time altering the company's computer system.

Cost: *Installation time:*

9.20 Notify the Customer and Salesperson of Credit Holds

Despite all of the actions taken by the collections staff to collect funds from customers, the basic intent with all but fraudulent customers is to still find a way to sell to them again at some later date. This is extremely difficult to do when it becomes necessary to put a customer on credit hold, because a stoppage in goods or services delivery may interfere to a significant extent in the conduct of the customer's business. However, a much worse scenario is when customers do not even know that they are on credit hold and continue to expect deliveries that never arrive. The company's salespeople will take the brunt of irate customer calls when this happens and will in turn inflict their ire on the credit and collections people responsible for the credit hold.

The solution is to notify both the customer and salesperson as soon as a credit hold is imposed, and there are several ways to do so. First, the salesperson should be notified before the credit hold is imposed, thereby giving fair warning and a last chance to argue against the credit hold. One should then make a personal phone call to the customer to issue the notification. However, this call should not be to the accounts payable person with whom the collections staff has probably been dealing; instead, call the most senior person possible in the organization. By doing so, the odds of having immediate action taken will increase dramatically. Phone calls or personal visits are the only way to communicate this information. Do not use letters, because they are too slow, or e-mail, because the messages may not be read for some time or may be inadvertently deleted.

Cost: *Installation time:* 🕐

9.21 Inform the Sales Staff When Accounts Are Sent to a Collection Agency

Despite a company's best efforts to screen collection agencies with reference checks and specific instructions on how to treat customers, some agencies are still likely to use a more vigorous style when attempting to collect funds on behalf of the company than the company would like. If customers are put off by these practices, they will probably communicate their displeasure back to the company sales representatives, who may then adopt the same vigorous attitude as the collection agency in confronting the collections department over the issue. This scenario spreads a considerable amount of ill will throughout the organization.

The solution is to always inform the sales staff in advance when accounts are about to be sent to a collection agency. This gives the sales staff one last chance to either argue on the customer's behalf or forewarn the customer of the impending raft of phone calls heading their way. In the latter case, this call may spring loose a payment by a customer who is unwilling to deal with a collection agency. This approach also creates another avenue for communications between the collections and sales staffs.

The only downside of this approach is a slight delay in forwarding accounts for collection, because the sales contact and any resulting discussions may require a few days to complete. In case a salesperson is nonresponsive when a notice is sent, be sure to include in the initial message the date on which the account will be sent to collection, so the salesperson cannot create a further delay by not issuing an acknowledgment. If the sales department states that they are not given sufficient notice, include the length of the notice period in the credit policy and communicate the policy to the sales department through training sessions or short presentations during sales department events.

Cost: Installation time:

9.22 Have Both Parties to a Settlement Sign a Mutual Release Agreement

Sometimes the only way to obtain a payment is to arrive at a negotiated settlement that results in the company writing off some portion of a receivable. Unfortunately, this may not be the end of the matter, because the customer may decide that it has sufficient grounds for complaint to file suit against the company and pursue additional compensation. Thus, the company has jumped from one settlement to the prospect of another, each one costing the company more money. The solution is to require both parties to sign a mutual release agreement as part of any initial settlement. This agreement states that the company gives up its right to sue the customer over the unpaid receivable balance, while the customer cannot sue the company in regard to the goods or services provided.

Do not use a boilerplate mutual release agreement in this situation. Instead, have an attorney draft a document that follows the laws of the state in which the company does business. Also, the mutual release agreement works only if the customer is obtaining some consideration in exchange for giving up its right to sue, so make sure the consideration is noted within the agreement.

Cost: Installation time:

9.23 Send the Customer a Completed Small Claims Court Complaint Form

Some customers do not intend to pay without a major threat from the company. They are used to all of the usual collection approaches of phone calls, faxes, e-mails, and overnight deliveries, and they shrug them all off with ease. At this point, most companies give up and hand over the accounts to a collection agency, mentally giving up the large fee charged by the collection agency.

One more technique that is sufficiently different to rattle a customer is the threat of a small claims court filing. Even if the company has no real intent to take an issue to court, just obtain the complaint documentation from the appropriate court, fill it out, and send a copy to the customer, with a note attached stating when the cash has to be in the company's hands or else the paperwork will be filed with the court.

It helps to build a reference library of small claims court forms, which vary by state (and sometimes by county), thereby making the filing process faster. Claims of this type are generally filed in the county where the customer resides, so a great many forms may be required to cover the locations of the entire customer base.

Cost: Installation time:

9.24 Sue Customers in Small Claims Court

If the previously noted attempt to obtain payment by sending a small claims complaint to a customer does not work, the next step is to actually file the complaint with a small claims court. This is usually filed in the county where the customer resides, but can also be where the action over which a complaint is filed took place. In either case, check with the court to verify the maximum amount of money it will address. If the amount being claimed is higher, waive the difference in order to fit under the court's maximum cap. Also pull a credit report on the customer to verify its official legal name and corporate status, so this information can be correctly listed on the complaint form. Finally, locate a collection attorney near the small claims court and request representation at the court for a modest fee and percentage of any proceeds.

These steps are not difficult, and the cost of continuing the process into small claims court is typically far less than the amount of the debt. Also, because a local attorney represents the company in court, the collections staff does not waste time traveling to court. To make the process even more efficient, create a procedure for this process and maintain a list of local attorneys to contact for representation in court. With these steps in place, collecting through small claims court becomes a mechanical and efficient process.

Cost: Installation time:

9.25 Prescreen Customers before Initiating Legal Action

Initiating legal action against a customer is an enormously expensive and prolonged undertaking that is almost never worth the effort. The only party that is assured to come out ahead on the situation is the lawyer. Even if the court awards a substantial settlement, the customer may go to great lengths to hide assets, so the company never collects a dime.

The solution is to always prescreen a customer's debts before initiating a legal action. This should at least involve purchasing a credit report on the customer to determine the number of judgments and tax liens already filed against it, as well as other types of outstanding debt. Some collection agencies can provide a more detailed analysis. This type of investigation may reveal that the customer has so many calls on its assets already that an investment in legal action is completely uneconomical. This simple best practice is highly recommended.

Cost: 💵💵   Installation time: ⏰

9.26 Have a Court Issue a Restraining Notice

Even if a court issues a judgment against a customer and in favor of the company, the customer may illegally attempt to dispose of corporate assets, so there is nothing left for the company to attach. Thus, after all the time and expense of court proceedings, a company still receives nothing for its efforts.

Consider having the court issue a restraining notice to the customer. This is a document stating that the customer cannot dispose of any assets. It is especially effective when used to freeze the customer's bank account, because the receiving bank will block all account access at once. This approach is only useful after a legal judgment has been obtained, so a customer will have already had plenty of time (possibly years) to fraudulently dispose of assets.

Cost: 💵   Installation time: ⏰

9.27 Retain Lawyers Who Are Experienced in Money Judgment Collection

Although the average lawyer can be counted on to have training and expertise in the general conduct of a lawsuit, this does not mean that he or she has any idea of how to collect the money judgment in the event of a successful lawsuit. Collection requires tracking down the location of assets (possibly through a court-ordered interrogatory), filing the correct paperwork to attach them, and assisting in asset liquidation. Few lawyers have taken the time to acquire this level of expertise.

Clearly, finding a lawyer with money judgment collection expertise is of paramount importance if a company regularly finds itself with money judgments but no way to collect. Although one can find the right lawyer through references from other attorneys or collection agencies, this can involve a long process of trying out a succession of lawyers until a productive one is found.

Cost: *Installation time:* 🕑

9.28 Reclaim Goods from Insolvent Customers

When a company ships goods to a customer and then learns that the customer has gone bankrupt, the collections department usually settles in for a long period of filing claims in bankruptcy court and attempting to extract a few pennies on the dollar after many months of waiting.

However, there is an alternative if the company acts promptly following the customer's declaration of bankruptcy. The company can reclaim any of its goods already delivered to the customer, but only if it is a credit transaction, the customer is insolvent when it *receives* the goods, the company demands that the goods be returned within ten business days of the customer's receipt of them, and the customer still has possession of the goods when the company demands their return. This is obviously a restrictive set of conditions, so reclamation is not a legally viable alternative under the following conditions:

- The customer pays cash for the goods
- The customer becomes insolvent *after* receiving the goods

- The customer has already sold the goods to a third party
- The customer has converted the goods through some internal processing into another product
- The company demands return of the goods too late

If the collections department thinks a reclamation is possible under these rules, it should demand return of the goods in writing, and preferably by an overnight delivery service that requires a signature for package receipt, thereby establishing a firm receipt date that will hold up in court.

If the company makes its claim in a timely manner and this is upheld by the bankruptcy court, the company can expect either a cash payment for the goods, return of the goods, or at least a security interest in the goods resulting in a priority claim.

Cost: *Installation time:* 🕐 🕐 🕐

9.29 File an Involuntary Bankruptcy Petition for a Customer

Sometimes a customer is completely unwilling to pay a debt and also appears to be ridding itself of assets, potentially leaving nothing for a company to obtain in payment. In this situation, all assets will likely be gone before a company can obtain a judgment through the court system, especially if its claim is contested by the customer.

A possible solution is to find two other creditors of the customer (all with unsecured claims) and jointly file an involuntary bankruptcy petition. The threat of doing so may be a sufficient incentive for a customer to pay its debt. If not, the court can then force the customer into bankruptcy and appoint a trustee to oversee the business, thereby keeping additional assets from being liquidated.

A problem is that 10 days can pass between the involuntary filing and the issuance of a summons, and then another 20 days during which the customer has an opportunity to file an answer, as well as more time if there is a court backlog. During this interval, the customer can continue to liquidate assets. Admittedly, all of these assets can be pulled back into the corporate entity if they occur within 90 days of the bankruptcy event, but it can be extremely difficult to track down the assets. Another issue is that the court may throw out the petition and award court costs and attorney fees to the customer, and possibly even punitive damages. Thus, be certain of your case before filing an involuntary bankruptcy petition.

Cost: 💰   *Installation time:* ⏰ ⏰

9.30 Report a Customer to the Internal Revenue Service

When it becomes apparent that a customer will not pay for an overdue invoice no matter what action a company takes, it may be time for the most extreme collection activity of all, which is reporting the customer to the Internal Revenue Service (IRS) in hopes of obtaining a reward for turning in this information. To do so, one must have significant evidence that the customer is defrauding the government in some manner, assemble this information, and turn it in to the IRS at one of the locations noted in Exhibit 9.2. If the IRS uses this information to collect funds from the customer, it can award from 1% to 15% of the collected funds to the company, depending on the relevance of the forwarded information to the investigation. To claim an award, one must complete IRS Form 211, which is also noted in Exhibit 9.2.

This is a last-resort collection activity, because the IRS may take several years to achieve a collection, the award percentage is small, and the odds of success are generally low. Also, it is a foregone conclusion that the customer, if it ever learns of the company's involvement in this action, will never do business with the company again.

Cost: 💰   *Installation time:* ⏰ ⏰

9.31 Use the Collections Department to Collect Loans to Former Employees

Employees sometimes leave a company suddenly with unpaid loans or advances. Although the payroll department does its best to offset these liabilities against a final paycheck, some liabilities may be so large that a balance remains. If so, the human resources department usually requests payment. Because this department has no experience in collecting debts, payments tend to be both few in number and late in coming.

Exhibit 9.2 *Application for Reward for Original Information*

Form 211 (Rev. 7-2003) Department of the Treasury **Internal Revenue Service**	**Application for Reward for** **Original Information**	OMB Clearance No. 1545-0409
		Claim No.

This application is voluntary and the information requested enables us to determine and pay rewards. We use the information to record a claimant's reward as taxable income and to identify any tax outstanding (including taxes on a joint return filed with a spouse) against which the reward would first be applied. We need taxpayer identification numbers, i.e., social security number (SSN) or employer identification number (EIN), as applicable, in order to process it. Failure to provide the information requested may result in suspension of processing this application. Our authority for asking for the information on this form is 26 USC 6001, 6011, 6109, 7602, 7623, 7802, and 5 USC 301.

Name of claimant. If an individual, provide date of birth	Date of Birth Month Day Year	Claimant's Tax Identification Number, SSN or EIN:
Name of spouse (if applicable)	Date of Birth Month Day Year	Social Security Number

Address of claimant, including zip code, and telephone number (telephone number is optional)

I am applying for a reward, in accordance with the law and regulations, for original information furnished, which led to the detection of a violation of the internal revenue laws of the United States and the collection of taxes, penalties, and fines. I was not an employee of the Department of the Treasury at the time I came into possession of the information nor at the time I divulged it.

Name of IRS employee to whom violation was reported	Title of IRS employee	Date violation reported (Month/day/year)

Method of reporting the information check applicable box   [   ] Telephone   [   ] Mail   [   ] In person

Name of taxpayer who committed the violation and, if known, the taxpayer's SSN or EIN

Address of taxpayer, including zip code if known

Relative to information I furnished on the above taxpayer, the Internal Revenue Service made the following payments to me or on my behalf

Date of Payment   Amount   Name of Person/Entity to Whom Payment was made

Under penalties of perjury, I declare that I have examined this application and my accompanying statements, if any, and to the best of my knowledge and belief, they are true, correct, and complete. I understand the amount of any reward will represent what the Area Director/Compliance Services Field Director considers appropriate in this particular case. I agree to repay the reward, or an appropriate percentage thereof, if the collection on which it is based is subsequently reduced.

Signature of Claimant	Date

The following is to be completed by the Internal Revenue Service

Authorization of Reward

Area Director/Compliance Services Field Director	Sum Recovered $	Amount of Reward $

In consideration of the original information that was furnished by the claimant named above, which concerns a violation of the internal revenue laws and which led to the collection of taxes, penalties, and fines in the sum shown above, I approve payment of a reward in the amount stated.

Signature of the Compliance Services Field Director	Date

MAIL COMPLETED FORM TO THE APPROPRIATE ADDRESS SHOWN ON THE BACK

Form **211** (Rev. 7-2003)   Cat. No. 16571S   publish.no.irs.gov   Department of Treasury - **Internal Revenue Service**

Exhibit 9.2 *(continued)*

Send the completed Form 211 to the Internal Revenue Service Campus for your area shown below.

Name of Campus	Address	
Brookhaven Campus	Internal Revenue Service Attention: ICE Holtsville, NY 00501-0002	If you live in: Connecticut, Maine, Massachusetts, New Hampshire, New York, Rhode Island, Vermont
Cincinnati Campus	Internal Revenue Service Attention: ICE Cincinnati, OH 45999-0002	If you live in: Illinois, Indiana, Iowa, Kansas, Kentucky, Michigan, Minnesota, Missouri, Nebraska, North Dakota, Ohio, South Dakota, West Virginia, Wisconsin
Memphis Campus	Internal Revenue Service Attention: ICE Memphis, TN 37501-0002	If you live in: Alabama, Arkansas, Florida, Georgia, Louisiana, Mississippi, Oklahoma, Tennessee, Texas
Philadelphia Campus	Internal Revenue Service Attention: ICE Philadelphia, PA 19255-0002	If you live in: Delaware, Maryland, New Jersey, North Carolina, Pennsylvania, South Carolina, Virginia, Washington DC, Puerto Rico
Ogden Campus	Internal Revenue Service Attention: ICE Ogden, UT 84201-0002	If you live in: Alaska, Arizona, California, Colorado, Hawaii, Idaho, Montana, Nevada, New Mexico, Oregon, Utah, Washington, Wyoming

PAPERWORK REDUCTION ACT NOTICE: We ask for the information on this form to carry out the internal revenue laws of the United States. We need it to insure that taxpayers are complying with these laws and to allow us to figure and collect the right amount of tax.

You are required to give us the information if you are applying for a reward.

You are not required to provide the information requested on a form that is subject to the Paperwork Reduction Act unless the form displays a valid OMB control number. Books or records relating to a form or its instructions must be retained as long as their contents may become material in the administration of any internal revenue law. Generally, tax returns and return information are confidential, as required by Code section 6103.

The time needed to complete this form will vary depending on individual circumstances. The estimated average time is 15 minutes. If you have comments concerning the accuracy of these time estimates or suggestions for making this form simpler, we would be happy to hear from you. You can write to the Tax Forms Committee, Western Area Distribution Center, Rancho Cordova, CA 95743-0001.

Do NOT send the completed Form 211 to the Tax Forms Committee. Instead, send it to the IRS Campus for your area shown above.

Form 211 (Rev. 7-2003)   Cat. No. 16571S   publish.no.irs.gov   Department of Treasury - **Internal Revenue Service**

Consider shifting this collection task to the collections department. Its staff is accustomed to doggedly pursuing late payments and has a large bag of tricks into which it can delve for the most appropriate method to collect debts from a former employee. This will likely result in much more prompt payment. The only downside is that the collections staff may know the person in question, which may lead them to be more lenient in negotiating payment terms than would normally be the case.

Cost: *Installation time:*

9.32 Contact Customers Regarding Credit Balances

On occasion, a customer will overpay or double pay an invoice. Unless a company has a policy of returning these payments to customers at once, there will likely be a credit sitting on the company's books for some time of which the customer is not aware. Depending on local state laws, these credit balances may eventually have to be turned over to the state as unclaimed property. This benefits neither the company nor its customers.

A better approach is to regularly contact customers about these balances and ask them if they want the credit balance returned or if they would prefer to place an order and have the credit applied against it. In the latter case, the company earns a profit on any sale made. No matter which alternative a customer chooses, the company gains the customer's goodwill through its honesty. To ensure that this best practice is followed, enter it on the accounting department's activities calendar. Once a quarter is a sufficient interval for making this contact.

Cost: *Installation time:*

9.33 Negotiate with the Customer

Many of the earlier best practices may have left the impression that there is a clear process to be followed in order to achieve a full collection: dunning letters, phone calls, collection agency, lawsuit, and so on. Although this checklist approach works well in many cases, it can also take many months (if not years) to run through the entire process. Because a company wants its money as soon as possible, following a set collection path may not always be in its best interests. Instead, train the collections staff in the more subtle art of negotiation. This involves listening carefully to what a customer says regarding its financial situation and ability to pay a debt and using this information to obtain some sort of payment as soon as possible. Although negotiation may not result in full payment, it can frequently result in a rapid settlement that allows the collections staff to take a small write-off and move on to other collection problems in short order.

Negotiation skills are not innate. The collections manager must arrange for training sessions, as well as counsel the collections staff on problem accounts and sit in on collection calls and meetings to instill in the staff the right negotiation perspective. For a large collections department, this calls for the services of a full-time trainer. It can take a long time to achieve a uniformly high level of negotiation expertise, and some collectors will simply never get the knack.

Cost: *Installation time:*

10

Deduction Management

This chapter contains 12 best practices related to the management of deductions. The first three involve the use of centralization and standard systems to improve the efficiency of the process, while the next six address several approaches for resolving deduction issues. The final three best practices cover miscellaneous deduction topics. These best practices are summarized in Exhibit 10.1.

It is no accident that the bulk of the best practices in this chapter address procedures for determining who is to resolve deduction problems, how much authority they are allowed to do so, and the order in which deductions should be resolved. If a company is suffering from an overabundance of unresolved deductions, close

Exhibit 10.1 *Summary of Deduction Management Best Practices*

10.1	Centrally manage the deductions resolution process
10.2	Enforce a standard procedure for handling unauthorized deductions
10.3	Confirm and document customer insurance requirements
10.4	Summarize and resolve underlying issues causing deductions
10.5	Resolve deductions by declining order of dollar volume
10.6	Resolve pricing issues before approving orders
10.7	Resolve significant deduction issues in person
10.8	Place deduction resolution responsibility on the salesperson
10.9	Allow the customer service staff limited authority to resolve deductions
10.10	Discuss open deductions with the repairs department
10.11	Obtain better access to trade promotion information
10.12	Cut off customers based on the size of unauthorized deductions

attention to these five best practices (10.4 through 10.9) is key to bringing the problem under control.

10.1 Centrally Manage the Deductions Resolution Process

An aggravating problem with deductions is how they are passed from person to person within the company without ever reaching resolution. The usual problem is that the initial reviewer passes the deduction along to the person who initially appears to be most likely to resolve the problem, and then forgets that the deduction exists, having only achieved the short-term goal of removing it from his or her desk. Then the recipient either passes the issue along to a third person or requests a response from the customer, promptly forgetting about the issue. This constant transfer of responsibility inevitably results in very long deduction resolution periods, annoyed customers, and slow cash flow.

The solution is to centrally manage the deductions resolution process. A single person should be assigned responsibility for the deductions of a small group of customers and should monitor the status of each open deduction on a daily basis, no matter which person within the company is currently handling resolution issues. By doing so, one can apply constant pressure to deduction resolution, thereby shrinking the number of receivable days outstanding.

A problem with this approach is when the person responsible for a specific set of customer deductions is absent for multiple days. Without that person driving the resolution process, it is likely that deduction resolution will slow down at once. To avoid this problem, one can either assign a backup person or use workflow management software to automatically monitor the status of deductions and route open issues to the correct people within the company.

 *Cost:*   *Installation time:*

10.2 Enforce a Standard Procedure for Handling Unauthorized Deductions

Unauthorized deductions are the bane of the collections department. Many are so small that they seem too minor to bother with and are written off. Others are so large that they incur the immediate attention of the collection manager, resulting in prompt follow-up. The bulk of deductions fall somewhere between these two extremes, resulting in a muddle of deductions that no one wants to deal with, but that are cumulatively too large to write off. A common result is a great deal of management time spent reviewing individual deductions to determine a course of action.

The creation and enforcement of a standard procedure for unauthorized deductions is the answer. The procedure tends to follow a tiered approach, in which very small deductions are not worth the effort of even a single customer contact and are immediately written off. For larger deductions, a company may require immediate follow-up or only follow-up after the second deduction, or an immediate rebilling—the choice is up to the individual company. The procedure should include such basic steps as the following:

1. Ensuring that the customer has provided adequate documentation of the problem
2. Collecting data needed to substantiate or refute the claim
3. Contacting the customer to obtain missing information
4. Once collected, reviewing all information to determine a recommended course of action
5. Depending on the size of the deduction, obtaining necessary approvals
6. Contacting the customer with resolution information
7. If approved, entering credit information into the accounting system to clear debit balances representing valid deductions

The main point is to be consistent. The collections staff must be drilled in the use of this procedure, so there is absolutely no question about how to handle a deduction. This best practice will favorably increase departmental efficiency and require less management time to pass judgment on individual deduction problems.

When creating the procedure, keep it as simple as possible, especially in regard to tracking deductions. For example, if the procedure calls for a customer warning only after the second deduction is received, the accounting system must have a way to track deductions and report this information back to the collections staff. If this capability does not exist, it is better to adopt a simpler policy, such as billing back all deductions at once.

Consider posting the deduction handling procedure on the company intranet site. By doing so, it is easy to make changes to the procedure, post the altered document, and then issue an e-mail to interested staff regarding the changes and where the document can be found.

A final point is that any procedure needs to be reviewed occasionally to ensure that current business practices are still adequately met by the procedure. For example, if a company acquires another entity with an entirely different deduction resolution system, it may be worthwhile to compare the two and merge the best features into a common system, or at least impose the corporate procedure on the new acquisition in order to ensure process consistency throughout the organization. To ensure that procedures are reviewed, include it as a task on the annual department calendar at least once a year. Also, include a procedures review on an acquisition activities checklist, so the procedures of both entities can be combined as part of the initial restructuring.

Cost: *Installation time:*

10.3 Confirm and Document Customer Insurance Requirements

A key source of deduction disputes is the insurance charge that a company sometimes includes on its invoices to cover the risk of shipment damage. Even though this may be a direct cost pass-through with no profit to the company at all, some customers view this charge as unnecessary and a way for the company to earn additional profit. However, the level of product damage in transit may be sufficiently high that the company would incur significant deductions for damaged goods if it did not insure the shipments. Thus, a company is stuck between the proverbial rock and a hard place—either it must deal with deductions for insurance or deductions for damaged goods.

The solution is to have customers sign a statement authorizing the company to not obtain insurance for goods shipped to them. By retaining this statement in the customer's file, the collections staff can produce it whenever a customer tries to obtain a deduction for a damaged delivery. The downside to this solution is that this is yet one more piece of paper required as part of the ordering process. To save time, consider including it in the initial credit application package, or even as a check-off within the credit application document.

Cost: *Installation time:*

10.4 Summarize and Resolve Underlying Issues Causing Deductions

Although some customers take deductions for the sole goal of reducing the amount they owe, most customers have an actual complaint (e.g., damaged goods, late delivery, wrong item shipped). Most collections departments focus only on resolving deductions as they arrive in order to clear them from the accounts receivable aging report and never attempt to resolve the underlying problems causing the deductions. If they did so, deduction volumes would decline, resulting in a significant cost savings not only in the collections department but also in the production and logistics areas, where returned goods are handled.

An easy solution to this irritating problem is to have the collections staff summarize all deductions regularly and forward this information to management. The management team can then review the data to see what problems are causing the deductions, and correct them. The summary report can be sorted several ways: by customer, by dollar volume, by product, by date, and so on. It may be best to issue the report sorted in several formats, because problems hidden within one reporting format are more visible in others.

This best practice calls for the use of a central deductions database, which can be as simple as an electronic spreadsheet for smaller organizations or a database constituting part of a larger enterprise resources planning system, as is used in large companies.

Cost: *Installation time:* 🕐 🕐

10.5 Resolve Deductions by Declining Order of Dollar Volume

A collections manager may inherit a large deductions problem where there are hundreds of deductions sitting on the accounts receivable aging. The manager needs to address the backlog, but does not have the resources to do so within a short time period. The result is typically continuing problems with all customers who take deductions, not only because old receivables are still on the books, but also because the underlying reasons for the deductions have not been fixed, resulting in even more ongoing deductions.

The solution is to resolve deductions for the largest-dollar items first, and then work down through the deductions list in declining dollar order. This approach is initially designed to take out of the accounts receivable list the largest deductions, but more important, it allows the collections staff to research the reasons why the largest deductions are occurring and to put a stop to them. As the staff gradually fixes these issues and moves down to small deductions, it can address relatively smaller underlying deduction issues. Thus, this approach is designed to use deduction dollar volume as the criterion for determining the relative importance of fixes needed to resolve problems causing deductions.

This approach may have the initial reverse result of actually *increasing* the number of unresolved deductions on the books, because the collections staff is now focusing on the largest and therefore most time-consuming deduction problems. Although this outcome is likely, the underlying problem resolutions implemented by the collections team should gradually eliminate source problems that will dry up the flood of incoming deductions, so the situation will improve some months into the future.

Cost: Installation time: 🕰 🕰 🕰

10.6 Resolve Pricing Issues before Approving Orders

A common source of deduction issues is a dispute between the company and customer regarding the correct price to be paid. Customers typically only pay based on the price they listed in their purchase orders issued to the company. This is a particular problem when a customer uses an automated payment system that issues checks based on purchase orders, because they do not even bother to use or review invoices issued by the company.

The solution is to compare the prices listed on customer purchase orders to the official company price list and resolve pricing discrepancies in advance before any orders are approved for shipment. In low transaction volume situations, one can assign a staff person to manually conduct this comparison. Higher-volume situations call for a more expensive automated solution, where the computer system automatically conducts the comparison. Many commercially available accounting systems do not have this comparison function built into them and require expensive customization. No matter which approach is used, the process is eased if the company pricing structure is as simple as possible.

The resolution of pricing issues is not a credit management function. Instead, the customer service staff should be responsible for contacting customers about this issue.

Cost: 💵 💵   *Installation time:* ⏰

10.7 Resolve Significant Deduction Issues in Person

Some customers have massive numbers of deductions, frequently involving a wide array of reasons. Resolving these issues can require many phone calls, as well as faxes back and forth of such supporting documentation as purchase orders and bills of lading. The volume of information required for resolution virtually mandates a lengthy period to reach settlement. The number of issues and resulting contacts involved can also make both parties testy, which adversely impacts the ongoing business relationship.

A solution is to schedule regular face-to-face meetings with the customer to address the deductions. Not only does this approach allow both parties to settle many issues in one meeting, but everyone involved also gets to meet each other, which greatly enhances communications and makes future deduction resolution easier. The main problem with personal visits is the cost of the trip, not only in terms of travel costs but also in the time spent away from the office. Thus, this approach works better for local customers.

Cost: 💵 💵   *Installation time:* ⏰

10.8 Place Deduction Resolution Responsibility on the Salesperson

A small proportion of all customers is usually responsible for the bulk of the deduction problems that a company must resolve. This may be caused by a picky customer receiving staff, a propensity to delay payment unless all paperwork is perfectly in order, or simply a general orientation toward using any excuse to delay payment. Whatever the reason for the deductions, the amount of labor required to resolve these problems may be far out of proportion to the amount of profit earned from all sales to those customers.

A reasonable solution is to shift the deduction resolution problem onto the salesperson who is responsible for the account. The reasoning is that if the salesperson wants to earn a commission by selling to these difficult customers, he or she must compare the time wasted on deduction resolution to the amount of commission earned. A common result is either a rapid decline in sales to these customers or, if sales volume is sufficiently high, a considerable reduction in deduction issues.

The collections staff can easily convey deduction information to the sales staff with a weekly deduction summarization report, listing invoice numbers and the amounts of deductions taken. If the sales staff has e-mail access, this information can be sent to them even if they are in the field and can be accompanied by digitized images of the invoices, checks, and any related notices received from customers.

A problem with this approach is for the salesperson to take the customer's side in deduction resolution in order to quickly reduce the deduction resolution workload. If this occurs, company managers can cut the salesperson's commission or periodic bonus until such time as greater attention is paid to the deductions issue. An alternative is to have the sales staff resolve only smaller deductions, thereby saving the collections staff from dealing with the paperwork for many inconsequential deductions while also keeping the sales staff from settling large deductions too much in favor of customers.

It is also common to hear loud complaints from the sales staff about the amount of their time being wasted on deductions resolution when their time could be better spent selling, so management must strongly support this policy in order to override the complaints.

Cost: 🖋️   Installation time: ⏰

10.9 Allow the Customer Service Staff Limited Authority to Resolve Deductions

When customers find a problem with a company's delivery to them, they typically contact the customer service department first. If so, there is nothing more irritating than to wait while the customer service staff bumps the deduction request up through an interminable chain of command before finally reaching someone with the authority to resolve the issue. These delays can contribute many days to the resolution of even the most insignificant deductions.

The solution is to give the customer service staff the authority to resolve deductions on the spot. By doing so, many deductions are handled so fast that the collections staff never sees a problem and can profitably spend the bulk of its time working on larger-dollar collection issues.

The main difficulty with this approach is determining at what point extra approval of a proposed deduction is allowed. Typically, 80% of all deduction issues can be resolved by the customer service staff on the first customer contact, because the dollar amounts involved are so small that even a disproportionate amount of settlements in the customers' favor will not have much of a negative financial impact on the company. Larger deduction issues should normally be handed over to a specialized team of senior collections staff who have more experience in handling these issues.

Cost: *Installation time:* 🕐

10.10 Discuss Open Deductions with the Repairs Department

The repairs department is usually an overworked group that either repairs products returned by customers or elects to entirely replace them. They may also be called on to rework items that were damaged during the production process. If some items require special parts, this group may also place orders with suppliers for the parts, which causes a repair delay until the parts arrive. The result is conflicting requirements to service internal and external customers at the same time, possibly resulting in excessive delays for customer deductions taken to offset items sent back for repair.

Although the collections staff will not always succeed in having the repairs department fix customer products ahead of all other priority items, it can at least bring the most recent list of deductions to them and discuss what can be done to resolve the problems as expeditiously as possible. The focus of these meetings should be on completing those repairs interfering with collection of the largest deductions. It may also result in the repairs staff replacing more returned products with new ones, rather than waiting extra days for the arrival of parts to attempt a repair.

Cost: *Installation time:* 🕐

10.11 Obtain Better Access to Trade Promotion Information

Customers may not be taking deductions based on the usual pricing, quantity, or quality reasons. Instead, the marketing department may be offering them a variety of trade promotions for which they are taking entirely valid deductions. Because the collections staff may not have ready access to this information, they must go through a considerable amount of research to see if the deductions are correct.

A range of solutions is available to obtain better information about trade promotions. At the most manual level, the marketing manager can prepare and distribute a memo whenever trade promotions arise, summarizing the terms of each offered promotion and its duration; this is probably sufficient if few promotions are offered. For more active marketing departments, this may require the development of a networked database that the collections staff can access, showing not only the details of each promotion but also the customers to whom it applies. This latter approach usually requires one to assign a customer class code to each customer in the computer system and then link promotion deals to the class code for indexing purposes. Also, if a database is set up for this purpose, expect a significant expenditure of programming time to complete the project.

Cost:    *Installation time:* 🕐 🕐

10.12 Cut Off Customers Based on the Size of Unauthorized Deductions

Most managers will put up with customers who take unauthorized deductions. By doing so, they may preserve a considerable amount of top-line revenue. However, an activity-based costing (ABC) analysis often reveals that the time taken by internal staff to resolve deduction disputes is so expensive that the company realizes no profit at all on sales to these customers.

The solution is to conduct a periodic ABC analysis to compile the cost to resolve deduction issues. By comparing this deduction cost to the profit earned by customer, a company can readily determine which customers to cut off in order to improve the overall level of profitability. The result may not be a complete stoppage in business with a customer, but rather a change in credit terms to cash in advance, so the customer cannot continue to make deductions from payments.

An ABC review can be so time consuming that it should be completed no more than once a year. Also, even if the comparison of ABC deduction costs to customer profits results in the conclusion that a customer should be cut off, this is not necessarily the case when step-costing problems arise. Under the step-costing concept, if there is sufficient work to keep a staff person busy even if a customer and its attendant deduction problems are cut off, then the customer should not be cut off. Otherwise, the company loses the contribution margin earned from the customer without losing any related costs. Thus, this best practice is more valid when clear evidence exists that company labor costs will drop as a result of dropping a customer.

Cost: *Installation time:* 🕐

11

Outsourcing Collections

This chapter contains 18 best practices related to outsourcing and controlling various aspects of the collections function. The first six describe different types of outsourcing, ranging from the complete shifting of collections to an agency (not usually recommended), through the more limited outsourcing of credit checking, dunning letters, and not sufficient funds (NSF) collections, and on to the outright sale of accounts receivable. Four more best practices involve the criteria one should use to select a collections agency, and the remaining eight cover a range of outsourcing topics, including the timing of sending accounts to collection, using an in-house collection agency, and measuring agency performance. These best practices are summarized in Exhibit 11.1.

Although outsourcing a large amount of collections work is generally not the direction most companies take, it is still a valid approach when used judiciously. Some collection agencies have exceptional experience with customers in specific industries, and thus enjoy a high degree of collection success. Consequently, do not blanche at a collection agency's fee structure and refuse to use them; instead, consider the cost to the company if an invoice is *never* collected. Also, collection agencies can be useful during periods when the in-house and collections staff is completely overwhelmed with work and needs to offload some tasks for a limited period.

11.1 Outsource Collections

Some companies have a difficult time creating an effective collections department. Perhaps management of the function is poor, or the staff is not well trained, or it does not have sufficient sway over other departments, such as sales, to garner support in changing underlying systems in a way that will reduce the amount of

---

Exhibit 11.1 *Summary of Outsourcing Best Practices*

11.1   Outsource collections

11.2   Outsource credit checking

11.3   Outsource dunning letters to a credit reporting agency

11.4   Outsource NSF collections

11.5   Sell accounts receivable to a factoring organization

11.6   Sell uncollectible invoices to a debt buyer

11.7   Select agencies based on performance rather than fees

11.8   Select agencies based on references

11.9   Select agencies based on prior experience with specific customers

11.10 Use only collection agencies that have integrated legal services

11.11 Use an attorney first to obtain repayment of "reasonable attorney's fees"

11.12 Use several collection agencies at once

11.13 Create an in-house collection agency

11.14 Shift smaller accounts to collection agencies immediately

11.15 Refer accounts to collection agencies sooner

11.16 Do not shift fraudulent accounts to a collection agency

11.17 Periodically verify that the collection agency is bonded

11.18 Track the regularity of collection agency remittances

---

accounts receivable to collect. Whatever the reason or combination of reasons may be, there are times when the function simply does not work. A variation on this situation is when a collections staff is so overwhelmed with work that it cannot pay a sufficient amount of attention to the most difficult collection issues. This problem is much more common. In either case, the solution may be to go outside the company for help.

The best practice that solves this problem is to outsource the entire function or some portion of it. When doing so, a company sends its accounts receivable aging report to a collections agency, which contacts all customers with overdue invoices having reached a prespecified age—perhaps 60 days old, or whatever the agreement with the agency may specify. The agency is then responsible for bringing in the funds. In exchange, the agency either requires a percentage of each collected invoice (typically one-third) as payment for its services or charges an hourly rate for its services.

Despite the common perception that collection agencies only go after larger outstanding invoices, a few specialize in the more difficult types of collections, such as discounts for pricing discrepancies, damaged goods, promotional allowances, quality problems, quantity delivered variances, unearned cash discounts, and the like. Although collection agencies charge high fees for these specialized services to compensate them for the extra effort required, this option may still be better than a complete write-off of the deductions. Examples of collection agencies in this line of business are the Pyramid Group (*www.pyramidgroup.com*) and IAB (*www.iabinc.com*).

It is almost always less expensive to pay an hourly fee for collection services, rather than a percentage of the amounts collected. However, going with an hourly payment approach gives the supplier less initiative to collect payments. To counteract the reduced level of incentive, it is useful to continually measure the collection effectiveness of the supplier and switch to a new supplier if only a low percentages of invoices is being collected. This approach can be effective for quickly bringing a trained group of collection professionals to bear on an existing collections problem.

Before deciding on the outsourcing route, one must consider a variety of issues that make this solution appropriate for only a minority of situations. The first problem is cost. It is nearly always cheaper to keep the collections function in-house because the fees charged by any supplier must include a profit, which automatically makes its services more expensive. This problem is particularly important if the payment method is a percentage of the cash collected, because the percentage can be considerable. Also, this approach does not allow one to use most of the other best practices discussed in this book—by moving the entire function elsewhere, there is no longer any reason to improve the department's efficiency. Only a few best practices, those involving other departments (such as the sales and credit departments), are still available for implementation. Finally and most important, outsourcing the collections function puts the department's emphasis squarely on collecting money, rather than on the equally important issue of correcting the underlying problems that are causing customers to not pay their bills on time.

A collections supplier has absolutely no incentive to inform a company of why customers are not paying, because by doing so it is giving the company information that will reduce the number of overdue invoices and therefore the amount of the supplier's collection business. For example, if a customer does not pay its bills because a company repeatedly misprices its products, the collections agency will not inform the company of its error because then the invoice issue will be fixed and there will be fewer invoices to collect. All of these issues are major ones, requiring considerable deliberation before a company decides to outsource its collections function. Typically, this best practice should only be used in situations where a company wants to outsource the collection of a few of its most difficult collection problems. In most other cases, it is infinitely less expensive to search for a qualified manager who can bring the collections department up to a peak level of efficiency.

If a company elects to outsource its collections function, it is critical to maintain an in-house team that handles the determination of credit policy and the issuance of credit to customers. Management should be required to continuously review and revise credit levels granted, so a company maintains the correct balance of added sales versus bad debts incurred. The credit management function is too critical to ever be outsourced.

Cost: 💵 💵 💵   *Installation time:* ⏰

11.2 Outsource Credit Checking

Some companies operate under the policy that they will use the smallest possible number of employees, only grudgingly adding staff. Although this approach is useful for keeping overhead down and protecting a company from excessive losses if revenue takes a downward turn, the credit manager can become seriously backed up when a large quantity of credit applications arrive and there is no staff time to review them. The result can be delayed credit approvals, resulting in lost sales.

One possibility is to outsource the time-consuming credit checking task. Several collection agencies offer this service. The agency assigns a staff person to contact the bank and trade references listed on the application and returns the completed form to the credit manager, who now spends a small amount of quality time reviewing the application and deciding on the most appropriate credit arrangement. Some collection agencies can provide this service for less than the cost of doing it in-house, because they may have a database of collection and trade reference information already built up for the company's industry.

Even if this service is more expensive than doing it in-house, using it allows the credit manager to offload excessive workloads during peak periods of transaction volume, rather than having to hire an additional full-time person who will subsequently be underutilized. Some companies prefer to outsource all credit checking, on the grounds that they would rather spend their time analyzing credit information than accumulating it.

Cost: *Installation time:* 🕐

11.3 Outsource Dunning Letters to a Credit Reporting Agency

Customers are all too used to seeing dunning letters sent by a company. This only tells them that the company has not yet gotten serious enough about collection to have someone call them, much less consider sending the account to a collection agency. Thus, a dunning letter can be construed as a prewarning that money will be payable in the near future, but not just yet.

A good, inexpensive way to jolt complacent customers into making a payment is to have a credit reporting agency write a dunning letter on behalf of the company. The letter goes out on the reporting agency's letterhead, so the customer thinks its account has been turned over to the agency. Furthermore, because the letter is coming from a *credit reporting agency* and not just a collection agency, a customer realizes that this action is now being added to its credit report for all to see.

As an example, Dun & Bradstreet offers the DunsDemand Letter, which (as of the publication date) costs $12.50 per letter issued or somewhat less on a subscription basis. The letter goes out on Dun & Bradstreet letterhead and includes a remittance allowing customers to send their payments back to the company, rather than to Dun & Bradstreet. For $25, Dun & Bradstreet will instead send a series of three letters to one's customers.

Cost: 💵   *Installation time:* 🕐 🕐

11.4 Outsource NSF Collections

In some industries, an uncomfortably high proportion of all credit sales made will result in a not sufficient funds (NSF) check, for which the depositing bank will charge a fee back to the company. The company then has the choice of either redepositing the check or pursuing the customer for a new payment, and also of whether to charge the NSF fee back to the customer. Furthermore, an NSF demands additional accounting to back it out of the cash receipts journal. No matter what collection approach is used, the handling of NSFs, especially in high volume, represents a major efficiency reduction for the accounting department.

One solution is to convert these paper checks into electronic checks on-site and transmit the information to a service bureau specializing in NSF collections. They resubmit the checks through the Automated Clearing House (ACH) Network system. The company can also add an NSF fee to the resubmitted check amounts, so there is no trouble collecting the additional amount. In addition, the company can time the resubmission of these electronic checks to the period when it thinks cash is most likely to be in customer bank accounts.

A transaction fee is associated with the ACH submissions, which varies by service bureau. One must also purchase or lease the check reader and related software from the service bureau. The fees involved generally make this option viable only for companies experiencing large NSF volumes.

Cost: *Installation time:*

11.5 Sell Accounts Receivable to a Factoring Organization

A company may wrestle with collection problems for many months while its cash flow problems mount. One can become desperate in these situations, caving in on all sorts of deduction or discounting demands from customers in order to rake in sufficient cash to meet the company's own cash requirements. Underfunded companies constantly face this situation.

One solution is to sell accounts receivable to a factoring organization. This can involve several types, ranging from the receipt of a loan from the factor that is collateralized by one's accounts receivable, through a sale of receivables that allows the right of return for uncollectible invoices, to the outright sale of receivables. This approach brings in ready cash for those companies requiring it right away.

The problem with factoring is its expense. The interest rate is reasonable only if the arrangement is actually a loan with receivables used as collateral. It is vastly more expensive to sell receivables outright, because the factor is taking on the risk of collection. The price paid will decline rapidly as receivables age, possibly declining to a few cents on the dollar for the oldest receivables. Thus, the outright sale of receivables is usually only practiced by those companies with either serious cash flow problems or an unwillingness to invest in a sufficiently large collections department to handle the volume of collections work. See the next best practice for an additional discussion of selling invoices.

Cost: 💵 💵 💵   *Installation time:* ⏰

11.6 Sell Uncollectible Invoices to a Debt Buyer

What should one do when the collections staff cannot collect a debt, neither can a collection agency, and the company is not willing to spend the money for legal resolution? The usual response is to write off the invoice as a bad debt.

A possible alternative for larger companies is to sell these invoices to debt buyers. By doing so, the company realizes a few pennies on the dollar while the debt buyer takes on the collection task in exchange for the chance to earn a substantial return if even a few customers can be forced to pay. Examples of debt buyers of consumer receivables are Asta Funding and Portfolio Recovery Associates, and the NCO Group also purchases commercial receivables.

This approach can be considered either an extremely expensive one or nearly free, depending on the company's point of view—it is selling off assets for next to nothing and must recognize a substantial loss as part of the deal; however, it is gaining a small amount of cash flow from the transaction that it would otherwise never have obtained. The amount earned from a sale to a debt buyer can go up substantially if the accounts sold are relatively new, so the collections manager must be willing to promptly make the sale decision if no other collection possibility is apparent.

Selling receivables is not a viable option for smaller firms, because debt buyers prefer to purchase receivables in large blocks, from which they can selectively mine a small number of higher-probability collection targets.

Cost: 💵 💵 💵   *Installation time:* ⏰

11.7 Select Agencies Based on Performance Rather than Fees

The one issue that arises every time a company contemplates shifting overdue invoices to an agency is the extremely high cost of doing so—usually between

20% and 33% of the invoice amount will be paid to the agency in the event of collection. Given the high price, credit managers have a tendency to shop around for the lowest-priced agency, including some that work on an hourly basis. The result is frequently contracting with an agency that achieves a lower rate of collection success. Collection agencies working for less money tend to pick from the available invoices in order to maximize their profitability, and so will quickly drop any invoices for which there is not a high chance of collectibility.

The answer is to not base the outsourcing decision solely on cost, but rather on the total cost-effectiveness of an agency. This means one should compare the fees charged by an agency to the amount of dollars it has succeeded in collecting and make an agency retention decision based on that ratio. For this best practice to succeed, one should use several collection agencies at once, so one can compare the cost-benefit ratio for several agencies and gradually winnow out the poor performers. A likely outcome is that the company retains the most expensive agency instead of the cheapest, because the best collectors charge top dollar for their services.

Be sure to document the cost-benefit comparison, because senior managers may go on a cost-cutting tear and attempt to force the collection manager to drop the expensive agencies in favor of some less expensive solution.

Cost: Installation time:

11.8 Select Agencies Based on References

When a collection agency engages in illegal practices to collect a debt on one's behalf, the company is technically liable for the agency's actions, because the agency is acting as the company's agent. Although this occurrence is rare, a company can be forced to pay penalties or civil judgments if these illegal practices become known.

The solution is to conduct a thorough reference check on all collection agencies one plans to use, verifying the experiences that other companies have had. Another indicator is the length of time the agency has been in business (easily verified through a credit report), because an agency operating on the borders of the law is not likely to last long. The illegal practices issue alone scares many companies into using the same collection agency for years, on the grounds that they do not want to take the risk of using an unknown agency. This reaction is extreme—at a minimum, maintain business with a small group of agencies, so one can see how they perform in comparison to each other.

Cost: *Installation time:* 🕑

11.9 Select Agencies Based on Prior Experience with Specific Customers

It is always more efficient to collect from customers with whom the company has a considerable amount of prior collection experience. For these customers, a personal relationship may exist between the collection person and the customer's accounts payable staff, the company has adequate information about various contacts within the company, or there is some knowledge of what collection activities have resulted in payments in the past.

This same principle applies to the assignment of an overdue invoice to a collection agency. If the company hands over an account to an agency that has never dealt with a customer before, the agency must progress through a ramp-up period ranging anywhere from a few minutes to multiple weeks, while it gathers information about the customer. This ramp-up period costs the company in uncollected funds. Consequently, one should consider contacting a collection agency located near the customer and asking if they have experience with the customer. Because this practice may result in a vast number of collection agencies working for the company, only do so for the largest-dollar outstanding invoices, where prior experience with specific customers will have the largest potential pay-off.

Cost: *Installation time:* 🕑

11.10 Use Only Collection Agencies that Have Integrated Legal Services

Once a company refers an overdue account to a collection agency, it should not have to deal with the additional tasks of lining up lawyers to assist the collection agency's staff in taking action against customers. Yet this problem sometimes occurs, because some of the smaller collection agencies are just a few people with a fax machine and telephones; once they determine that collection is unlikely, they simply dump invoices back onto the referring company.

A better solution is to locate collection agencies that not only handle the initial customer contacts but who also have connections with law firms sufficient to immediately refer the invoices to the lawyers for appropriate legal action. This approach not only prevents a company from having to deal directly with lawyers but also keeps overdue invoices from being bounced back by a collection agency unless there is absolutely no hope of collection. Also, this approach keeps a company from having to run through several law firms before finding one with sufficient expertise to deal efficiently with overdue customer accounts. A final benefit is that collection agencies that have set up these legal connections are typically those that have been in business the longest and have the most professional methods for dealing with customers, so a company will probably obtain the best overall collection service by following this best practice.

Cost:    *Installation time:*

11.11 Use an Attorney First to Obtain Repayment of "Reasonable Attorney's Fees"

Some customers will not be dislodged from their money unless the collections manager turns over the account to a collections agency that uses more frequent and vigorous collection methods. However, the company must then pay a substantial fee for this service. Is there a less expensive collection approach?

There may be if the customer signed a credit application requiring it to pay for "reasonable attorney's fees" to collect a debt, which is standard contract language in many instances. If so, consider bypassing the collection agency and passing the account directly to an attorney for collection. Of course, there is still the issue of obtaining reimbursement for the attorney's fees, which may be a prolonged affair. However, because the customer agreed to the legal fee reimbursement on the credit application, the company should eventually succeed in collecting.

Cost: *Installation time:*

11.12 Use Several Collection Agencies at Once

It can become excessively comfortable to build up a long-term relationship with a single collection agency and automatically forward problem accounts to it. The problem is that the collection agency may become more focused on maintaining a good relationship with the collections manager than on collecting the referred accounts. The result is an increased bad debt percentage.

A solution is to form relationships with multiple collection agencies and dole out business to all of them. By doing so, one can monitor and compare results by agency, shifting new business away from the worst performers. If an agency does such a poor job that the best alternative is to drop them, always add a new agency to the mix. By doing so, there is always a new organization against which to benchmark the performance of the group and the other designated collection agencies will be kept on their toes.

The only downside is the extra effort of monitoring which agency is responsible for which customer account. To make this chore less burdensome, always concentrate all overdue invoices for a specific customer with the same collection agency. By doing so, tracking is only by customer and not by invoice (a potentially much larger number), while customers do not have to accept calls from multiple collection agencies, and the agencies can concentrate their efforts on a smaller number of accounts.

 *Cost:* *Installation time:*

11.13 Create an In-House Collection Agency

A third-party collection agency presents two problems: it is expensive and one has no control over how collection activities are handled. The first problem leads to a natural tendency to issue the smallest number of accounts to a collection agency as late as possible, leading to a small proportion of collections. The second issue is particularly important in terms of customer relations, because a collection agency using strong-arm tactics can alienate a customer forever.

One solution is to create an in-house collection agency that works only on the company's overdue collections. For maximum effect, one should create a name independent of the company's and use separate letterhead, so customers will really think they have been turned over to a dreaded collection agency. Sometimes just the concept of having been turned over for collection will break free a payment! Also, because this agency is a subsidiary of the company, the collection manager has direct control over how collections are conducted, so there is no question about alienating collection activities being used. Finally, there will be no need to pay large collection fees to anyone, because the company owns the captive agency.

The best approach is to set up an in-house agency in fact, which calls for incorporation, legal use of a separate name, and the periodic filing of tax returns. All administrative functions can be maintained by the parent company in order to reduce costs, although a few collections staff should be switched over to the subsidiary in order to make customers more firmly believe that a collection agency is now at work.

Cost: 💵   *Installation time:* 🕐 🕐

11.14 Shift Smaller Accounts to Collection Agencies Immediately

It is not uncommon to see a collections department that appears to be understaffed in proportion to the amount of invoice payments to be collected. Although companies sometimes experience trouble attracting and retaining staff in this department, the problem is not necessarily the departmental headcount. An additional issue is that the staff is frequently spending a large proportion of its time contacting customers and researching payment issues for accounts that are quite small, so large invoice balances do not receive sufficient attention to ensure the most rapid collection speed.

A solution is to not even attempt collecting smaller invoices with the in-house staff. Instead, refer these accounts to a collections agency immediately. Although the company will still incur a significant collection fee in exchange for this service, the invoices being referred are so small that the total expense incurred is not that large. This also gives the collections staff vastly more time to deal with the largest accounts, including such activities as calling before invoice due dates to verify upcoming payment dates and making personal visits to customer sites. If handled correctly, the much greater speed of collection on larger accounts should more than offset the incremental increase in collection agency fees.

The invoice size below which all invoices are sent to a collection agency will vary by individual company circumstances. A reasonable approach is to hand over the bottom 20% of invoices based on dollar size and gradually alter this amount over time in order to achieve the best balance of increased expenses and greater in-house servicing of large accounts. If the in-house collections staff is small, the proportion of referred invoices could eventually reach 80% of all over-due invoices, although this proportion may not be cost-effective.

Another issue is ensuring that collection agencies treat customers appropri-ately, so they will still be interested in using the company for future orders. To find collection agencies falling into this level of support, one should intensively prescreen agencies, including checking multiple referrals, and also periodically surveying customers to ensure that contacts by the collection agency are suffi-ciently polite. It is a particularly important issue if the company has required the collection agency to identify itself to customers as though it is the company's col-lection department.

Cost:    *Installation time:* 🕐

11.15 Refer Accounts to Collection Agencies Sooner

The typical company keeps trying to collect on overdue accounts for a long time before finally referring them to a collection agency. This is sometimes a matter of disorganization, with no formal method for determining how many times a cus-tomer has been contacted or when there appears to be no further approach to be taken in-house for achieving a collection. Consequently, invoices tend to gather dust on the receivables aging report for several months before they are finally shifted to a collections agency. As a result, collection agencies must deal with issues so old that it is extremely difficult to achieve a collection, either because the customer is no longer in business, the customer's business has declined so substantially that there is no remaining cash from which a payment can be made, or because so many personnel changes have occurred at either the company or the customer that it is extremely difficult to determine who the agency should even speak to.

The solution is to set a hard date by which all outstanding accounts receivable must be evaluated and referred to a collection agency. The exact review date will vary by industry and company. However, to put the issue in perspective, it should be much closer to an invoice aging date of 90 days than the half-year or more that is frequently used. By doing so, the collection agency may agree to charge a lower collection fee, because it realizes that more recent invoices are typically easier to collect.

This does not mean that every invoice still on the receivables aging report must be shifted to a collections agency as of the review date, because it is always less expensive to make an in-house collection. However, if there is clearly no progress made by the in-house staff as of the review date, then this is an appropriate time to make a referral.

Cost: 💵 💵 💵   *Installation time:* 🕑

11.16 Do Not Shift Fraudulent Accounts to a Collection Agency

When a company realizes that it has extended credit to a fraudulent customer, it frequently gives up on the account at once and hands it over to a collection agency. However, the collection percentage from this action is typically close to zero. Collection agencies are not in the business of going after fraudulent customers and do not usually have the resources to do so. Consequently, they park these invoices in a pending file and pursue other accounts with a higher chance of successful collection.

The fraudulent account must be kept in-house. Although the odds of success in these cases are always low, there may still be a slight chance of payment recovery if the company works diligently with a legal team and its internal resources to pursue such customers over a long period. Given the resources required, even this approach is useful only for the largest overdue invoices, where the size of the potential pay-off outweighs the substantial cost of continuing investigation.

Cost: 💵   *Installation time:* 🕑 🕑 🕑

11.17 Periodically Verify that the Collection Agency Is Bonded

A collection agency usually requires a customer to send payment on an overdue invoice to the agency, not the company. The agency then extracts its fee from the payment and forwards the remaining funds to the company. Alternately, the agency holds the customer's check until it is paid in full by the company and then forwards the check to the company. An agency's least-favorite approach is for the customer to send payment directly to the company, which then adds a significant interval before the agency is paid by the company. The first of these three approaches presents the risk that the agency could fraudulently walk away with the entire amount of a company's funds.

The solution is to require the collection agency to be bonded. This inquiry can occur during the agency selection process. In addition, the collection manager should have a note in the annual activity calendar to ask for a copy of the annual bonding agreement, to verify that the agency continues to be fully bonded. This requirement is also a good way to eliminate from consideration those collection agencies with minimal funding and focuses the company's attention on working solely with those agencies with a good reputation and that are intent on being in the business for a long time.

Cost: 💵   Installation time: ⏰ ⏰ ⏰

11.18 Track the Regularity of Collection Agency Remittances

The collection agency industry is a large one with low barriers to entry, so agencies come and go at an alarmingly high rate. Many collection agencies are underfunded and tend to hold onto collected funds for longer than they should in order to meet their own expense obligations. Not only does this practice keep funds away from the referring company, but it also puts the company at risk of losing its funds for the second time—first from the original customer and now from the agency that collected the funds.

A solution is to track the date on which cash is supposed to be remitted to the company and vigorously pursue late payments from agencies. For example, if an agency is supposed to remit all funds collected on the last day of the month and the company has not received those funds within five additional business days, the accounting department activities calendar should indicate that an immediate call to the agency is in order. A persistently late payment history without a reasonable excuse is clear grounds for agency dismissal.

Cost: 💵   Installation time:

12

Billing and Collections Measurements

Besides the best practices noted in the previous chapters, one should determine the extent of any resulting changes on internal operations. This chapter contains 11 measurements that can be used to determine changes in the efficiency and effectiveness with which best practices have altered the accounting department. This chapter also includes six measurements that can be used to determine the creditworthiness of customers.*

Do not feel compelled to use all of the measurements in this chapter. Instead, use only those measurements that are most useful for tracking key internal operational functions and those customer measures most relevant to a company's customer base. Too many measurements constitute an overflow of information and certainly require an excessive amount of effort to calculate. Exhibit 12.1 itemizes all of the measurements listed in this chapter.

12.1 Operational Measurement: Average Time to Issue Invoices

The accounting department can have a considerable impact on the timing of cash receipts, based on its ability to issue invoices to customers as soon as possible after shipments or services have been completed. If this critical step is delayed, then the processing time needed by customers to approve invoices and set them up for payment will *not* change, meaning that the date on which payments are made back to the company will be delayed. This can potentially put a company in

---

* Selected measurements in this chapter are adapted with permission from Bragg, *Business Ratios and Formulas* (Hoboken, NJ: John Wiley & Sons, 2002).

Exhibit 12.1 *Billing and Collections Measurements*

12.1   Average time to issue invoices

12.2   Percentage of cash applied on day of receipt

12.3   Number of cash transactions processed per person

12.4   Number of active customers per credit/collection staff

12.5   Collections cost percentage

12.6   Percentage collected of dollar volume assigned

12.7   Days sales outstanding

12.8   Sales-weighted days sales outstanding

12.9   Days delinquent sales outstanding

12.10   Percentage of receivables over XX days old

12.11   Bad debt percentage

12.12   Altman's Z-score bankruptcy prediction formula

12.13   Sales-to–working capital ratio

12.14   Debt-to-equity ratio

12.15   Quick ratio

12.16   Accounts receivable turnover

12.17   Inventory turnover

---

a dangerously low cash-flow position, or at least reduce the amount of interest income it can earn on its excess cash. For these reasons, one should constantly monitor the average time needed to issue invoices.

To calculate this ratio, subtract the shipment date from the invoice date for each invoice, and summarize the number of days required for all invoices issued during the period. Then divide the result by the total number of invoices issued. One can choose to include or exclude the number of days on weekends and holidays, depending on a company's emphasis on issuing invoices even during these traditional days off. Also, one can modify the measurement to include only those 10% or 20% of the invoices with the longest delays following shipment, which focuses management attention on the worst problems in the invoicing process. The formula is:

$$\frac{\text{(Sum of invoice dates)} - \text{(Sum of shipment dates)}}{\text{Number of invoices issued}}$$

As noted under the formula description, the calculation can be thrown off if weekends or holidays are included, because they can result in a calculation that shows an inordinate length of time between shipment and invoicing. For example, if the shipping department sends out a delivery at the end of the day before a three-day holiday, then the accounting department will not see the paperwork until the following Monday, at which point three days have already passed and will be counted in the measurement. Thus, one must either discount these days from the calculation or assume that invoices will be issued on *all* days, irrespective of the presence of a holiday or weekend.

12.2 Operational Measurement: Percentage of Cash Applied on Day of Receipt

There is nothing more irritating for a collections person than to contact a customer about an overdue payment, just to find that the customer has already paid and that the company has already received the money without updating its accounts receivable records. This causes a considerable amount of inefficiency within the collections staff. One can track this problem by measuring the percentage of cash receipts applied to the accounts receivable records on the day of cash receipt.

To determine this ratio, summarize the dollars of cash applied on the day of cash receipt (which should be available in the cash receipts journal) by the total dollars of incoming cash on the day of receipt (which comes from the bank deposit slip for that day). If wire transfers are also made directly to the company's bank account, then these can be discovered by completing an online bank reconciliation on a daily basis; this information should then be included in the measurement. The formula is:

$$\frac{\text{Dollars of cash receipts applied on day of receipt}}{\text{Total dollars of incoming cash on day of receipt}}$$

As noted in the example, it may not be possible to apply cash to the receivable records, because customers have not indicated which invoices are to be paid with the cash. The amount of these funds must then be recorded in a holding account until the customers can be contacted about the problem. On the grounds that a missing cash application is the customer's fault, one can exclude the amount of this unapplied cash from the measurement. However, one can also include this cash in the measurement, on the grounds that this will force the cash applications staff to more rapidly resolve the problem with customers in order to achieve the highest possible measurement result.

12.3 Operational Measurement: Number of Cash Transactions Processed Per Person

If a company receives a large number of cash receipts on a regular basis, its accounting staff will spend a considerable amount of time matching cash receipts to open accounts receivable. As the transaction volume increases, the efficiency of this operation will become of increasing importance to management—both because a great deal of labor is required and because the cash should be matched to open receivables as soon as possible. A good measurement for tracking the efficiency of this function is the number of cash transactions processed per person.

To calculate the measurement, accumulate the total number of invoices against which payments are applied during the measurement period and divide it by the total number of full-time equivalents processing cash receipts. The formula is:

$$\frac{\text{Number of cash receipt transactions processed}}{\text{Number of full-time equivalents processing cash receipt transactions}}$$

It is not accurate to use the total number of checks received in the numerator, because a single check may call for the application of cash to multiple invoices. Instead, be sure to use in the numerator the total number of invoices against which cash has been applied.

12.4 Operational Measurement: Number of Active Customers Per Credit/Collection Staff

If a company has a large collections staff, managers should be interested in the average number of customers assigned to each employee. When tracked over time, this is a good indicator of the efficiency of the collections department. To calculate the number of active customers per credit/collections staff, divide the number of active customers by the number of in-house credit/collections full-time equivalents. The formula is:

$$\frac{\text{Number of active customers}}{\text{Number of in-house credit/collections full-time equivalents}}$$

This measurement can be manipulated by reducing the number of collections employees, even though this action may result in reduced amounts of dollars collected. To guard against this issue, always pair this measurement with some calculation of collection effectiveness, such as days sales outstanding, to see the complete picture of collections effectiveness *and* efficiency.

The calculation can also be manipulated by including in the numerator all inactive customers, thereby making the staff appear to be far more efficient than is really the case. To avoid this problem, institute a policy of deleting from the accounting database all customers with whom the company has done no business in a prespecified number of months or years.

One further method for manipulating this measurement is to offload many customers to outside collection agencies while still recording the customers in the numerator. If this is the case, either remove offloaded customers from the numerator or add the collection agency's staff to the denominator.

12.5 Operational Measurement: Collections Cost Percentage

The preceding measures addressed specific efficiency issues within the accounting or credit/collections departments. However, they did not address the overall cost of the collections function. This issue is best addressed by determining the proportion of collection costs to the dollars of overdue funds collected. To calculate the measurement, add the cost of internal collections to attorney costs and outsourced collection costs, and divide the sum by the total amount of collected funds. The formula is:

$$\frac{(\text{Cost of internal collections} + \text{Attorney cost} + \text{Outsourced collections cost})}{\text{Collected funds}}$$

Several calculation problems are associated with this measurement. One is the disparity between the timing of collection costs incurred and the amount of funds collected. The costs may be incurred a month or two before cash receipt, so the measurement may look inadequate in one month and superb the next. This is less of an issue when most collection tasks are handled by a collections agency that works on a contingency basis, because it charges the company only when it succeeds in making a collection, thereby matching cash receipts to expenses incurred. If timing issues appear to be causing problems with the measurement, aggregate the information and report it over several months, such as a rolling three-month average.

Another calculation problem is the nature of the denominator. Should it be all funds collected from credit sales or just funds received from past-due accounts receivable? The latter yields a more accurate comparison of collection costs to results, but the determination of an overdue receivable can be subject to some debate, making the calculation difficult to quantify. A reasonable solution is to include in the denominator only those funds collected from receivables that passed a certain age before being collected, such as 45 days.

12.6 Operational Measurement: Percentage Collected of Dollar Volume Assigned

The collections function is a difficult one to manage, because it depends largely on the hiring and support of a skilled group of collections personnel. This requires one to constantly monitor the staff's collection results and replace those who are not performing above a minimum level. To do so, a good measure is the percentage of overdue invoices assigned to each of the collections staff that have been collected. The measure can be used to monitor the performance of either an internal collections staff or that of a collections agency to which accounts have been assigned.

If a collections agency is being monitored, divide the cash received back from the agency by the total amount of accounts receivable assigned to the agency. However, because the numerator will include the collection agency's fee (which is subtracted from any funds collected), it will tend to show an unusually low percentage; one may consider removing the fee deduction when running the calculation in order to get a better idea of the collection agency's performance. The formula is:

$$\frac{\text{Cash received from collection agency}}{\text{Total accounts receivable assigned to collection agency}}$$

If the entity being measured is the internal collections staff, the same measurement is used; however, it is more common to calculate the measure for individual employees within the department so the most precise determination can be made of performance levels by person.

This measurement can yield misleading results if the accounts receivable assigned to a collection agency or in-house collections staff are not compared to cash receipts related to those same receivables. For example, if a collection agency were given $100,000 to collect, followed by another $100,000 two months later, the cash received from its efforts should only be linked to the first $100,000 until a sufficient amount of time has passed for it to have made reasonable collection efforts on the second $100,000. If this problem is not addressed, a common result is an excessively low percentage collected, because cash receipts are being compared to additional new receivables, as well as the original base of receivables from which they were collected.

12.7 Operational Measurement: Days Sales Outstanding

The average age of accounts receivable is easier to understand if it is expressed in terms of the average number of days that accounts receivable are outstanding. This format is particularly useful when it is compared to the standard number of days of credit granted to customers. For example, if the average collection period is 60 days and the standard days of credit is 30, then customers are taking much too long to pay their invoices. A sign of good performance is when the average receivable collection period is only a few days longer than the standard days of credit. To calculate days sales outstanding, divide annual credit sales by 365 days, and divide the result into average accounts receivable. The formula is:

$$\frac{\text{Average accounts receivable}}{(\text{Annual sales} \div 365)}$$

The main issue is what figure to use for annual sales. If the total sales for the year are used, this may result in a skewed measurement, because the sales associated with the current outstanding accounts receivable may be significantly higher or lower than the average level of sales represented by the annual sales figure. This problem is especially common when sales are highly seasonal. A better approach is to annualize the sales figure for the period covered by the bulk of the existing accounts receivable.

12.8 Operational Measurement: Sales-Weighted Days Sales Outstanding

The trouble with most measures comparing revenues to sales is the assumption that sales are the same from month-to-month, so that old receivables are matched to an assumed level of sales approximating sales in the current month. When prior-month sales are substantially different, this can skew the resulting performance calculation. For example, if prior-month sales were much higher than those in the current month and if the proportion of unpaid invoices to sales were the same in the prior and current months, the residual unpaid invoices from the prior month would make a days of receivables calculation look inordinately high. Thus, variations in sales volume from month to month can make the performance of the collections department look better or worse than it really is, even if its performance has not changed at all.

One can apply sales weighting to the standard days sales outstanding measurement in order to adjust for variations in sales levels from month to month. To do so, divide the number of receivable dollars outstanding in the current month by the credit sales incurred in that month, plus the receivable dollars outstanding for the preceding month divided by the credit sales incurred in that month, and so on for as many months as are represented in the aging report. Then multiply the sum of all these fractions by 30 days. The formula is:

$$30 \text{ days} \times \left(\frac{\text{Current month receivables outstanding}}{\text{Current month credit sales}} + \frac{\text{Preceding month receivables outstanding}}{\text{Preceding month credit sales}} + \frac{\text{Next preceding month receivables outstanding}}{\text{Next preceding month credit sales}} \right)$$

12.9 Operational Measurement: Days Delinquent Sales Outstanding

There is no collection problem with the vast majority of accounts receivable. Recognizing this fact, some managers prefer to focus the attention of their collection staffs more precisely on their ability to collect money from those few accounts that do not pay on time. The days delinquent sales outstanding measure is an effective way to use this calculation, because it addresses only those invoices that are overdue. To calculate this ratio, divide annualized credit sales from delinquent accounts by the average amount of delinquent accounts receivable, and then divide the result into 365 days. The formula is:

$$\frac{365}{(\text{Annualized credit sales from delinquent accounts} \div \text{Average delinquent accounts receivable})}$$

One problem with this measure is determining the point at which an account receivable is considered to be delinquent. For example, if the allowable payment period for an invoice is 30 days, most customers will pay the bill on the 30th day, so that it will not arrive in the mail for several more days—consequently, using 30 days as the cut-off period will still include nearly all unpaid invoices. There is no standard approach to determining the cut-off point, but it is reasonable to allow up to a week of extra time beyond the allowed payment period before classifying an invoice as delinquent.

Another problem with this measurement is determining the amount of the *average* delinquent account receivable. If the subject company is a small one, it probably has only a few delinquent invoices, so the collection of just a few of them will significantly alter the average amount; this is less of an issue for large companies, which have so many more outstanding invoices that the collection of one or two will not have a significant impact on the average amount outstanding.

12.10 Operational Measurement: Percentage of Receivables Over XX Days Old

A company can precisely tailor its accounts receivable measurements by calculating only that portion of receivables that are older than a specific date. This is particularly useful in industries in which it is customary to pay late, so that a conventional days of receivables measurement will not tell an accounting manager if a problem with collections actually exists. For example, if the traditional payment period is 65 days, then it is difficult to tell from a days of receivables measurement of 60 days if all invoices are not due for payment or if some proportion of them are well past the customary payment date. The percent of receivables of XX days old is a good way to more clearly define this problem.

To calculate this percentage, divide the total dollar amount of all outstanding receivables exceeding a user-specified age by the total amount of all accounts receivable outstanding. The measurement is more accurate if all bad debts for which a credit has already been created can be netted against their corresponding credits, thereby eliminating them from the numerator. Otherwise, an old bad debt may still appear in the numerator, because its corresponding credit is much newer and so will not be listed in the numerator, and therefore cannot offset it. The formula is:

$$\frac{\text{Dollar amount of outstanding receivables} > \text{XX days old}}{\text{Total dollars of outstanding receivables}}$$

A self-serving collections manager can alter the number of days used in the formula, so that the amount overdue always looks insignificant. For example, if a large unpaid invoice is 69 days old, the measurement can be set to anything over 69 days in order to exclude it, thereby making the collections department's performance look better than it really is. This problem can be avoided by consistently using the same number of days in the measurement for many periods, thereby also giving a better period-to-period comparison of results.

12.11 Operational Measurement: Bad Debt Percentage

A company should keep track not only of the total amount of bad debts incurred each year, but also their trend line, the specific reasons why each one became a bad debt, the relationship between corporate credit policy and the amount of bad debts incurred, and the company's bad debt experience in relation to the rest of the industry. All of these comparisons are needed in order to determine how bad debt levels are being controlled. The most basic of these measurements is the bad debt percentage, which compares the amount of bad debt incurred to either the total amount of credit sales or total outstanding accounts receivable.

To calculate this percentage, divide total bad debt dollars by the total amount of accounts receivable. The formula is:

$$\frac{\text{Total bad debt dollars recognized}}{\text{Total outstanding accounts receivable}}$$

The problem with using accounts receivable as the denominator for this calculation is that it shows only the relationship of bad debts to a small proportion of sales, which are represented by the accounts receivable balance. An alternative approach is to divide total bad debt dollars by total annualized credit sales; however, if this approach is used, then the numerator will only be comparable to the denominator if the bad debt figure is annualized, either by using the last 12 months of bad debts on a rolling basis or by annualizing the amount of bad debts incurred over a shorter period. The formula is:

$$\frac{\text{Total bad debt dollars recognized}}{\text{Total credit sales}}$$

This measurement can be easily altered by anyone who does not want to have a high bad debt percentage. The key problem is that the numerator consists of the total bad debt dollars recognized. If the controller does not want to recognize a bad debt, the amount is simply left in accounts receivable. Another problem is that previously recognized bad debts that are later paid by customers must be backed out of the bad debt expense, rather than being reinvoiced as new sales. In the first case, the bad debt percentage will be too low; in the latter case, it will be too high.

12.12 Credit Review Measurement: Altman's Z-Score Bankruptcy Prediction Formula

The Z-score bankruptcy predictor combines five common business ratios, using a weighting system that was statistically calculated by Dr. Edward Altman to determine the likelihood of a company going bankrupt at some point in the future. It was derived based on data from manufacturing firms, but has since proven to be highly effective in determining the risk that a services firm will go bankrupt as well. The calculation can also be used by a lender to determine the creditworthiness of a company.

If the calculation results in a score above 2.99, a company is probably in safe financial condition. A score between 3.0 and 2.7 is a gray area, indicating that a company is in acceptable condition at the moment but could slide into a more difficult financial condition in the future. A score between 2.7 and 1.8 indicates that a company will probably be bankrupt within two years. Any score below 1.8 indicates a high risk of bankruptcy in the near future.

To determine a company's score using this system, add together the following five ratios, multiplied by the indicated weighting factors:

1. Return on total assets × 3.3 weighting factor
2. Sales to total assets × 0.999 weighting factor
3. Equity to debt × 0.6 weighting factor
4. Working capital to total assets × 1.2 weighting factor
5. Retained earnings to total assets × 1.4 weighting factor

The formula, using more detailed derivations for each of these ratios, is as follows:

$$(\text{Operating income} \div \text{Total assets}) \times 3.3$$

$$+$$

$$(\text{Sales} \div \text{Total assets}) \times 0.999$$

$$+$$

$$(\text{Market value of common stock} + \text{Preferred stock}) \div (\text{Total liabilities}) \times 0.6$$

$$+$$

$$(\text{Working capital} \div \text{Total assets}) \times 1.2$$

$$+$$

$$(\text{Retained earnings} \div \text{Total assets}) \times 1.4$$

This derivation of the Z-score uses weighting factors that are applicable to publicly held companies. If one is calculating the score for a privately held company, the weighting factors change slightly and are:

1. Return on total assets × 3.1 weighting factor
2. Sales to total assets × 0.998 weighting factor
3. Equity to debt × 0.42 weighting factor
4. Working capital to total assets × 0.71 weighting factor
5. Retained earnings to total assets × 0.84 weighting factor

The results of this calculation are only reliable if there is no fraudulent financial reporting by a company that results in a higher Z-score than would otherwise be the case. Also, a sudden downturn in the economy, or some other factor affecting profits, such as a price war, can send a company's financial condition spiraling downward, irrespective of a high Z-score.

12.13 Credit Review Measurement: Sales-to–Working Capital Ratio

It is exceedingly important to keep the amount of cash used by an organization to a minimum, so that its financing needs are reduced. One of the best ways to determine changes in the overall usage of cash over time is the ratio of sales to working capital. This ratio shows the amount of cash required to maintain a certain level of sales. It is most effective when tracked on a trend line, so the credit staff can see if there is a long-term change in the amount of cash required by a customer in order to generate the same amount of sales. For instance, if a company has elected to increase its sales to less creditworthy customers, it is likely that these customers will pay more slowly than regular customers, thereby increasing the company's investment in accounts receivable. Similarly, if the management team decides to increase the speed of order fulfillment by increasing the amount of inventory for certain items, then the inventory investment will increase. In both cases, the ratio of working capital to sales will worsen as a result of specific management decisions. The credit staff should pay particularly close attention to this measurement on a trend line, because a decline in the proportion of working capital to sales generated is a strong indicator that a customer may suddenly run out of cash.

To calculate the ratio, annualized net sales are compared to working capital, which is accounts receivable, plus inventory, minus accounts payable. One should not use annualized *gross* sales in the calculation, because this would include in the sales figure the amount of any sales that have already been returned and are therefore already included in the inventory figure. The formula is:

$$\frac{\text{Annualized net sales}}{(\text{Accounts receivable} + \text{Inventory} - \text{Accounts payable})}$$

12.14 Credit Review Measurement: Debt-to-Equity Ratio

This ratio reveals the extent to which company management is willing to fund its operations with debt, rather than equity. For example, a company that wants to increase its return on equity can do so by obtaining debt, which it then uses to buy back stock, thereby shrinking the amount of equity that is used to calculate the return on equity. This strategy works for as long as the after-tax interest cost of the debt does not exceed the benefit of the increased earnings per share resulting from the reduction in shares. A high debt-to-equity ratio indicates to a credit manager a significant amount of customer credit risk, because debt payments can interfere with a customer's ability to pay its bills.

To calculate this ratio, divide total debt by total equity. For a true picture of the amount of debt that a company has obtained, the debt figure should include all operating and capital lease payments. The formula is:

$$\frac{\text{Debt}}{\text{Equity}}$$

A more restrictive view of the formula is to only include long-term debt in the numerator, on the assumption that this variation gives a better picture of a company's long-term debt-to-equity structure. However, this view excludes situations where short-term debt, such as revolving credit lines, cannot be paid off in the short term and must eventually be converted into long-term debt, thereby increasing the amount of long-term debt.

One should consider calculating the debt-to-equity ratio for several years into the future, focusing on the relationship between interest and principal payments (rather than total debt) and equity for each year. The reason for this approach is that a large amount of total debt on the balance sheet may not reveal a true picture of a company's ability to pay off the debt if the debt is not due for payment until a required balloon payment at some point well into the future. However, a much smaller amount of debt on the balance sheet may be completely unsupportable if the bulk of it is due for payment in the near term.

12.15 Credit Review Measurement: Quick Ratio

This ratio is heavily used by credit departments to see if a company has a sufficient level of liquidity to pay its liabilities. By using this ratio, one can gain a better understanding of a company's very short-term ability to generate cash from its most liquid assets, such as accounts receivable and marketable securities.

To calculate the ratio, add together cash, marketable securities, and accounts receivable, and divide the result by current liabilities. Be sure to include only those marketable securities that can be liquidated in the short term and those receivables that are not significantly overdue. The formula is:

$$\frac{(\text{Cash} + \text{Marketable securities} + \text{Accounts receivable})}{\text{Current liabilities}}$$

The measure may still not give a true measure of corporate liquidity if most of the accounts receivable are not due for some weeks yet, while accounts payable may be due immediately.

12.16 Credit Review Measurement: Accounts Receivable Turnover

The speed with which a company can obtain payment from customers for outstanding receivable balances is crucial for the reduction of cash requirements. A very high level of accounts receivable turnover indicates that a customer's credit and collections function is very good at avoiding potentially delinquent customers, as well as collecting overdue funds.

To calculate the ratio, divide annualized credit sales by the sum of average accounts receivable and notes due from customers. The key issue in this calculation is the concept of annualized credit sales. If a company is estimating very high sales levels later in the year, this can result in an inordinately large figure in the numerator, against which current receivables are compared, which results in an inaccurately high level of turnover. A better approach is to simply multiply the current month's sales by 12 to derive the annualized credit sales figure. Another alternative is to annualize the last two months of sales, on the grounds that the receivables balance relates primarily to sales in those two months. The exact measurement method used can result in some variation in the reported level of turnover, so one should model the results using several different approaches in order to arrive at the one that most closely approximates reality. The basic formula is:

$$\frac{\text{Annualized credit sales}}{(\text{Average accounts receivable} + \text{Notes payable by customers})}$$

12.17 Credit Review Measurement: Inventory Turnover

Inventory is frequently the largest component of a company's working capital; in such situations, if inventory is not being used by operations at a reasonable pace, then a customer has invested a large part of its cash in an asset that may be difficult to liquidate in short order. Accordingly, keeping close track of the rate of customer inventory turnover can be important to a credit department. This section describes two inventory turnover measurements, which may be combined to yield the most complete turnover reporting for management to peruse. In all cases, these measurements should be tracked on a trend line in order to see if there are gradual changes in the rate of turnover.

The most simple turnover calculation is to divide the period-end inventory into the annualized cost of sales. One can also use an *average* inventory figure in the denominator, which avoids sudden changes in the inventory level that are likely to occur on any specific period-end date. The formula is:

$$\frac{\text{Cost of goods sold}}{\text{Inventory}}$$

A variation on the formula is to divide it into 365 days, which yields the number of days of inventory on hand. This may be more understandable to the layperson; for example, 43 days of inventory is more clear than 8.5 inventory turns, even though they represent the same situation. The formula is:

$$\frac{365}{\text{Cost of goods sold} \div \text{Inventory}}$$

The turnover ratio can be skewed by changes in the underlying costing methods used to allocate direct labor and especially overhead cost pools to the inventory. For example, if additional categories of costs are added to the overhead cost pool, then the allocation to inventory will increase, which will reduce the reported level of inventory turnover, even though the turnover level under the original calculation method has not changed at all. The problem can also arise if the method of allocating costs is changed; for example, it may be shifted from an allocation based on labor hours worked to one based on machine hours worked, which can alter the total amount of overhead costs assigned to inventory. The problem can also arise if the inventory valuation is based on standard costs and the underlying standards are altered. In all three cases, the amount of inventory on hand has not changed, but the costing systems used have altered the reported level of inventory costs, which affects the reported level of turnover.

Appendix
Summary of Best Practices

Chapter 2

2.1   Create a credit policy

2.2   Modify the credit policy based on product margins

2.3   Modify the credit policy based on changing economic conditions

2.4   Modify the credit policy based on potential product obsolescence

2.5   Train the credit staff about credit procedures

2.6   Create a credit scoring model

2.7   Use a third-party credit scoring model

2.8   Create a credit decision table

2.9   Arrange for automatic notification of credit rating changes

2.10 Create a customer credit file

2.11 Include a requirement for multiple contacts in the credit application

2.12 Modify the terms of the credit application in the company's favor

2.13 Do not accept any order unless a credit application is completed

2.14 Require a new credit application if customers have not ordered in some time

2.15 Require a new credit application if credit limits are exceeded

2.16 Set a short time limit for the duration of credit reviews

2.17 Enter the last credit review date in the computer system

2.18 Call new customers and explain credit terms

2.19 Issue a payment procedure to customers

2.20 Create and periodically review a report showing credit levels exceeded

2.21 Uniformly administer late fees

2.22 Install an automated credit reference system

Chapter 3

3.1 Automatically grant minor credit lines to new customers

3.2 Assign new account processing to one person

3.3 Preapprove customer credit

3.4 Verify the existence of a prospective customer

3.5 Investigate unanswered questions on the credit application

3.6 Obtain credit reports on customers

3.7 Obtain additional credit application information through a customer visit

3.8 Join an industry credit group

3.9 Access the SEC filings of public customers

3.10 Refer a potential customer to a distributor

3.11 Require salesperson collection assistance in advance

3.12 Require partial cash-in.advance payments

3.13 Use COD terms sparingly

3.14 Combine COD terms with a surcharge

3.15 Offer a lease-purchase option to customers

3.16 Install a financing program for marginal customers

3.17 Perfect a security interest in personal property sold to a customer

3.18 Obtain a purchase money security interest in goods shipped

3.19 Enter into a consignment arrangement with a customer

3.20 Require senior lien holders to subordinate their liens below the company's lien

3.21 Require personal guarantees

3.22 Require intercorporate guarantees

3.23 Obtain a letter of credit

3.24 Obtain credit insurance

3.25 Obtain an export credit guarantee

3.26 Obtain a surety bond

3.27 Shorten the terms of sale

3.28 Review the credit levels of the top 20% of customers each year

3.29 Review the credit levels of all customers issuing multiple NSF checks

3.30 Review the credit levels of all customers who skip payments

3.31 Review the credit levels of all customers who stop taking cash discounts

Chapter 4

4.1   Add contact information to the invoice

4.2   Add credit card contact information to the invoice

4.3   Clearly state the payment due date on the invoice

4.4   Clearly state the discount amount on the invoice

4.5   Remove unnecessary information from invoices

4.6   Add a receipt signature to the invoice

4.7   Add carrier route codes to billing addresses

4.8   Train the billing staff in the invoicing process

4.9   Mark all envelopes as "address correction requested"

4.10   Immediately update the customer file with address changes

4.11   Have the sales staff review contact information for recurring invoices

4.12   Automatically check errors during invoice data entry

4.13   Computerize the shipping log

4.14   Track exceptions between the shipping log and invoice register

4.15   Proofread the invoices

4.16   Reduce the number of parts in multipart invoices

4.17   Eliminate month-end statements

4.18   Replace intercompany invoicing with operating transactions

4.19   Use automated bank account deductions

4.20   Use fingerprint verification for credit card and check payments

Chapter 5

5.1   Submit early billing of recurring invoices

5.2   Print invoices every day

5.3   Print separate invoices for each line item

5.4   Issue single, summarized invoices each period

5.5   Issue invoices to coincide with customer payment dates

5.6   Have delivery person create the invoice

5.7   Have delivery person deliver the invoice

5.8   E-mail invoices in Acrobat format

5.9   Issue electronic invoices through the Internet

5.10 Transmit transactions via electronic data interchange

Chapter 6

6.1   Have a salesperson pick up the check in person

6.2   Send a messenger to pick up the check

6.3   Institute lockbox collections

6.4   Install a lockbox truncation system

6.5   Periodically review lockbox locations

6.6   Access online check images from a lockbox

6.7   Issue the corporate overnight delivery account number to customers

6.8   Accept credit card payments

6.9   Offer customers secure Internet payment options

6.10 Conduct immediate review of unapplied cash

6.11 Review restrictive endorsements before cashing checks

Chapter 7

7.1   Create an integrated customer service department

7.2   Hire a credit and collection manager

7.3   Create collection specialists

7.4   Train the collections staff in collection techniques

7.5   Assign new collectors to payment confirmation tasks

7.6   Assign the best collector to the worst customers

7.7   Clearly define account ownership

7.8   Utilize collection call stratification

7.9   Periodically assign collectors to different territories

7.10 Structure the collections work day around prime calling hours

7.11 Join the sales staff on customer visits

7.12 Maintain an ongoing relationship with customers' payables managers

7.13 Schedule a regular accounts review with key managers

7.14 Meet with the sales staff regularly

7.15 E-mail the accounts receivable aging to the sales staff

7.16 Write off small balances with no approval

7.17 Access customer payment information over the internet

7.18 Simplify the pricing structure

7.19 Grant percentage discounts for early payment

7.20 Periodically reevaluate the discount percentage offered

7.21 Only pay commissions from cash received

7.22 Route cash-in-advance orders straight to the collections staff

7.23 Conduct bad debt postmortems

7.24 Review confirming purchase orders

7.25 Offer bonuses to the collections staff

7.26 Offer bonuses to the sales staff

7.27 Report on bad debts by salesperson

7.28 Post collection results by collector

Chapter 8

8.1 Create a collection policies and procedures manual

8.2 Train the sales staff in credit policies and procedures

8.3 Use a collection call database

8.4 Link to a comprehensive collections software package

8.5 Create an on-line document management system for credit information

8.6 Maintain a database of customer emergency contacts

8.7 Maintain a database of personal information about contacts

8.8 Maintain a customer orders database

8.9 Compile a customer assets database

8.10 Install a payment deduction investigation system

8.11 Implement a customer order exception tracking system

8.12 Set up automatic fax of overdue invoices

8.13 Issue dunning letters automatically

8.14 Trace individuals through an online tracking service

8.15 Lock access to the credit hold flag

8.16 Flag slow-paying customers for early contact

8.17   Periodically alter the mode of communication with customers

8.18   Periodically alter dunning letters and issuance intervals

8.19   Issue a notification letter before the due date for large invoices

8.20   Do everything required by customers' payables systems

Chapter 9

9.1   Thank customers who pay on time

9.2   Set up customers with EFT agreements

9.3   Require a signed purchase agreement for all major sales

9.4   Eliminate grace periods

9.5   Use dunning letters only for small overdue balances

9.6   Issue dunning letters by e-mail

9.7   Issue dunning letters to management positions outside accounts payable

9.8   Issue attorney letters

9.9   Stamp a reminder notice on late invoices

9.10   Send invoices by certified mail to customers who repeatedly lose their invoices

9.11   Insist on payment of undisputed balances

9.12   Insist on a wire transfer when payments are repeatedly reported to be "in the mail"

9.13   Offset an overdue receivable against a payable to a customer

9.14   Send a letter confirming payment commitments

9.15   Set up a periodic payment schedule

9.16   Convert a receivable into a promissory note

9.17   Accept a merchandise return

9.18   Accept payment in kind

9.19   Add the overdue customer balance to cash-on-delivery shipments for crucial items

9.20   Notify the customer and salesperson of credit holds

9.21   Inform the sales staff when accounts are sent to a collection agency

9.22   Have both parties to a settlement sign a mutual release agreement

9.23   Send the customer a completed small claims court complaint form

9.24   Sue customers in small claims court

9.25   Prescreen customers before initiating legal action

9.26   Have a court issue a restraining notice

9.27   Retain lawyers who are experienced in money judgment collection

9.28   Reclaim goods from insolvent customers

9.29   File an involuntary bankruptcy petition for a customer

9.30   Report a customer to the Internal Revenue Service

9.31   Use the collections department to collect loans to former employees

9.32   Contact customers regarding credit balances

9.33   Negotiate with the customer

Chapter 10

10.1   Centrally manage the deduction resolution process

10.2   Enforce a standard procedure for handling unauthorized deductions

10.3   Confirm and document customer insurance requirements

10.4   Summarize and resolve underlying issues causing deductions

10.5   Resolve deductions by declining order of dollar volume

10.6   Resolve pricing issues before approving orders

10.7   Resolve significant deduction issues in person

10.8   Place deduction resolution responsibility on the salesperson

10.9   Allow the customer service staff limited authority to resolve deductions

10.10 Discuss open deductions with the repairs department

10.11 Obtain better access to trade promotion information

10.12 Cut off customers based on the size of unauthorized deductions

Chapter 11

11.1   Outsource collections

11.2   Outsource credit checking

11.3   Outsource dunning letters to a credit reporting agency

11.4   Outsource NSF collections

11.5   Sell accounts receivable to a factoring organization

11.6   Sell uncollectible invoices to a debt buyer

11.7 Select agencies based on performance rather than fees

11.8 Select agencies based on references

11.9 Select agencies based on prior experience with specific customers

11.10 Use only collection agencies that have integrated legal services

11.11 Use an attorney first to obtain repayment of "reasonable attorney's fees"

11.12 Use several collection agencies at once

11.13 Create an in-house collection agency

11.14 Shift smaller accounts to collection agencies immediately

11.15 Refer accounts to collection agencies sooner

11.16 Do not shift fraudulent accounts to a collection agency

11.17 Periodically verify that the collection agency is bonded

11.18 Track the regularity of collection agency remittances

Chapter 12

Average time to issue invoices	$\dfrac{\text{(Sum of invoice dates)} - \text{(Sum of shipment dates)}}{\text{Number of invoices issued}}$
Percentage of cash applied on day of receipt	$\dfrac{\text{Dollars of cash receipts applied on day of receipt}}{\text{Total dollars of incoming cash on day of receipt}}$
Number of cash transactions processed per person	$\dfrac{\text{Number of cash receipt transactions processed}}{\text{Number of full-time equivalents processing cash receipt transactions}}$
Number of active customers per credit/collection staff	$\dfrac{\text{Number of active customers}}{\text{Number of in-house credit/collections full-time equivalents}}$
Collections cost percentage	$\dfrac{\text{(Cost of internal collections} + \text{Attorney cost} + \text{Outsourced collections cost)}}{\text{Collected funds}}$
Percentage collected of dollar volume assigned	$\dfrac{\text{Cash received from collection agency}}{\text{Total accounts receivable assigned to collection agency}}$

Days sales outstanding	$$\frac{\text{Average accounts receivable}}{(\text{Annual sales} \div 365)}$$
Sales-weighted days sales outstanding	$30 \text{ days} \times$ $$\left(\frac{\text{Current month receivables outstanding}}{\text{Current month credit sales}} \right.$$ $+$ $$\frac{\text{Preceding month receivables outstanding}}{\text{Preceding month credit sales}}$$ $+$ $$\left. \frac{\text{Next preceding month receivables outstanding}}{\text{Next preceding month credit sales}} \right)$$
Days delinquent sales outstanding	$$\frac{365}{\left(\begin{array}{c}\text{Annualized credit sales from delinquent accounts} \div \\ \text{Average delinquent accounts receivable}\end{array}\right)}$$
Percentage of receivables over XX days old	$$\frac{\text{Dollar amount of outstanding receivables} > \text{XX days old}}{\text{Total dollars of outstanding receivables}}$$
Bad debt percentage	$$\frac{\text{Total bad debt dollars recognized}}{\text{Total outstanding accounts receivable}}$$ $$\frac{\text{Total bad debt dollars recognized}}{\text{Total credit sales}}$$
Altman's Z-score bankruptcy prediction formula	$(\text{Operating income} \div \text{Total assets}) \times 3.3$ $+$ $(\text{Sales} \div \text{Total assets}) \times 0.999$ $+$ $(\text{Market value of common stock} + \text{Preferred stock}) \div$ $(\text{Total liabilities}) \times 0.6$ $+$ $(\text{Working capital} \div \text{Total assets}) \times 1.2$ $+$ $(\text{Retained earnings} \div \text{Total assets}) \times 1.4$
Sales-to–working capital ratio	$$\frac{\text{Annualized net sales}}{(\text{Accounts receivable} + \text{Inventory} - \text{Accounts payable})}$$

Debt-to-equity ratio	$$\frac{\text{Debt}}{\text{Equity}}$$
Quick ratio	$$\frac{(\text{Cash} + \text{Marketable securities} + \text{Accounts receivable})}{\text{Current liabilities}}$$
Accounts receivable turnover	$$\frac{\text{Annualized credit sales}}{(\text{Average accounts receivable} + \text{Notes payable by customers})}$$
Inventory turnover	$$\frac{\text{Cost of goods sold}}{\text{Inventory}}$$ $$\frac{365}{\text{Cost of goods sold} \div \text{Inventory}}$$

Glossary

NOTE: Definitions followed by an asterisk (*) are reprinted with permission from Bragg, *Ultimate Accountant's Reference* (Hoboken, NJ: John Wiley & Sons, Inc., 2004), Appendix E.

Accounts payable A current liability on the balance sheet, representing short-term obligations to pay suppliers.*

Accounts receivable A current asset on the balance sheet, representing short-term amounts due from customers who have purchased on account.*

Active customer account A customer having recently transacted business with a company.

Age category A date range used for each column in the aged accounts receivable report, in which invoices are listed based on their age.

Allowance for bad debts An offset to the accounts receivable balance, against which bad debts are charged. The presence of this allowance allows one to avoid severe changes in the period-to-period bad debt expense by expensing a steady amount to the allowance account in every period, rather than writing off large bad debts to expense on an infrequent basis.*

Assignment A transfer of property to be held as collateral for a debt, or the transfer of title to receivables to a debt buyer.

Bad debt An account receivable or promissory note that is judged to be uncollectible.

Bankruptcy The condition of being supervised by a bankruptcy court because of a company having become unable to meet its current liabilities.

Bankruptcy discharge A bankruptcy court's official release of a debtor from liability for its debts, no matter the extent to which they have been paid.

Beginning receivables The amount of outstanding accounts receivable, as well as unapplied credits, deductions, and payments outstanding at the beginning of a reporting period.

Bill of Sale A legal document stating that title to an asset has been transferred to a buyer.

Cash All petty cash, currency, held checks, certificates of deposit, traveler's checks, money orders, letters of credit, bank drafts, cashier's checks, and demand deposits that are held by a company without restriction, and which are readily available on demand.*

Cash in advance A full or partial payment by a customer at the time of ordering for goods or services to be delivered at a later date.

Cash on delivery Delivery terms under which the customer must pay cash at the time of receipt.

Chapter 11 The restructuring of a company's liabilities to allow it to continue as a going concern.

Chapter 7 Complete liquidation of a business through the bankruptcy process.

Chargeoff The act of charging a receivable to the bad debt expense account.

Collateral A debtor asset pledged to a creditor in case the debtor cannot fulfill an obligation.

Collection agency A third-party firm specializing in collecting overdue accounts receivable on behalf of a company.

Collection letter A letter sent to customers whose invoices are overdue for payment, reminding them of the amount overdue, stating payment terms, and detailing additional actions to be taken by the company if payment is not made by the customer.

Collection policy A standard policy detailing the treatment of customers who are late in paying amounts owed to a company.

Collector A person whose primary job responsibility is collecting payment on accounts receivable.

Cost of goods sold The accumulated total of all costs used to create a product or service, which is then sold.

Cram-down The confirmation of a bankruptcy plan over the objections of some shareholders or creditors.

Credit file A file maintained by the credit department about each customer, generally containing customer financial statements, corporate information, contact addresses, collateral pledged, and credit reports.

Credit hold Freezing the amount of credit offered to customers, thereby forcing them to pay for goods or services in cash.

Credit limit The maximum amount of outstanding accounts receivable a company will allow a customer to attain.

Credit report A report issued by a third-party reporting agency, detailing the financial status and payment history of a company.

Credit sale A sale made with a promise of delayed payment by the customer.

Credit scoring The process of creating a scoring system for determining the credit-worthiness of customers based on a variety of quantitative and qualitative factors.

Creditors committee A committee comprised of some company creditors, who represent all creditors in a bankruptcy proceeding.

Current asset The cash, accounts receivable, and inventory accounts on the balance sheet, or any other assets that are expected to be liquidated within a short time interval.*

Current balance The unpaid accounts receivable owed by a customer, possibly including any late payment fees.

Current liability The accounts payable, short-term notes payable, and accrued expenses accounts on the balance sheet, or any other liabilities that are expected to be liquidated within a short time interval.*

Cut-off date The date listed on an account receivable statement, after which no account activity for additional debts or payments are listed.

Days outstanding The number of days elapsed between invoice issuance and receipt of full payment.

Debt Funds owed to another entity.*

Deduction A reduction in the cash payment made by a customer for an outstanding invoice.

Default The failure by a debtor to make a principal or interest payment in a timely manner.*

Delinquent account The set of outstanding invoices for a specific customer that have not been paid within payment terms.

Discount A percentage reduction in the face value of an invoice, offered in conjunction with early payment of the invoice.

Due date The date by which payment is due on an invoice. This is the invoice issuance date plus the number of days credit allowed to the customer.

Ending receivables The amount of outstanding accounts receivable, as well as unapplied credits, deductions, and payments outstanding at the end of a reporting period.

Equity The difference between the total of all recorded assets and liabilities on the balance sheet.*

Factoring The sale of accounts receivable to a third party, with the third party bearing the risk of loss if the accounts receivable cannot be collected.*

Fraud   A party's intentional misstatement of information in order to obtain consideration from another party that would not normally have been given.

Gross sales   The total sales recorded prior to sales discounts and returns.[*]

Inventory   Those items included categorized as either raw materials, work-in-process, or finished goods, and involved in either the creation of products or service supplies for customers.[*]

Invoice   A document submitted to a customer, identifying a transaction for which the customer owes payment to the issuer.[*]

Last contact date   The last date on which the collections staff either directly contacted a customer or sent it notification information regarding an overdue payment.

Late fee   An interest rate or flat fee charged on the remaining overdue balance on an invoice.

Letter of credit   A bank guarantee of a customer's ability to pay for a specific liability for a specific period.

Lien   A security interest established against an asset in order to give the lien holder the ability to liquidate the asset to settle an outstanding debt.

Marketable security   An easily traded investment, such as treasury bills, and is recorded as a current asset, because it is easily convertible into cash.[*]

Net sales   Total revenue, less the cost of sales returns, allowances, and discounts.[*]

NSF check   A check payment for which there are not sufficient funds in the customer account for the bank to issue funds to the entity to whom the check was paid.

Obligor   Any guarantor of a debt who has not been released from a payment obligation.

Open account   Allowing a customer to accept goods or services in exchange for an invoice, which will be paid at a later date.

Outstanding balance   The unpaid accounts receivable owed by a customer, possibly including any late payment fees.

Paid in full   Complete payment for a liability. This can be construed as payment of the remaining liability after the creditor cancels part of a debt resulting from a negotiated settlement.

Personal guarantee   A pledge by an individual to pay for a company liability if the company cannot pay.

Proof of claim   Documentation provided to a bankruptcy court of a creditor's right to a payment from the bankrupt estate.

Purchase order   An authorization by a customer's purchasing function to acquire goods or services from a supplier.

Quick ratio   A comparison of a company's short-term liabilities and short-term assets, with the intent of determining the company's ability to pay its short-term liabilities with its existing short-term assets.

Re-aged account   An overdue customer account whose overdue status flag has been reset to current status in the computer system, usually as part of a partial payment deal with the customer.

Receivable   The uncollected portion of amounts owed by a customer for goods delivered or services received.

Recourse   The right of a creditor under a factoring arrangement to be paid by the debtor for any uncollectible accounts receivable sold to the creditor.*

Recovery rate   The percentage paid of gross account receivable. This percentage can be calculated for a single account or for the entire receivables balance for all customers.

Restrictive endorsement   A notation on a check, typically stating that the payment represents full payment of an entire obligation.

Revenue   An inflow of cash, accounts receivable, or barter from a customer in exchange for the provision of a service or product to that customer by a company.*

Sales allowance   A reduction in a price that is allowed by the seller, as a result of a problem with the sold product or service.*

Sales discount   A reduction in the price of a product or service that is offered by the seller in exchange for early payment by the buyer.*

Security interest   A lien on customer assets, usually terminating upon payment of a receivable balance or other debt.

Settled in full   Total payment of an account receivable.

Settlement   A payment made to settle a debt, sometimes for less than the full amount of the debt, with the remaining balance being written off by the creditor.

Trade reference   A reference given by a company's suppliers, who give one a reference regarding their credit experience with the company.

UCC   The Uniform Commercial Code.

UCC-1   A statement filed with the Secretary of State's office of the state in which a debtor's assets are located, perfecting a creditor's claim to specific assets or groups of assets.

Uncollectible account   An account receivable for which there is no chance of obtaining payment.

Unearned discount   When a customer takes an early payment deduction on an invoice payment, despite not having paid the invoice by the date specified to earn the discount.

Working capital   The amount of a company's current assets minus its current liabilities, and is considered to be a prime measure of its level of liquidity.[*]

Index